TWENTIETH CENTURY
BALTIMORE

*A Native Son's Casual History of the
City on the Patapsco*

JACK BURKERT

ISBN: 979-8-35095-974-1

Dedication

*There are so many people to thank for their kind assistance, inspiration, and encouragement
in creating this casual history of Baltimore.
I have tried to list most of them in the acknowledgements at the end of this volume.
I have probably missed some of them. Mea culpa.*

*But there is one person who stands out above all others, who needs a special mention,
Cynthia Horn Burkert:
wife, friend, life companion, part-time editor, frequent listener, grammarian resource. Most
importantly, when the writing task seemed overwhelming, she kept me motivated.*

AUTHOR'S NOTE

SOME YEARS AGO, I BEGAN work as a Museum Educator at the Baltimore Museum of Industry, the start of another episode in my life-long career as an educator. I was assigned a special project: another local museum had requested a presentation of the "life and times" of a prominent Baltimorean, focusing on business and industry during his lifetime. I did the research, learned all about this fascinating individual, Mendes Cohen, and completed the presentation. Soon, another similar request came along. Museums across the city were coordinating a "War on the Homefront" series. Could we offer a program detailing Baltimore's commercial and industrial contribution during World War Two? Yes! The history research bug had once again bitten me. Topic after topic was researched and created until here, twelve years later, there are two dozen different programs.

Along the way, I became a Senior Museum Educator. The topics I spoke and wrote about had more of the air of authority. (Titles shouldn't but they do influence.) For guidance I always relied upon the responsibility of being a museum educator. Museums are trusted institutions. Truth and facts matter. And any person who conveys messages on their own or on behalf of another has an enormous responsibility to facts and to the truth. Everything I say and write must be responsibly researched and reported. I believe I've done my best to honor that principle, to keep it factual, to write historic truth and not opinion. Some of the history, I lived. I know those things to be accurate to the best of my ability.

This is not an academic work, and there are no footnotes. However, the bibliography reflects some of the extensive research that forms the foundation of this book. I have learned that curiosity is very much an ally. The stories are told after researching primary sources, conducting personal interviews, and combing through historic newspapers. I took the work seriously, wanted it to be right, and spent many hours poring over newly purchased materials, doing internet digging (beware, rabbit holes), and meeting with experts, folks who lived the experience, and professional associates for advice or specialized knowledge.

Is everything included? Of course not! If one were to try, failure would always lurk, and this book would be triple its size and probably unreadable. Then where would we be? I have created this work with the help, assistance, and suggestions of many including friends and associates at the Museum and beyond, hopefully all of them noted later in the acknowledgements. I would be remiss if I didn't especially acknowledge Baltimore Museum of Industry Executive Director Anita Kasoff, who made it possible for me to delve into the museum files to find just the right images for inclusion in this text.

If you want a readable history of the Queen City of the Patapsco River and its 20th century story, you have come to the right place. Read on!

Jack Burkert
April 2024

TABLE OF CONTENTS

INTRODUCTION

THIS IS THE STORY OF a city: Baltimore, Maryland, my hometown. It is a direct result of my work in developing and presenting a series of popular Baltimore history lectures beginning in 2011. Over time, more and more social history – how people worked and lived, what issues concerned them – began to emerge. Jobs, industry, and work were always the core material, but increasingly the life of the city and the stories of its people became the focus of my programs.

Audience members asked, "When are you going to write all of this down?" Well, here you have it: a story of a city and its people, a history from the perspective of a fellow Baltimorean, one native son who is also an amateur historian. It is a story of Baltimore in the 20th century, no more and no less, the history of a place and its people from many walks of life. In telling the stories, there were constant efforts to be aware of cultural differences, of differing perspectives, and of how events impacted the diverse people that make Baltimore, well, Baltimore.

Though the 20th century revealed here is a Baltimore story, the events of the nation are reflected within that story. Some will feel I've strayed from the local history I set out to write, but how does one explain the Catonsville Nine, for instance, unless the Vietnam War story has been told as context? Through the decades, two World Wars, the Roaring Twenties, and a handful hard times, always there was a "this was Baltimore" story nearby, only a sentence or two away. Civil rights stories are here, stories important to Baltimore regardless of the reader's or participant's race or ethnicity. I am aware that I have treated events of consequence (blockbusting, highway wars, Baltimore's market system, and others) with less detail than might be desired. These and many other topics are treated effectively and extensively in the research and writing of authors and historians of far greater ability than mine. If you want to know more, go where I went, to the research, the contemporary news reports, the interviews with those who would retell their experiences.

This may be unlike any history you have ever read. I've told the story in the hope that it is readable and interesting. So many people who love (or ought to love) history are driven away by dry-as-dust narrative, more data than necessary or than one could absorb, and story lines lost amidst excruciating detail. This book is intended to be a fun read. I think I got it right, but only pure hubris would allow a claim of perfection. When you question something, check it first, then let me know what you find, so the second edition is better than this first: nativesonbaltimore@gmail.com.

Enjoy the story....

CHAPTER ONE:
TURNING THE CENTURY

The 1900s

Ⓘ**T WAS NEW YEAR'S EVE**, 1899. The beginning of a new century was welcomed on a cold, crisp night. The 19th century was ended, and its cares and woes would surely go with it. Celebration was on the minds of the people, and Baltimoreans were in the streets, greeting one another with handshakes, hugs, and "Happy New Year" messages. Baltimore had become a big city, over half a million souls, and was still growing. The 19th century had seen an explosion of growth as the city's agrarian economy turned more and more industrial, and the need for workers was answered by immigrants, most from rural Europe, learning the skills to survive in a city. Like other cities, Baltimore was not an easy place for newcomers: new customs, a new language, and all new surroundings, each took their toll.

It was a challenging time. Electricity ran the trolleys, while homes were still lit with candles and kerosene. A water utility was operating, but purification had yet to arrive, and the city lacked a sanitary sewer system. Horses trudged through the crowded port-side streets, dropping waste. Automobiles were just appearing, simply adding to the confusion on the streets. The Port of Baltimore, once a backwater lacking a reliable export and insufficient citizens to justify much import, had grown so that cargo of all sorts came and went. Grain, tobacco, metals, tools, machines, all made their way around the world from Baltimore's harbor, as raw materials and workers arrived. The city had grown into the nation's second largest immigration center.

And now it was about to be the 20th century. As the clock struck midnight, ships' whistles sounded the welcoming news: a new century had arrived. It was a time of optimism for many, and America was riding high after recent military victories and land acquisition. A war with Spain had just ended and in the process, the country had gained colonial possessions: Cuba, the Philippines, and Puerto Rico. President William McKinley, presiding over a prosperous era, would soon be re-elected. Entertainment at a multitude of theaters was available. Amusement parks powered by electricity were opening. Travel was faster and easier as coal-powered steamships and railroads sped travelers to their destinations. Life could only get better!

It had been reported that the departing 19th century was so successful that the U. S. Patent Office could be closed. Surely everything needed for comfort, convenience, and commerce had already been invented. Not everyone agreed, of course, but such was the optimism of the time. Prognosticators issued their view of the changes sure to occur in the 20th century. In the *Ladies Home Journal*, predictions ranged from practical, to outlandish, with a few eerily foreshadowing future technologies. Among the practical: automobiles were predicted to be everywhere, doing everything, for everyone from farmers to children at play, with the horse in harness scarce; the end of bugs was on the way, as extermination would be so effective, there would be no houseflies, mosquitos, or horse flies; the letters C, X, and Q were declared useless, and they would soon be eliminated from the alphabet; deliveries would be made by pneumatic tubes from stores and shops, and mail would surely arrive by tube (though perhaps with automobiles to move goods the last mile.)

More far-fetched: photographs would be transmitted by wire, and people would be able to view far-away lands using cameras and viewing on large theater screens. Optimistically, everyone would be fit from exercise by walking ten miles a day, and with improved sanitation and medical progress, people would have a life expectancy of 50 years of age.

THE GILDED AGE ENDS

At the beginning of the 20th century the years known as the "Gilded Age", a monopoly-driven era of powerful tycoons and unparalleled corruption, was drawing to a close. The Gilded Age, a descriptive term coined by Mark Twain, was no boon to the working man. A set of fabulously wealthy businessmen had wrested control of industries, established exploitive monopolies, mechanized industry to the detriment of skilled labor, and abandoned 92 percent of American families to living below the poverty line. These leaders had earned the soubriquet, "robber barons", for indeed they had exploited for personal gain all that they touched. Their corporations conspired to control the nation's rail transportation network, aspiring even to control trans-Atlantic travel and commerce, as well as gaining control of complete industries such as steel, copper, banking, oil, and more. In Baltimore, owners of the mills in the Jones Falls Valley had successfully conspired to monopolize the canvas or "duck cloth" market. If a buyer wanted canvas, Baltimore was the source, and the price was fixed. Nationwide, there were few restrictions on business monopolies, limitations that were in place were seldom enforced, and a non-confrontational government allowed business generally to do as it pleased.

On September 6, 1901, President William McKinley was assassinated. Suddenly, his vice president, Theodore Roosevelt, had become president. The days of the Gilded Age were from that moment destined to come to an end. When Theodore Roosevelt took over and remade the presidency, the Gilded Age and its tycoons and monopolies had more than met their match. His policy was activist: breaking up the combines and monopolies of the era, or trust-busting. In Baltimore, at the time a major canning center, the prosecution and elimination of the "tin can" monopoly as created by the American Can Company would have a local impact. American Can Company's policy had been to buy can-making competitors and instead of operating them, simply shut them down. With fewer can suppliers there would be less competition, creating an ability for American Can to charge higher prices. By 1910, American Can supplied 90 percent of the nation's need for tin cans. This market control would soon end as government trust-busting forced change upon the company, allowing new competitors to enter the market. As a result, the supply of cans increased, the price of food in cans declined, and the consumer had won a small victory. When Republican candidate Roosevelt sought re-election in 1904, he even carried Democratic-leaning Maryland (though by a mere fifty-one vote margin out of two-hundred-eighteen thousand cast). He didn't please everyone, least of all budding Baltimore journalist Henry L. Mencken, who conferred upon him the sarcastic title "Roosevelt the First". This was the first inkling of what would be Mencken's lifelong propensity toward presidential critique.

Henry Louis Mencken found his way into his calling, journalism, in the first decade of the 20th century. Born in Baltimore in 1880, he made his way through the Polytechnic High School and into his father's cigar sales business. On the passing of his father, nineteen-year-old Henry took a position with *The Baltimore Herald* newspaper, reporting news and offering opinion. By 1906, he had joined *The Baltimore Sun*, and opinion pieces became his signature. His first attack in 1910 on pending prohibition legislation assured his reputation. As his fame grew, he published beyond the city's newspapers, becoming the co-editor of the *Smart Set Magazine*, followed by *The American Mercury*. Although published in New York, Mencken worked from his home on Hollins Street in Baltimore, regularly journeying to New York for editorial meetings. He had earned the title "The Sage of Baltimore".

A BUSINESS-FRIENDLY CITY

As the northern-most of Southern cities, Baltimore had long positioned itself as an appealing marketplace for consumers to the south. The city catered to the needs for manufactured goods of rural, agrarian states, and a continuing influx of immigrants allowed employers to hire workers at lower wages. The port put the world close at hand, with easy and efficient access to raw materials from around the world. The city was truly a first-tier choice for business. Through political policy and power favorable to business, the city was to be a business powerhouse for decades to come. In the first decade of the 20th century, the city worked metal: the largest copper smelting operation in the world was located on the east side. It forged iron and steel at a southwest foundry into cast iron stoves, iron-fronted buildings, and more. The Maryland Steel Company plant at Sparrow's Point, in its second decade of operation, was becoming a model of "how to". The sewing trades had been thriving since the Civil war and were getting more robust. Men's suits dominated the garment industry. Local umbrella makers led that industry and straw hats became a Baltimore specialty, millions of them shading men's heads for the next sixty years. While family businesses continued, mostly in small specialty shops, this was the beginning of a century of domination by corporations, of which Baltimore hosted more than two hundred.

The city boasted an amazing array of businesses, serving consumers near and far. There was money in the city to be loaned, borrowed, saved, and paid, thus banking interests proliferated. Nine local banks offered service to the community, outnumbered by the twenty-one national banks that established operations in the city. The city was a true passenger and cargo hub. The home-town railroad company was the Baltimore and Ohio, operating from multiple stations, with competing services offered by the Pennsylvania, the Western Maryland, the Maryland and Pennsylvania, and the interurban Washington, Baltimore, and Annapolis Company. Port operations would dominate commerce at the beginning of the 20th century and into the next, with six intercontinental shipping companies and thirteen more local, coastal and Chesapeake Bay service providers. The city was a corporate headquarters center as dozens of businesses called Baltimore their home.

The future of the city was ultimately in the hands of its working citizens. Willing immigrants continued to arrive in great numbers so that the work and the growth continued. Corporations can buy machines, build buildings, and seek clients, but it is the workers who deliver the products and services. Businesses such as the canning and the garment industries were each significant to Baltimore as they competed with the Port of Baltimore and one another to become the biggest business in Baltimore. Businesses relied upon both highly skilled and less skilled hands to fill the cans, sew the seams, and perform hundreds of other tasks. Some would work in high rise factories, some in the sweat shop conditions of the attics and homes of Fell's Point and beyond. Some work was seasonal, some was year-round. The workdays were long when work was available, cold in the winter, sweltering in the summer. When work was not available, there was only community charity to fall back upon.

Immigration to America, specifically to Baltimore, had been meeting the labor needs of business and industry since colonial times. In Baltimore, early immigrants paved the streets with Belgian blocks and built the houses that lined them. They hewed the sailing ships which made Baltimore famous, loaded them with cargo, and manned their decks as they sailed away. They came from England, Ireland, Scotland, and Germany in those early years, but by the beginning of the 20th century, the new arrivals came from further east in Europe, speaking languages less understood. From Poland, from Russia, from Lithuania and more they came, sailing the Atlantic in the steel, steam powered ships that had replaced the wooden sailing ships of previous generations. They leaned on the help of one another, with aid from prior arrivals, churches, and fraternal groups. Some were Catholic, some were Jewish, some escaped poverty, some escaped persecution, but all were bold enough to depart their homeland with its familiar life to sail thousands of miles to find a new place, in a new home. They took the jobs and built the economy, learning English as quickly as they could, slowly becoming Americans and Baltimoreans.

Life for these immigrants was not often easy, as families all toiled to eke out an existence. Dads worked jobs at trades if they had them, as laborers if they didn't, while moms often took in work as the opportunity arose. Sewing buttons at home for the garment makers was a common vocation, children working alongside parents. For some women, employment meant time at a factory. They often worked with their children beside them, by design to create a bit more family income or by circumstance, as childcare was not often available. Factory owners were of mixed minds on the issue of children in the workplace. But if the women were to be able to work, the children had to be tolerated, despite the lower quality of work done by the children. So frequent were the occasions of children laboring in the workplace that the Maryland Legislature began to restrict times and places where children could work, beginning in April 1902. Children under the age of fourteen were no longer permitted to work, and children between the ages of eight and twelve had to attend school.

THE PORT OF BALTIMORE

When Captain John Smith entered the Patapsco River and its natural harbor in 1600, he declared, "Heaven and earth never agreed better to frame a place for man's habitation". Since those earliest days of exploration, the river has been a dominant feature in the settlement, growth, and development of the City of Baltimore. The Port of Baltimore and its shipbuilding industry have seen clipper ships, sailing vessels, and vessels of iron and steel. Callers at the port have included ships of peace and commerce, ships of misery filled with slaves being sold to plantations in the south, domestic ships of war, and on occasion, foreign ships of war, not always arriving with peaceful intention. More than a million immigrants and thousands of enslaved persons arrived by water. Local shipments came and went onboard coastal vessels calling on the ports of the Chesapeake and cities of the Atlantic Coast. International trade came and went by multiple ship lines to the Caribbean, Europe, South America, and even Asia. The North German Lloyd Line moved tobacco east and immigrants west, to and from Bremen in Germany. The Allen Line brought cargo and immigrants from Liverpool, while the A.H. Bull Line connected Baltimore with Puerto Rico.

A local shipping company, the Atlantic Transport Line, competed with other service providers traversing the waters of the North Atlantic. Its founder, Bernard Baker operated the company to transport passengers from New York, Baltimore, and Philadelphia to European ports, mostly in Britain. Baker, a philanthropic Baltimorean, led the company until it was sold to the International Mercantile Marine Company, J.P. Morgan's unsuccessful 1902 effort to monopolize the trans-Atlantic shipping business. Baker had accepted stock in payment for his company and suffered major financial losses when Morgan's company went broke, but continued his maritime role, advising government and industry, and later becoming a trustee of the Johns Hopkins University.

The Port of Baltimore grew decisively along the Middle Branch of the Patapsco River in 1902. Vacant swampy land along the Patapsco's Middle Branch attracted the eye of the newly formed Western Maryland Railroad. At the behest of financier owner George Gould (son of railroad magnate Jay Gould), the railroad then built Port Covington, a yard and terminal as its international outlet for transporting grain and coal. The Western Maryland built piers for freight and coal and laid seventy-five miles of railroad track in a two thousand railcar storage yard, thus creating the railroad's "Junction with the World."

GETTING AROUND THE CITY

The 20th century saw the coming of the automobile age with Baltimore adopting and adapting to this latest invention. Baltimore became a modest automotive center, responding to changing times with custom manufacturing in small carriage shops that once made horse drawn carriages and buggies. Enterprising carriage builders expanded their modest shops, building a new style of carriage now powered not by horse but instead equipped with small gasoline engines, steam engines, even electric motors using battery power. These automobiles and the convenience they offered became the transport of the future. A half dozen or more entered the cottage industry of automaking, led by two of note: Carl Spoerer's Sons, and the Sinclair Scott Company. Each saw opportunity in the "horseless carriage" trade.

Carl Spoerer's Sons Company was a carriage builder located on South Carey Street near the center of the city. When Carl passed away at the end of the 19th century, his sons saw the future no longer in carriages, but in automobiles. They began around 1910 to build roadsters and enclosed vehicles, adding a gasoline engine to their knowledge of carriages and mechanics. The price of the handmade cars they built was about $2,500 (about $80,000 in 2023 dollars.) They would soon be forced to compete, unsuccessfully, with Henry Ford's mass production assembly lines and the resulting $600 Model T. Still, the company persisted as a parts and service provider until the 1930s.

Sinclair Scott, located near the southside area of Port Covington, renamed the Baltimore Peninsula, was a metal working company specializing in kitchen appliances and tools. They began manufacturing automobile parts early in the 20th century. When the Ariel Automobile Company of Massachusetts was unable to pay an invoice to Sinclair Scott for goods they had received, they proposed a trade to satisfy the debt. Their design and tooling for the Ariel would be shipped south to Baltimore. Sinclair Scott was suddenly in the automobile business. The automobile was renamed the Maryland and though they proved unprofitable, 871 of them were made until production was halted in 1910.

Automobiles, the first of which were built in Germany, were very experimental in this first decade of the 20th century. The newly founded American Automobile Association (1902) undertook a highly visible testing program that found its way to Baltimore in 1907. The Glidden Tours took various makes and models on a long-distance route, from Cleveland, Ohio, south to Tennessee, then northward through Baltimore to the finish line in New York. It was an endurance contest, a long-distance road rally style race with check-in points, checkers waving black and white flags to the vehicles as they arrived. This was to be the first use of racing style checkered flags (1906). In Baltimore, the cars and drivers overnighted before continuing north.

Road improvements were desperately needed. In 1900, just 1,300 of the state's 14,000 miles of road were improved. The era used a very loose definition of improved: if a road was graded, it was improved. Enhancements such as paving, often gravel or perhaps oyster shells, placed that road in the top tier of highways. Mud in the winter and dust in the summer was the rule. A national Good Roads Movement had been founded in 1880, a coalition of road users that was energized at the time by the new craze of bicycling. By 1900, *Good Roads* magazine gave the movement a voice for citizen demands for roadway improvement. Maryland responded to the demands of the "Good Roads Coalition" by creating and funding the State Roads Commission in 1908. The City of Baltimore had long since been hardscaping the urban scene with paving blocks on the streets around the city. As early as the late 1700s, the city had funded road improvements with a lottery, later adding streetcar tracks to the rights of way.

The 1900s were also the first decade of mass access to the benefits of electrification. Charles Brush had in the 1880s created a reliable electrical generator, attached "arc street lighting" to the power source, and Brush Electric Company illuminated the city. With lighting power lines in place, the trolley system followed with its own power line network. America's first-ever electrified trolley system appeared in Baltimore in 1885 when the Baltimore and Hampden line began operating. Factories soon joined the electrification movement, enjoying the flexibility of electric power tools. Private home electrification came in the 1900s, with wealthy Baltimoreans connecting for very expensive but convenient interior lighting. The demand for electric power set off a generation of electrical retrofitting, and by the late 19-teens and 1920s new home designs were specifically adapted to home electrification needs. Home appliances began to appear in the same period, the electric stove as early as 1896, with toasters, heaters, even vacuum cleaners soon adding their convenience, producing lifestyle changes in even modest homes.

A new company was formed at the very end of the 19th century, the United Railways Company, when other smaller streetcar companies merged into one cohesive group. In years past, small streetcar companies such as the Baltimore and Hampden operated independent of one another using their own utility lines and power plants. The individual companies each operated within their own small service radius, leaving passengers little to no long-distance travel options. When these smaller lines were consolidated as United Railways, longer distance travel via connecting services was only one public benefit. The company constructed a new power plant (1902) on Pratt Street in the approximate geographic center of the company's track system, a coal fired utility plant that powered the company's three hundred miles of track and was capable of running as many as four hundred street cars at any one time. Located harborside, the coal to create the steam to turn the generating turbines was delivered by barge. To cool the equipment, water from the harbor was pumped in and circulated. United Railways operated an ever-expanding trackage system, typically transporting over 100,000 passengers annually. The company's operations were later hampered only by the disruption of the Great Baltimore Fire in 1904, followed by construction designed to increase the power capacity of the facility. The plant would later be sold to the Consolidated Gas, Electric Light, and Power Company.

CALAMITY

Sunday, February 7, 1904, started cold and bright but quite windy. It was a typically quiet Sunday when it began, but in Baltimore history, it would become a memorable day. At 20 South Hopkins Place, the John E. Hurst Dry Goods Company occupied a six-story brick building in the front of which was a basement delivery elevator, extending under the sidewalk. Wisps of smoke rising from the building were noted by passersby around 10 a.m., and soon after an automatic alarm in the building sounded, summoning the Baltimore Fire Department to combat the Great Baltimore Fire.

It is theorized that a carelessly discarded cigar or cigarette found its way through openings in the elevator shaft into the building's basement where it landed on bundles of stored fabric. Firemen, including Captain John Kahl, broke open the building with a crowbar. He described what he found: "I couldn't see much smoke, and I remember thinking that we'd be back in the firehouse in no time." It would be late Monday before he finally got back to the firehouse. The basement was soon engulfed in flame, and shortly after the entire building exploded into a ball of fire and smoke, throwing firebrands, debris, and sparks into the wind. The hot debris landed on and set into flames the adjacent buildings. Thus began a thirty-hour fight to stop the fire, to control the direction, to extinguish the ongoing catastrophe. The fire burned east, then a bit north, before resolutely turning southeast overnight toward the waterfront and the west side of the Jones Falls waterway. In the end, the heart of the city was destroyed, with over 1,500 buildings gone, 1,000 more heavily damaged, encompassing over eighty city blocks.

The Baltimore Fire Department was outmatched. This was a 20th century fire fought with 19th century equipment: tall buildings versus horse drawn equipment, water pressure from hoses capable of reaching only the lower floors as fire raced upward. Adjacent jurisdictions were summoned, the first firefighters coming from Washington, D.C. Nearby counties, cities, even cities in nearby states responded with equipment and personnel, arriving by carriage, rail, and in the case of the Sparrow's Point Steel Mill Fire Company, by United Railways trolley. On arrival many of their hose connections, in the absence of standardization, could not connect to the Baltimore fire hydrants, as the couplings were of different diameters. To deliver water to the fire, the misfit connections were wrapped in canvas, a leaky and inadequate solution. As the fire neared the Baltimore waterfront, the hoses of the New York fire companies were dropped directly into the harbor, thus the only connection needed was from their hoses to their own pumps. In all, seventy-two fire companies arrived to help extinguish the thirty-hour fire.

The impact of the fire was as wide as it was quick. Banks, offices, and shops, the 35,000 jobs they hosted and fully 2,500 businesses were virtually wiped out in a weekend. Valuables lay in the street, those that the 2,000-degree heat had somehow spared. The brick construction of downtown was no match for the intense heart, as mortar simply crumbled under the assault. The Maryland Militia was called out to guard the debris. Newspapers were unable to publish, their offices and presses laid to waste. Reporters wrote the stories, rushed them to nearby Washington and later to Philadelphia for printing, then the papers were returned to Baltimore by train. Baltimore's Custom House, under construction, was damaged but survived as did the "fireproof" Continental Building, the tallest in Baltimore at the time which proved to be as advertised, fireproof. With the gutted interior refurbished, the building was soon back in use. The Alexander Brown Building sustained a few cracks in its façade as the fire moved past its doors, protected perhaps by the updraft from the burning Sun Iron Building across Baltimore Street. With good fortune, the human toll was small. The fire had started on a quiet Sunday morning with downtown largely unoccupied, a few churchgoers the exception. While the fire attracted on-lookers and observers, and desperate business-owners trying to rescue documents, equipment, and cash from buildings in the path of the fire, they eluded the fire as it leapt from building to building, block to block, throughout the day and night. In one turn of events, to save his brother's cash and documents, Holly Smith entered an endangered building, but misunderstood the directions he had been given, turned left instead of right at the top of a flight of stairs, and rescued papers, cash, and books from the wrong office. For ten-year-old Althea Stroup, the day was a different sort of adventure. She was headed toward her home on Fort Avenue aboard a southbound trolley when the fire broke out. Unable to get through, the trolley was first diverted, then rerouted to the Druid Hill trolley barn with Althea still aboard. Refusing to abandon his charge, the conductor walked the youngster the several miles to her home on the south side of the city. A single unidentified body was later found floating in the harbor. A few who had fought the fire succumbed to the stress of the event in the following days. One businessman lost his life a week later when a building collapsed on him.

A massive effort would be needed to start the city on the road to recovery. The financial toll was large, as measured in 2023 dollars a loss totaling $4.2 billion. Young Mayor Robert McLane had been a cheerleader for the firemen, moving about the city encouraging their efforts. In office for just under a year, McLane started the recovery effort declaring, "Baltimore will take care of its own, thank you" and returned unsolicited financial aid to the donors. Under his leadership, the Burnt District Commission was created, an oversight body that would have broad powers to condemn, exercise eminent domain authority, and remake the burnt district along a more organized and orderly plan. Sadly, McLane did not long figure into the future of the city. The newly married mayor was dead before the month of May ended. Some said he had committed suicide, others suspected murder, but the rebuilding of the city would have to proceed without his leadership. He was succeeded by Republican E. Clay Timanus, who served only the remainder of McLane's term of office, presiding over the rebuilding of the city, then losing to Democrat J. Barry Mahool in the 1907 election.

The pace of the rebuild of Baltimore was nothing short of miraculous. The fire had consumed 140 acres of the city. The Burnt District Commission authorized by the Maryland General Assembly helped to quickly facilitate the city's recovery, leading to an entire restoration of the city in ten years, with most of the work completed in half that time. The Burnt District Commission was able to access funding for its work from the earlier sale of Baltimore's interest in the Western Maryland Railroad. The Commission had the ability to modify property lines; to realign, rebuild, or widen streets, especially the congested waterfront Pratt Street; to open public squares and marketplaces; and to disburse state-provided relief funds. The General Assembly also authorized the Citizens Relief Commission to provide funding of $250,000 ($7,500,000 in 2023 dollars) for distribution to impacted citizens, though only $23,000 was spent.

A pre-fire Pratt Street was narrow and chronically congested. It connected the city's more prominent cargo piers, on a right-of-way that was shared by carts, wagons, new motorized trucks, buggies, and the Baltimore and Ohio trains serving business and commerce. Placement of utility wires underground had long been a desire of city government, but the utility company had argued that underground wires would duplicate those already above ground. That argument was settled when the above ground wires were lost to the fire and the central city's utility wires went underground. With the efforts of Mayor Timanus, an enclosed sewer system received the voters' approval for a $10,000,000 bond issue. Sewer construction soon began. Baltimore was among the last large urban areas without this basic public health need. The flood-prone Jones Falls was tamed with covers, to be expanded to a complete roadway (the Fallsway) in the next decade, with new retaining walls and higher bridges that would not be swept away when the Falls was in flood stage. The piers along Pratt Street were rebuilt as publicly owned facilities, replacing private ownership, all wider and deeper to accommodate larger vessels.

Street Cleaning Commissioner Joseph Wickes endeavored to control the dust in the streets, where it lay several inches thick in places, an accumulation from the fire's destruction of masonry buildings. The B&O Railroad laid temporary tracks nearby so train loads of debris could be moved away. Amidst it all, the life of the city struggled to return to a degree of normalcy. A few blocks south a freighter docked, one of many to call on the port in these days, unloading bananas. Examining the rebuild of the unit block of South Gay Street can offer insight into the processes at work in the city in the years immediately after the fire. Two property owners, Samuel Sexton, a stove manufacturer, and Napoleon Bonaparte Loeb, known as an auctioneer and investor, each built a new building to house his company and the offices of smaller businesses. Both began rebuilding, almost competing with one another, on adjacent lots. Architects were employed by each of the business owners to create new headquarters for them. The Sexton Building was five stories high with two store fronts facing Gay Street. Loeb's would be a more traditional office tower also of five stories, including both an elevator and a rathskeller in the basement, at a cost of $30,000 (about $900,000 in 2023 dollars). Before he could complete his project, tragedy struck Samuel Sexton. Apparently under the pressure of a completing the rebuild as quickly as possible, he was stricken with apoplexy, a term in more common use in the era to indicate a hemorrhagic stroke, the result of a ruptured brain blood vessel. He died the next day, November 22, 1904, just over 9 months from the date his business and building had burned in the Great Fire.

Later maps drawn by the Sanborn Map Company portray the Sexton building as the home of General Electric Supply Company. The Sexton building was directly across Gay Street from the High-Pressure Fire Department House, a project initiated in the aftermath of the fire. The fire department began a standardization and modernization process, including creating a high-pressure water system that could supply water well above the Baltimore Fire-era limit of the third floor of flaming buildings. City building codes were also changed at the behest of the fire department, demanding more fireproofing in new construction and the use of improved materials.

Two years after the fire, in September 1906 the many fire companies that had come from near and far to assist the Baltimore Fire Department in extinguishing the 1904 fire were invited back to the city to join in a Baltimore Jubilee. Many came by train, just as they had two years before, from Philadelphia, Washington, D.C., Atlantic City, New Jersey, Wilmington, Delaware, and several other Pennsylvania and Maryland cities, including Annapolis. They were joined by virtually the entire Baltimore Fire Department for a celebratory parade. In sweltering heat, they marched from Lower Broadway north to Baltimore Street, westward across the city to pass the reviewing stand, through the recovering Burnt District where the fire they had fought remained only partly in evidence, to Mount Vernon Square where the parade was disbanded. Many of the visitors remained overnight, visiting the Electric Park in Northwest Baltimore, others returning late at night to their home cities. The city was in recovery, the Jubilee and parade offering clear evidence. The work of the Burnt District Commission was also drawing to a close. It had largely accomplished its goals, and while city rebuilding continued, its work in guiding and planning was complete by 1907.

A HEALTHIER CITY

By 1901, the continuing influx of immigrants had not yet been properly absorbed into the community. Large swaths of the city were identified as slums, many of them housing some of the four hundred garment industry sweat shop operations identified in a 1901 city government study. Public hygiene in those slums was such that typhoid was not uncommon, the city's sewer system was yet in the future, and muck-raking journalists had yet to impact food sanitation, particularly of the milk supply. Many citizens were mired in an inherited way-of-life that stressed racial and nativist discrimination that in 1910 was codified by Mayor Mahool and the City Council into a red-lining law that barred African Americans from living outside so-called "colored" districts, exacerbating overcrowding and the health problems arising from high density living conditions.

Baltimore, like most cities, was a blend of expensive and lavish homes, modest but well-maintained dwellings, and deficient housing stock, with older portions of the city where housing well past its prime was attractive only because it was surrounded by job opportunities in nearby industries. The 19th century had produced regular, and regularly erroneous, explanations of how the poor were by their own actions responsible for their "pauperism", attaching a racial bias to any conclusions drawn, and proposing action only when disease, crime, and presumed immorality began to impact the greater population. In the early years of the 20th century, a city-sponsored study of sweat shops and slums concluded that the city had large slum areas where the housing was in poor repair, dirty inside and out, and more often than not, overcrowded with multi-generational families crammed into small spaces. The occupants of these houses were most often recent immigrants, and in these early 1900s, many were recently arrived Russian Jews. Twenty thousand or more in number, they had fled czarist persecution which almost made slum life in Baltimore look good. The study detailed a lack of exterior repair, dirty basements, inadequate lighting, a lack of yard drainage, and overall, an unclean physical presence. Worse, space in these homes often doubled as garment industry sweat shop workplaces.

The Baltimore City Health Department, the oldest such agency in the United States (1797), with 19th century victories over smallpox and yellow fever behind them, turned their attention to diphtheria, tuberculosis, typhoid, and scarlet fever. A healthier environment was created with the post-Baltimore Fire construction of a city sewer system, completed by 1915. With many homes lacking laundry and bathroom facilities, Henry T. Walters, son of art collector William Walters, donated money to the city to build and operate several public bath houses (1901). These public bath houses replaced the warm weather use of a few 19th century city-created public harbor side beaches. Entering the bath houses for a few pennies (children for even less), bathers would be provided a small piece of soap, a towel, and as much hot water as they could enjoy. Showers for the men, showers and tubs for the women, and a basement laundry room for washing clothing were provided. Dora Silber, daughter of an immigrant baker, described how after working at the Sonneborn Clothing factory she would visit the Walters Public Bath in east Baltimore. Like other patrons, she would first wash the clothing she had arrived in, then hang it to dry while bathing herself. The heat inside the bath house would quickly dry her freshly washed clothes, making them ready to wear once her bath was over.

There were Baltimoreans who were dedicating their lives to the health needs of the city, and by extension, the entire country. Scientists and physicians at the Johns Hopkins Hospital, then in only its second decade of operation, were breaking new ground in medicine. Near the Hopkins facility were many overcrowded neighborhoods, communities of immigrants in densely packed housing. More than 600 people were living in the 70 houses on just a single block of East Lombard Street between Lloyd and Central Avenues. Two complete households lived in 1139 E. Lombard Street in 1910:

- The Bergers: Morris, a 55-year-old pants presser; his 50-year-old wife Eva; their 18-year-old daughter Fannie, a coat operator; their newlywed son, 26-year-old Harris, a pants maker; and Harris's wife Rebecca, aged 20.

- The Sundicks: Max, a 36-year-old pants presser; his 35-year-old wife Sarah; and their four children, ages 6 months to 10 years.

Such living conditions generated their own health epidemics. Amid this crowded housing were found garment industry sweat shops, their cramped and dirty workplaces creating yet more health risks. It was the City Health Department and the scientists and public health workers at Hopkins who began to address the health concerns that existed in these tenements. Their work was appropriately focused on hygiene and nutrition, addressed with both intervention and educational programs. Hopkins was also pioneering in specialty medical work, among them brain surgery and the creation of new social work and psychiatry departments. The city conducted a study of the sweat shops, at the time numbering almost 400, with an eye to limiting their unhealthy existence. Thousands of immigrants labored in these unsanitary, dark, and unsafe places where the work was hard, the hours long, and the pay low. Legislation that followed established standards for square footage per employee, maximum allowable room temperature, air circulation, and toilet accommodations, resulting in a great reduction in the number of such workplaces.

In 1908, the Baltimore City Health Department began its efforts to address the quality and safety of the milk supply. Milk was often an unsanitary and unreliable product. The first of the new milk regulations mandated pasteurization (1908), but milk safety demanded further steps. Within the city were some 3,000 dairy cows, some maintained in small yards sharing the space with outdoor privies. Following an infant cholera outbreak in 1907, health department inspections of the herds were increased, finding unsanitary conditions such as open milk containers with chickens roosting along their upper edge. Milk was sold from barrels on wagons rolling through the city streets. Housewives would await the wagon's arrival on their block, purchasing their day's supply from one of the estimated five hundred wagons plying this trade. Improving milk purification became a priority. To do so the Health Department mandated bottled milk, ending the bulk sale trade. Milk plants were licensed and inspected, and by the next decade milk safety regulations and inspections had been proven effective.

PROGRESS FOR WOMEN

Baltimore's early 20th century mirrored the issues in America, albeit often with a local slant on the problem. Most vexing it seemed was the slow, seventy-year march toward achieving for women the right to vote. Dating to the Seneca Falls (New York) Convention of 1848, women's suffrage became a national movement. Baltimore's women joined the battle but missed (perhaps only formally) the first forty plus years, not establishing the Baltimore City Suffrage Club until 1894. It was aligned with the Maryland Women's Suffrage Association and became one of several clubs that were formed to advance women's voting rights. The Maryland Women's Suffrage Association opened their Baltimore office in 1902, later hosting a national suffrage convention at the Lyric Theater in 1906.

Edith Houghton Hooker moved to Baltimore to attend the Johns Hopkins School of Medicine. In Baltimore she became a social worker where her interest in the women's suffrage movement changed the course of her life. She was convinced that for the movement to achieve the desired results, women would have to make their protests more united and more militant. She created the Just Government League of Maryland in 1907, a more militant group that through her leadership offered persuasive public presentations, advocacy newsletters, open air meetings, and took to the streets with protest marches. Hooker personally created, wrote, and published the *Maryland Suffrage News*, sharing news and events that would make the suffrage movement a more cohesive and persuasive force in the women's movement. While these events were transpiring, in a small village in rural Kent County, Maryland, local women made history. In the municipal election of 1908 in Still Pond, Maryland, the first women in the state cast ballots. Fourteen women were registered to vote, though just three cast their ballots: Mary Jane Clark Howard, Anne Baker Maxwell, and Lillie Deringer Kelley.

Hooker was effective in many ways, but the efforts of the Just Government League and Edith Hooker were not able to sway the very conservative Maryland House of Delegates. Despite multiple meetings and appearances, their work came to no avail. The Maryland House of Delegates, presented with a ratification vote for the 19th Constitutional Amendment that would grant the right to vote to women, rejected its passage on the basis of "states' rights", arguing that granting the privilege to vote was an issue for each individual state to determine for its residents. With the ratification of the amendment in a sufficient number of other states, the suffrage amendment became law. Conservative Marylanders then filed a lawsuit challenging the amendment, its passage, and the addition of women to the voting rolls. In 1922, the United States Supreme Court upheld the amendment, with an embarrassed Maryland finally ratifying the 19th amendment in 1941.

A CITY OF NEIGHBORHOODS

Neighborhoods are the building blocks of cities, a most basic social unit. Neighborhoods are residential districts where face-to-face interaction is the norm, driving the sense of community and often, trust. Baltimore became a city of over 200 neighborhoods where newly arrived immigrants as well as one-time slaves and free Blacks could find communities of trust in neighborhoods comprised of people like themselves, alike in language, foods, and religion. Neighborhoods in Baltimore formed ways of life, sustained habits of another time and place, and offered mutual support. The neighborhood offered support that including savings associations able to loan money into and for the benefit of the community. Religious institutions, churches, cathedrals, and synagogues, maintained religious ties and offered personal support. A small sampling:

East Lombard Street. Along and abutting Lombard Street, this neighborhood welcomed Jewish immigrants from central Europe throughout the 19th century. The community was centered upon a religious nucleus, growing with shopkeepers, educators, business owners, and business workers forming a community that offered familiar services, foods, languages, and religion. Close quarters living was typical, with a high density of residents crowded into modest housing. The community grew adjacent to and reliant upon the Lloyd Street Synagogue, a congregation formed in 1830, with its 1845 building the third oldest synagogue in the United States. The community endured, changing only as wealthier community members moved to more upscale, greener neighborhoods.

Hampden. A very different neighborhood grew up in the 19th century to house a different group, the families of those employed in the mills, first flour mills, then later the cotton and duck cloth factories of the Jones Falls Valley. The 400-acre village of Hampden was formed early in the 19th century on ridges above the valley, with workers from the factories living in mill-owned stone and frame housing. By 1900, the agreeable residential neighborhood expanded as vacant lands especially to the east were covered with Baltimore row houses. At its peak, the workers that resided in nearby Hampden made eighty percent of the world's supply of cotton duck cloth.

Little Italy. The neighborhood of Little Italy grew almost by accident. This modest community was built just east of the Pratt Street piers, near the B&O Railroad's President Street Station. The area was settled by successions of German, then Irish, followed by an overflow of Jewish immigrants from the nearby Lombard Street neighborhood. Italians began arriving in the late 19th century, and the district became an all-Italian enclave by the early days of the 20th century. Italians came to Baltimore by train, exiting at nearby President Street Station, where they found St. Leo's Roman Catholic Church nearby and settled into the community.

Roland Park. This was an entirely different sort of Baltimore community, created as a planned enclave nestled into the trees on the north side of Baltimore. The community was organized in 1903 as a residential community with covenants and restricted deeds. Early advertising for Roland Park promised that residents could live in "…a garden suburb, free of city grime and racial diversity." This was clearly-stated discrimination, a neighborhood where Black, foreign, and Jewish persons would not be permitted to purchase property or reside. Large custom-built electrified houses, artesian wells feeding a water system, gas mains, and a nearby six-store shopping center (reportedly the first in the country) marked the community as an upscale place to reside, if you could get in.

Neighborhood life in the early 20th century was convenient. The local grocery was indeed local, within walking distance. The corner grocery was king. Modest sized stores located throughout the city featured self-service and across-the-counter delivery. These groceries were family operated stores, with the family often living above the store. One chain, the J.W. Crook stores, grew to over two hundred convenient, friendly locations in the city and region. In their time, convenience on a first name basis with the grocer was the norm. By the 1950s, these corner groceries would yield to self-service, 25,000-square-foot "supermarkets". Local bakeries dotted the neighborhoods, descended from 19th century German or Jewish operated bakeries. Some became chain operations like Muhly's or Silber's. Others specialized in producing cookies or confections. Some neighborhoods were fortunate enough to have a specialty delivered to their door: Baltimore peach cake from cart vendors, selling slices and sections. And of course, until the health department intervened, milk was sold on neighborhood routes, salespersons travelling the streets and ladling out the quantities requested by housewives. A later descendent of this route salesman network was the door-to-door milkman with his clanking bottles.

JIM CROW BALTIMORE

The decade of 1900 to 1910 was, by any measure, a low point in racial justice, a high point for segregation and the southern sympathizers' flourishing. Fully forty years after America's Civil War, Baltimore's southern roots were very much on display during this period with segregationist leaning Democrats declaring Baltimore a "White Man's City", taking control of City Hall with the 1899 election of Democratic Mayor Thomas Hayes. Hayes was born in Maryland but spent the Civil War years fighting for the Confederacy. He had defeated William Malster, a Republican ship builder and businessman. Much of what was happening in the city was an extension of the culture of slavery, without the slaves. The lives of African American citizens were impacted by multiple laws demonstrating bias, beginning with the banning of interracial marriage. There were "bastardy laws" giving unwed mothers the right to seek support from a child's father, but only if they were White. Black mothers were not accorded the same right. The school board voted more money for Black teachers and Black schools, but the true agenda assured that White teachers never encountered a Black student or parent. Baltimore's large free Black population had few rights, few options, and few places to live.

Many of the attitudes creating this level of abusive discrimination came from the philosophy of the "Lost Cause", a literary and intellectual fiction designed to elevate the Confederacy to her former status. It was an aggressive effort, with books, essays, and conversations proliferating, all espousing the view that "The South" had been wronged. Statues of Confederate heroes were planned or erected, and in the city the Daughters of the Confederacy ccommissioned and erected in 1903 the Confederate Soldiers and Sailors Monument on Mount Royal Avenue.

The Lost Cause detailed the wrongs inflicted on the Confederacy and offered depictions of life in the rebellious states which clearly conflicted with reality. When detailed, the tenets of the Lost Cause offer insight into the mindset of those espousing it. They included:

- Slavery did not cause the war (despite multiple states naming slavery as the reason for seceding from the Union).

- Slavery was and is a benign practice for all involved, both master and slave.

- There was always a natural and undeniable superiority to traditional White Southern society.

- Southern nobility and chivalry were always evident, even in the times of war.

- The North started the war (clearly ignoring the shots fired at Fort Sumter).

- The South is Christian, the North merely materialistic.

This series of fabrications became the justification for racial segregation, discrimination, and violence. Efforts to reverse post-war reconstruction, intimidate Black citizens, and once again impose White supremacy were driven by the Lost Cause philosophy, visibly so in the early 1900s.

The Baltimore City Council codified into law the informal red-lining practice of segregated housing. The so-called "Negro district" of the city had become crowded and untenable for a healthy existence, despite many city progressives unsuccessfully seeking relief for the citizens residing there. When one successful Black lawyer, George McMechen, acted on his own and moved his family into a White neighborhood, he was met by gangs of thugs and neighborhood protests. The City Council responded by passing a restrictive law outlining who could move into which neighborhood, signed by Mayor Mahool in December 1910. Legal appeals caused the law to be rewritten and re-enacted three times over the ensuing months. The protests and appeals continued. In 1916, Mayor James Preston stated the law was "acting admirably in Baltimore". Despite his pronouncement, by 1917 the courts found the Baltimore law unconstitutional. For the Black community, red-lining real estate laws and segregated trains and boats became the new normal. Add to these new measures the longer standing abuses of inadequate schools, disenfranchisement, discrimination in employment, and a handful of murderous lynchings, and it is clear Baltimore's Jim Crow era reflected the majority White public opinion.

UNIQUELY BALTIMORE

For Baltimore in this era, the age of electrification began. Electrical power began to show promise and started to capture the population's interest. Electricity launched along its path to oblivion the age of gas lamps, kerosene lanterns, and candles. Trolley lines had harnessed electric power for some twenty years by mid-decade. Paralleling those power lines, electric streetlights appeared. Factories and businesses began to take a chance on the benefits of a convenient power source. Though expensive, Thomas Edison's light bulbs began to appear in the homes of the wealthy. It would be the 19-teens before demand for electricity became commonplace. Mass electrification would have to wait for convenience and cost to become manageable.

But electricity was becoming more familiar, led in many ways by trolley lines and by electrified amusement parks. Two of the earliest such parks, formed in the late 1890s, were the Electric Park and Gwynn Oak Park. These and other privately-owned parks offered local, outdoor, spacious, and novel recreation to city residents. A park-like setting, illuminated with the new incandescent lighting, provided simple amusement activities, often a ballroom with dancing or entertainment, and picnic grounds for individual and group outings. Gwynn Oak, built along the Gwynn's Falls, offered a carousel and a lake for boating. Newspaper reports promoted the Gwynn Oak as "the great picnic and Sunday school excursion ground of the city" (1909). The Electric Park was located along Belvedere Avenue in the Northwest corner of the city. Served directly by the North Avenue trolley line, the Electric Park offered more entertainment than the relaxing atmosphere of the early years of Gwynn Oak. Opened in 1896, the park added a carousel in 1900, followed by other amusements like a human roulette wheel and two roller coasters. The Casino restaurant, vaudeville acts and even a dirigible launch made Electric Park a busy place.

A notorious park also operated just outside the city limits in the first decade of the century. Jack Flood's Park was in Anne Arundel County, adjacent to the city on waterfront land that was later annexed by the city. It was a wide-open, anything goes location, where the beer flowed freely and the dancing girls were friendly. Flood operated his park with the belief that everyone should have an opportunity to "blow off steam", and they did. Helping with the process were "look the other direction" police and politicians. In an era when beer gardens seemed to be everywhere, Flood's Park went well beyond the norm. Jack Flood was politically well-connected, kept no books, operated on a cash basis, and locked the water fountains so thirsty patrons had to buy their drinks. Under the law at the time, Flood's liquor sales on Sunday were illegal unless the property was a hotel, so Flood obtained a county hotel license for $250, had patrons register as guests at the gate, and legally opened the bar. Flood stated simply, "intoxicating liquor *had never* been sold… to other than bona-fide guests." Temperance Leagues and churches were incensed by the Flood enterprise, demanding its license be revoked, but the wily Flood managed to ensure that evidence of wrongdoing never made it to liquor board hearings. Entertainment at the park included vaudeville names of the era: both Mae West and W.C. Fields are said to have appeared there, among many others. The park's closing hour led to a rush to the last United Railways streetcar departure, formally named "The Owl", but called the "Dirty Shirt" trip by the conductors who operated the cars, with patrons universally drunk and disorderly, willing to pay the fare with keys, collar buttons, penknives, or anything except the one thing they didn't have, the necessary nickel. On board "The Owl" were rival gang members, factions who would turn the trip into a fight-filled ride, with weapons of all sorts in use, but without police intervention on the Anne Arundel County portion of the trip. The county police department had closed at midnight. It was left to the Baltimore City police to sort out the conflict, annoyed at this gang battle they inherited from Flood's Park.

Flood's Park was not the only amusement point just south of the city in Anne Arundel County. In this era of segregation and Jim Crow laws, the African American community had few options for a local holiday excursion. Highland Beach, Sparrow's Beach, even Carr's Beach near Annapolis were options, but George Brown, who had himself endured bias in years past, was determined to provide a first-class experience for the Black community. He established Brown's Grove, located on Rock Creek, a tidal inlet off the Patapsco River, reached by the steamboat *Starlight*, also owned and operated by Brown. The park included a picnic grove, amusement rides like a carousel and roller coaster, a beach and bathhouse, and refreshment stands. Baltimore broadcaster Chuck Richards later recalled, "We boarded the excursion boat Starlight at the foot of Broadway every Sunday morning….in the evening, as dusk came on, we took the excursion boat back, often under the moon, there was a ballroom aboard, and dancing and always a good band." Brown's Grove survived through the next two decades. The park closed upon the death of George Brown in 1935 with a subsequent fire destroying the remaining buildings in 1938.

Designs for public parkland was dominated by the Olmstead firm, the company formally organized in 1865 after Frederick Law Olmstead and his partner Calvert Vaux won the competition for the design of Central Park in New York City. Partnerships and name changes came and went, with the Olmstead banner presiding over the design and construction of over 1,000 parks, among them the Capitol grounds in Washington, D.C., the Biltmore Estate in North Carolina, and in Baltimore, the design or inspiration for local parks such as the modest Latrobe Park in Locust Point to the much larger Carroll, Clifton, and Patterson Parks. For Baltimore's citizenry, city parks were a vital way to gain relief from the crowded, hot, congested city streets. Unlike the private amusement parks of Gwynn Oak, Carlin's, Brown's, or Flood, Baltimore's Olmstead parks followed a master plan developed in 1904 for an interconnected series of parks. The parks were seen as green havens with curving pathways, open vistas, and quiet groves, inviting the populace to enjoy, relax or share recreational facilities.

Vaudeville arrived in Baltimore with the turning of the century. Two theaters, both opened in 1904, would lead the way into this form of light entertainment. The Amusa Theater on East Baltimore Street was among the first, offering among its many acts the headliner, Johnny Jones and His Trained Dogs. The Maryland Theater on Franklin Street was James Kernan's offering to the city's theater, vaudeville, and film center. Kernan was a true Baltimore empresario, beginning after the Civil War with an outdoor summer garden featuring entertainment and refreshment, then graduating to more substantial and permanent efforts, culminating in his "million-dollar enterprise", three properties designed to offer and house entertainment for the masses. Adjacent to his Maryland Theater, Kernan built the upscale Kernan Hotel, featuring a Turkish bath for hotel guests, a 75-foot bar of solid white marble in the basement, and on stage and in the dining room the city's first jazz band. The third part of the "million-dollar enterprise" was the Auditorium Theater, another music and entertainment hall erected just a block to the south. The Auditorium Theater was ultimately renamed the Mayfair, continuing to entertain Baltimoreans until the mid-1980s. James Kernan's Maryland Theater paused its vaudeville programming to offer an early showing of the film *Birth of a Nation* (1915), acknowledged to have inspired a rebirth of the Ku Klux Klan. Perhaps that film had a special appeal to Kernan, who had been a Confederate soldier during the Civil War.

Rivaling the live performances of the vaudeville theaters was a new form of entertainment, motion pictures. Lantern shows, illuminated slides often accompanied by music, had offered exhibitions since the 1850s, but Edison's motion pictures were a modern upgrade. Baltimoreans could watch as people, places, and events were placed into motion on a screen, typically seen in local store front nickelodeons, theaters charging an affordable admission of five cents, a single nickel ($1.50 in 2023 dollars). By 1910, the latest movies could be seen at the Bijou, the Royal Moving Picture Parlor, the Fairyland, the Ideal, the Comic, and the Crescent, altogether no less than forty such venues across the city. Most nickelodeons were simple exhibition spaces, but many offered a larger seating capacity: the Theotorium on North Avenue seated 500, well beyond that of the usual storefront locations like the Dixie on West Baltimore Street (capacity 187) or The Royal on North Monroe, with just 100 seats. Messrs. Pearce and Schneck leased the Y.M.C.A. Hall on Carey Street, making it possible for them to offer patrons three different reels, about 30 minutes of viewing, for the usual five cent admission. Most of the nickelodeons changed shows each week, with the Horn Theater offering new movies that were just ten days old.

Baltimoreans were able to enjoy a quick lunch, with the most well-known of lunchrooms the Baltimore Dairy Lunch, a chain first opened in the 1880s by James Whitcomb and headquartered in Baltimore. Through a series of partnerships, the chain quickly numbered 120 locations, with locations beyond Baltimore from New England through the Mid-Atlantic, and later in southeastern states. The quick lunch concept soon spread to other cities, often as copycat operations: there was a Detroit Lunch located in New York City, and a New York Lunch with a location in Detroit. The lunchrooms were simple affairs, offering a standard menu: perhaps a chicken pie, baked beans with buttered bread, eggs, and oatmeal, each priced at about ten cents. The food was not a mysterious offering from a kitchen but was on display for customer inspection and selection, predating the cafeteria trend that would arrive years later. Seating was basic, a schoolroom style one-armed chair designed by Whitcomb for eating, not lingering. The Dairy Lunch usually had a distinct masculine atmosphere as a place for the working man to eat a quick meal, surrounded by both professional men and laborers. In a 1915 article in *National Magazine*, Whitcomb's Baltimore Lunchrooms are described as locations where sustenance is offered in "bright, clean, airy accommodations… tasteful array of food sold at reasonable prices…(with) the elimination of tipping and tired waiters."

City dwellers always had an interest in sports and sportsmen, among them Baltimorean Joe Gans, an African American lightweight boxer. Gans had worked in unskilled labor typical of the times, often as an oyster shucker, but boxing was his calling. He entered the ring at age 17, boxing in a scientific style (as it was known), studying his opponent, taking advantage of weaknesses, avoiding his strengths, a style very different from the out-and-out brawling fisticuffs of the time. Gans became world champion in 1902, holding that title until 1908 with a career record of 145 wins, and just ten losses, some of which were awarded to his White opponent regardless of the results in the boxing ring. His most famous fight took place in 1906 in the mining town of Goldfield, Nevada. Billed as the Fight of the Century, 8,000 attended the outdoor event, with Gans and Oscar "Battling" Nelson competing for their share of the $30,000 prize ($925,000 in 2023 dollars). Gans fought Nelson for forty-two rounds, ultimately winning but nonetheless taking home the smaller portion of the purse, $10,000. His White opponent, who had lost due to disqualification for personal fouls, took home twice as much. On his return to Baltimore, Gans bought a hotel on East Lexington Street, renaming it the Goldfield Hotel. At its opening in October 1907, he hired the services of a Baltimore piano player to entertain the crowds in attendance, a young Eubie Blake.

The Baltimore Orioles had been a championship caliber team though the late 1890s, dominating the National League. But at the end of the 1900 season, the league decided to reduce its number from twelve teams to eight. The Orioles were one of the teams that had lost their place in the now smaller National League. Good fortune and timing seemed to shine upon them as a new upstart league, the American League, had been created and the Orioles became one of their charter teams. The 1901 season saw them place fifth in the league, winning slightly more games than they lost, led by players such as pitchers Crazy Schmidt and Joe McGinnity, and in this era of dual roles, infielders John McGraw who was also the manager, and Jack Dunn, team owner. The 1902 season did not go as well with Mc Graw's form of aggressive play catching the critical eye of league officials. McGraw was suspended first temporarily, then permanently. He took off for the New York Giants. With the team deep in debt, the owner sold the Orioles to two National League team owners, whose teams began poaching some key Orioles players. Ultimately the Orioles were forced to forfeit a game as they had too few players to field a team. Such chaos could not continue, and after the 1902 season, the entire team was sold and moved to New York. The Baltimore Orioles became the New York Yankees.

This first decade of the 20th century saw many changes to the city, not the least of which was the Great Baltimore Fire with its cityscape modifying effects. With challenges yet to be met, the growth of businesses in this business-friendly city, response to a European war, and the prosperity that few doubted was on its way, a good decade would be followed by a great one. The great flow of immigrants to and through the city would surely continue, offering a labor force adequate to support the growth the city had been enjoying. One by one, those expectations became challenges for the years ahead, challenges that would need solutions. Most would be faced and some would be solved in the next decade, the 19-teens.

CHAPTER TWO:
CHANGING TIMES

The 19-Teens

To Baltimoreans, the momentum of growth, improvements, thriving businesses, and dominating industries in the first decade of the 20th century was surely a predictor to the future, the decade of the 19-teens. The amazing rebuild of the city in the aftermath of the Great Baltimore Fire (1904), was a miracle of these modern times. Optimism prevailed. Democrat James Preston had become mayor and would remain so for virtually the entire decade (1911-1919). Preston, supported by the Democratic Party establishment, was conservative, but his specialty seemed to be in remaking the city with transformative, lasting public works: a north-south throughway, The Fallsway; a waterside connector, the Key Highway; a new link to the southern reaches of the city, the Hanover Street Bridge; and other civic projects planned and built in the decade. Baltimoreans would soon see bigger changes, however, beyond those taking place in the growing infrastructure. The decade would bring a war and an epidemic, changing lives, changing Baltimore. It would become a decade to be endured.

CHANGE IN THE AIR

Women's Suffrage. This was the decade when the cause of women's voting rights, which began at Seneca Falls, New York, in 1848, marked 70 years of petitioning, requesting, demanding, and insisting women be granted the right to vote. Six western states, beginning with the territory of Wyoming in 1869, had taken action to grant suffrage to women, but the need was for a national standard. The movement began to see real progress when Woodrow Wilson, who had opposed suffrage in 1912, changed his stance before the election of 1916, advocating for granting the vote to women. This was a time that many had awaited, as a U. S. Constitutional amendment granting women the right to vote seemed more possible than ever. Baltimorean Mary Elizabeth Garrett, daughter of John W. Garrett, president of the B&O Railroad, was a philanthropist and a suffragist. She had secured the right of women to enter medical school by completing the funding for the new Johns Hopkins Hospital. It was her effort and financial support that opened Baltimore's female college preparatory school, Bryn Mawr. She took an active interest in the women's suffrage movement with other suffragists, including Susan B. Anthony and Julia Ward Howe, convening at her Mt. Vernon Place home to discuss strategy. Garrett donated as much as $20,000 per year to the movement ($600,000 in 2023 dollars) and was an active participant in a 1912 Baltimore Suffrage Parade, conducted during the presidential nominating convention in Baltimore. The cause of women's suffrage would be successful at the end of the decade, though Garrett would not live to see that victory as she died in 1915, a victim of leukemia.

Prohibition. The alcohol abstinence movement had reached maturity in this decade of the 19-teens. Banning the consumption of alcohol had been the dream of many since the 1830s. Their perseverance was paying off, as individual states began banning alcohol consumption and a pending U.S. Constitutional amendment that would make the ban national policy was proceeding toward ratification. The Sage of Baltimore, Henry L. Mencken, wrote in *The Baltimore Sun* repeatedly of his opposition to prohibition, in forty-two columns and countless editorials. His opposition came to naught, as the 18th Amendment became the law of the land January 16, 1919. Baltimore began to close its distilleries, its breweries, and its taverns; thousands of Baltimoreans working in those businesses lost their jobs. But alcohol would not be denied, and so an unintended consequence of prohibition soon arose with the creation of speakeasies, closed door clubs where a password allowed entry, opening to quench the demand for drink. Citizens imbibed more than ever, and local arrests for drunkenness went up, perhaps because people were drawn to indulging in the forbidden.

Neutrality. In Europe, the continent had become a tinderbox of alliances between nations with those alliances creating obligations to come to the aid of one another in the event of an adversary's aggression. Across the continent, mutual distrust existed disguised with a superficial politeness between the leaders, many of whom were related to one another through their connection to Britain's late Queen Victoria. An armaments race between adversaries had been underway since about 1898, especially in naval weaponry and battleships. With the launch of a new, more powerful battleship design, the HMS Dreadnaught (1906), Britain had raised the stakes. America was officially a non-combatant neutral, but circumstances and belligerent actions were slowly drawing neutral America into the conflict. In Baltimore, about 20 percent of the population was of German ancestry who generally looked with favor on their German homeland, but public opinion began to change when slow-to-arrive reports of German atrocities in Belgium surfaced: the city of Dinant had been burned after 674 of its civilians were massacred. The day would soon come when those of German ancestry would have to decide: were they Germans living in America or were they Americans?

POLITICAL THEATRE

In advance of the presidential election of 1912, the political parties convened their nominating conventions. The Democratic Party gathered its 1,100 delegates at Baltimore in the recently built (1901) 5th Regiment Armory. The convention was a traditional nominating event, with multiple candidates vying for the nomination, backroom negotiations seeking support, and the result hanging in the balance. Each nominee's supporters gathered at his headquarters hotel, with Governor Wilson holding forth at the city's newest hotel, the Emerson, while nominee Governor of Ohio Judson Harmon had the misfortune to select as his headquarters Baltimore's oldest hotel, the five-story Eutaw House. The Eutaw burned down just before the convention convened. In the convention hall, delegates shifted from nominee to nominee, some of them changing allegiance in accordance with the direction of a "king maker", delegate William Jennings Bryan. Bryan, the Democratic nominee in 1896, 1900, and 1908, had visions of winning the nomination once again, anticipating a complete voting deadlock. Bryan undid his chances at a deadlock when after the ninth ballot he changed his vote from Clark to Wilson. At the convention's outset Champ Clark of Missouri, Speaker of the U.S. House of Representatives, had been favored for the nomination, but Bryan's move undermined that possibility. Clark needed two-thirds of the delegates to be nominated. Bryan's shift, followed by other delegates, made the two-thirds for nomination beyond his reach. Governor Woodrow Wilson of New Jersey was nominated on the forty-sixth ballot.

Perhaps the greatest theatrical aspect of the Democratic convention was a parade in support of women's suffrage that wound through downtown Baltimore then headed north to the convention. The parade organizers petitioned for permission to end the parade inside the Armory, which was denied, to no one's surprise. Twenty thousand Baltimoreans watched the mile long procession led by Ida Neepier, costumed as Joan of Arc and riding astride a white stallion, a heroine triumphant, inspiring, pure, and righteous. That Joan was also tortured and executed seemed to be of no consequence. Among the parade's floats, there was one for motherhood, another for Margaret Brent, said to be the first woman who had demanded the vote in the 1640s. There were bands and marching units accompanied by six horse-drawn chariots, each one representing one of the western states that had already granted women the right to vote. The opinion of the conventioneers toward women's suffrage was not altered, nor was the position of the nominee, Woodrow Wilson. Women's suffrage was not supported in the 1912 party platform.

INDUSTRY AND COMMERCE

At the beginning of the decade, Baltimore's population of about 550,000 made it the 7th largest city in the country. It had become a manufacturing center as well as a transportation hub. A steel mill on the city's east side at Sparrow's Point had grown to be an employer of thousands. In addition, Baltimoreans worked refining oil, transporting it, or selling its products through both Standard and American Oil stations. Metalworking in many forms used copper and iron in local foundry and smelting operations. Noxzema was formulated locally to address sunburn and Isaac Emerson's workers made Bromo Seltzer to alleviate headaches in a downtown factory. Frank Schenuit began making automobile tires in 1912 in the Jones Falls Valley, a new neighbor to textile mills that had started in earlier decades and the monopolized canvas production for decades. Dwarfing each of these, however, was the city's garment trade, producing men's suits, shirts, shoes, down to BVD under garments. Twenty-seven thousand Baltimoreans worked in the city's needle trades, including umbrella manufacturing and the manufacture of straw hats.

The city had become an important railroad center, offering service for both freight and passengers. The home-town Baltimore and Ohio Railroad (B&O) had been joined by the Pennsylvania and smaller lines such as the Western Maryland and the Maryland and Pennsylvania. The B&O's Mount Clare shops built and repaired locomotives and rolling stock, employing over 3,000 by decade's end. Steel rails, from steel made at Sparrow's Point, radiated outward from the city to many points of the compass. Local warehouses like those of the Terminal Corporation, first owned by the Pennsylvania Railroad, then later sold to and operated by independent proprietors, bulged with raw materials and finished goods. Wagons and in time trucks gathered freight from across the city, transporting it to railroad warehouses where it was sorted and consolidated by destination, then loaded into outbound freight cars. The railroads seemed to have not a hint of the competition from the trucks that would appear in the future, not surprisingly given the lack of reliability of early trucks and the sad condition of the roads. Passenger rail stations were spread across the city for the Baltimore and Ohio and the Pennsylvania Railroads, plus one or more for each of the other lines, including a unique interurban facility in downtown that offered hourly service to both Annapolis and Washington, D.C. Eight stations and terminals were spread across the center city, from one on Calvert Street to the venerable President Street Station, from an Oak (later Howard) Street station near North Avenue to two of the stations operated by the B&O, one at each end of the Howard Street Tunnel. These and more formed a network of terminus points and enroute stations carrying both passengers and freight for passenger transportation and shipment of goods to virtually every corner of the state and nation.

Automobile manufacturing had become the next logical step for many carriage and wagon makers in the early years of the 20th century. Horses pulling wagons, carriages, and buggies were fading as gasoline powered vehicles became the transport of choice. Automobiles were being made in Baltimore by custom shops building a few vehicles at a time. Their process was slow and cumbersome, the products they produced expensive. By 1910, some makers had already been bankrupted, finding profitability elusive. Sinclair Scott, a canning equipment maker, had tried with their Maryland touring car. The Lord Baltimore Motor Car Company, 1910-1915, briefly built runabout models and trucks. For the vehicles on the streets of the city, in 1906 speed limits were raised to twelve miles per hour. Not everyone seemed to obey the limits as by 1919, some 13,000 drivers, almost all of them male, were cited and appeared in traffic court. By 1920, twenty-two automobile dealerships lined Mount Royal Avenue, with another twenty-eight spread elsewhere across the city. One company that endured for multiple years was Carl Spoerer's Sons Company on South Carey Street. Local manufacturing was phased out as customers opted for a lower cost, mass-produced option. The mass-produced vehicle of choice was Henry Ford's Model T, and as Ford's option became available nationwide, Baltimore's custom automobile shops faded away. The Spoerer's and Sons Company was an exception, remaining in business into the 1930s, offering automotive parts, supplies, and repairs.

If local automobile building was a cottage industry with a precarious future, ship building was the complete opposite. Shipbuilding was a long-standing Baltimore manufacturing strength and with few exceptions, a continuing source of local employment. At the foot of Federal Hill, along the north and east faces, most of the way east to Fort McHenry, ship builders and allied businesses lined the newly constructed Key Highway. Successive generations of local shipbuilders had maintained construction expertise that began with ships of wood, then iron, and finally steel. The early ships they built were powered by sail, which then became steam powered, with an odd, decades-long transition period when both were employed. Baltimore shipbuilders had designed new ships, with the Baltimore Clipper an early one; survived the hardship years of the Civil War; and saw, by the 20th century, dozens of yards consolidate into a mere handful. In southeast Baltimore County, a shipyard at the Sparrow's Point steel mill had been open since the late 1880s. The yard had been building tugs, barges, even dredges destined for the Panama Canal construction. By the 19-teens, cargo, passenger, and tanker ships were constructed, with tanker ships became something of a Sparrow's Point specialty. The first large tanker built at Sparrow's Point was the *James McGee*, built for Standard Oil, sliding down the ways into the Patapsco River, May 29, 1917.

Close to the center city, a long dominant shipbuilding operation was at the foot of Federal Hill, the Skinner Shipyard. Harry Skinner took the risk of purchasing a nearby large yard founded by former mayor William Malster, the Columbian Yard. Despite its long and continuing history, the business of ship building was precarious, as business rose and fell with the fortunes of the economy. Shipbuilding would boom in the good times, when many ships were ordered and built, while during subsequent harder times, orders would virtually come to a halt, and the shipyards barely survived with the few orders that did arrive, offering ship repairs just to maintain the yard and its workforce. Skinner had that experience at times in the past, and had endured prior recessionary times, but in this decade his over-extended business went into receivership. The yard passed through several hands late in the 19-teens before it was ultimately bought by the Bethlehem Steel Company and its Shipbuilding Division in 1921.

The expanding Bethlehem Steel Company saw the Maryland Steel Company steel mill at Sparrow's Point as an attractive property for purchase. Bethlehem Steel bought the entire operation in 1916. This was a mill with huge expansion possibilities on surrounding vacant lands using ore imported along the salt waters of the Patapsco River. The mill had begun producing steel in the late 1880s, initially under the name of its parent, the Pennsylvania Steel Company, owned in large part by the Pennsylvania Railroad. The mill, including an adjacent shipyard, was later renamed the Maryland Steel Company: same ownership, new name. In his introductory comments to the Baltimore business community, Charles Schwab, president of Bethlehem Steel, said he envisioned creating at Sparrow's Point the largest steel mill in the world. The newly purchased mill was immediately busy with war time orders for steel, armaments, and ships, becoming, it was said at the time, the American equivalent to the arms supplier to Germany, the "The Krupps of America." Schwab announced in that same speech a $50 million company investment ($850,000,000 in 2023 dollars) to increase the size and capacity of the plant. Thousands of workers made steel and built ships, living in the company town of Sparrow's Point or commuting on a Number 26 trolley, known as the Red Rocket, from Baltimore to the mill. Schwab finessed an arrangement prior to America's entry into the war, skirting neutrality laws to build British submarines in Canada using steel made at Sparrow's Point. Business was good, steel was the basic building block of America, and Schwab, living the high life, turned over the administration of the company to Eugene Grace, a Bethlehem Steel "lifer" who began his company career as a crane operator after graduating atop his class and as Lehigh University's class of 1899 valedictorian. Grace would remain in place for over fifty years as president, then Chairman of the Board. His was an insider's point of view, with a belief that the company could best function on its own with little or no outside input into company processes, neither the changing marketplace nor evolving employee management tools. This approach would be adequate, until it wasn't, as the post-World War Two world would catch Bethlehem and Grace unaware of the risk of ignoring change. Charles Schwab spent his time in this period, when not acting in his federally appointed position as the Director General of the Emergency Fleet Corporation, overseeing World War One ship building and utilization of the nation's merchant fleet in any of several locations: at a central Pennsylvania estate near his birthplace, at his New York mansion covering an entire Manhattan city block, or at least annually, at the tables in the sophisticated gambling center of Monte Carlo.

Bethlehem Steel watched the orders for war materials pour in. The company began to add workers, reaching 7,000 employees in the decade. These jobs paid well, the work was hard and there were but two shifts, day or night, with correspondingly long hours. Only a year after the plant was purchased, Schwab's promise of expansion was well under way. Among the changes, twelve new hot steel rolling mills were constructed. But the downside of this growth was the worker casualty rate: the work was dangerous. Hot iron or steel poured as liquid, carbon monoxide by-products, chemicals, hazardous wastes, cranes overhead, and so much more put workers at risk, every hour of every day. Industrial safety had become a subject of concern. Maryland had already created the nation's first worker compensation laws (1902), a subsistence payment to injured or incapacitated employees without regard to fault, thus putting a price, however modest, on worker injury. Estimates of worker casualties are limited, as recordkeeping in those early years was limited, but the company did keep a special streetcar ready for moving deceased workers to the morgue. One estimate by Mark Aldrich, a former economist at the Occupational Safety and Health Administration (O.S.H.A.) was that for a mill similar in size and operation in this period, 1,200 workers were injured or killed every year. As one writer commented in a magazine exposé of the dangers in a steel mill, "Steel is war".

A modest Baltimore oil refinery had been built along Boston Street adjacent to the harbor at the time of the Civil War, a well-positioned site for ships to deliver crude oil and export refined products. Baltimore expanded its position as an oil industry center when Standard Oil extended an oil pipeline to the Baltimore area in the 1880s. Oil arrived by pipeline and ship, often from Mexico, with the refinery handling all types of petroleum products, from gasoline to asphalt. Standard Oil opened the decade by controlling 64 percent of the petroleum business in the country but in 1911, was found in violation of anti-trust laws, leading to a break-up of the company into the "seven sisters", separate competing oil companies that shared the same origins. The Baltimore operation's parent was the original Standard Oil of New Jersey. In 1922, Standard Oil completed construction of a regional headquarters building in downtown Baltimore to oversee the company's Mid-Atlantic distribution and retail operations as well as the operations of the Boston Street refinery.

If Standard Oil was a giant oil company, Louis Blaustein began as very much the opposite, an immigrant peddler who edged his way into the oil business, who would ultimately stand alongside the giant company. His success story began when he noticed kerosene leaking from a retailer's wooden barrel. Recognizing the need for a better storage and sales system, he bought a metal tank wagon, filled it with kerosene, installed a spigot, and began selling the product to local retailers. When the automobile began making its presence felt, Blaustein switched to gasoline distribution. Louis' son Jacob formulated a "high test" gasoline by adding benzene to the gasoline, then naming it Amoco gasoline so customers could ask for it by brand name. The company soon incorporated as the American Oil Company. For modern distribution of the Amoco brand, a chain of 53 Lord Baltimore gasoline filling stations was built in Baltimore, with a comparable number in the Washington, D.C., area. The company had successfully carved out a local niche in the gasoline business.

The Port of Baltimore was the reason there was a Baltimore since before its official founding in 1729. As the city's economic engine, the port was looking forward to making a major positive impact in the anticipated upcoming decade. The Patapsco River's natural harbor welcomed hundreds of ships annually, as a wealth of products flowed to, through, and from the port, including coal, wheat, lumber, coffee, guano (for fertilizer), pineapple, and perhaps most critical to the city's growth, shiploads of immigrants, destined to be Baltimore's future labor force. Finished goods made in Baltimore were exported to and beyond domestic ports, to the West Indies, South America, and Europe. The city and the port anticipated new routes, new clients, new products from the west coast of South America. The Panama Canal would soon open, and Baltimore was in a direct sailing line southward to new countries and ports of call, ports that prior to the opening of the canal were far too distant for viable trade. Fate intervened. Though prosperity did arrive, it came from a place very different than expected and for an entirely different reason. A European war was starting, and all attention and trade was on the Atlantic, as all eyes were on Europe.

The Port of Baltimore became a major export center for the warring European countries. The Great War was underway. The Port shipped the materials of war to the limit of neutrality laws, providing sustenance but not weapons, even shipping steel with which others might make the weapons of war. As the war raged, civilians as well as armies found food scarce, with America through the Port of Baltimore becoming the provisioner for the people of Western Europe. Early in the hostilities, the first of 7,000 horses left the Port of Baltimore to supply motive power for artillery, supply wagons, and even perhaps mounts for senior officers. The first shipment, seven hundred equines, headed to the battlefields of France, where they were sure to meet their destiny. A local manufacturer, The Bartlett Hayward Company, had opened several plants in the Baltimore area to make artillery shells and ammunition, and they would all be loaded and shipped from the port. Virtually every product of Baltimore manufacturing found its way aboard a ship and on its way to the war zone: duck cloth for tents, backpacks and tarps; soldiers' uniforms made in Baltimore garment factories. Wheat, long a significant Baltimore export, left in massive quantities to help feed combatants and impacted citizens, after agricultural lands in Europe had become battlefields. The goods were bought through the availability of American bank loans, nationally as much as $10,000 per day ($300,000 in 2023 dollars), once the neutrality bans on financial transactions were lifted. Goods short of weaponry were made, then shipped, the perilous fate of the transporting ships left to the actions of war, subject once at sea to enemy ships, sabotage, and submarines.

From Baltimore and other ports massive amounts of coal were sent to Europe. Coal, the primary source of power, energy, heat, even fire for cooking, came to Baltimore after being mined in the mountains to the west, where it was loaded onto the Western Maryland or the B & O Railroad, then onto ships in the Baltimore harbor to be sent across the Atlantic. That the coal being shipped would create shortages at home was not recognized until the hard winter of 1917 arrived. Baltimore had two extremely harsh winters in the decade of the 19-teens, and with the first in 1912 that froze the Chesapeake Bay, the domestic coal supply remained adequate, as the European war had not yet begun. When a second bitter cold snap occurred in January-February 1917, there were far more serious repercussions as war-time exports had cut domestic supplies. Baltimoreans found coal hard to obtain and expensive when available. The lack of an adequate coal supply impacted the power company's ability to make electricity, resulting in further power shortages. Heating and cooking were constrained, as stoves and furnaces lacked the coal, the new electric stoves were often idled by power interruptions, and coal-hungry furnaces were fed more sparingly. Still, the coal shipments to Europe continued.

One ship among many made dramatic history: in March 1913, the steamer *Alum Chine* was being loaded near Fort Carroll, in mid-harbor, with 350 tons of dynamite destined for the Panama Canal construction site. The loading was behind schedule and in haste, a worker struck a case of dynamite caps with his bale hook, setting off a single cap and igniting a fire. Stevedores who saw and understood the risk began abandoning ship, but many of their workmates were unaware of the danger. Three explosions soon followed, the third disintegrating the *Alum Chine*, killing thirty-three, injuring sixty more. Just before the explosion, *Alum Chine* steward John Forrest jumped overboard, to be picked up by the U.S. Navy collier *Jerome*, itself damaged in the explosion. From on-board, Forrest saw the result of the blast and was later quoted saying that once the rain of debris had stopped falling, "there was simply nothing where the ship had been, but from her position a white-crested wave as big as a mountain was coming at us". The *Alum Chine* had been positioned for safety during loading in mid-harbor, but the blast was so intense that the debris was spread over a two-mile radius, with some of those on land thinking an earthquake had occurred. Windows were shattered miles away, doors were blown off hinges, and the explosive concussion was felt a hundred miles away in Atlantic City, New Jersey.

BALTIMORE CHANGING

The 19-teens became a decade of growth for Baltimore and its citizens. Baltimore grew vertically: Maryland Casualty Company built a skyscraper, as did the Emerson Drug Company. The Tower Building and the Bromo Seltzer Tower added to the skyline. In 1916, the Consolidated Gas, Electric Light and Power Company, the result of a 1906 merger of multiple utility providers, constructed its 21-story headquarters building on Lexington Street in central Baltimore.

Baltimore also grew horizontally, as the city's boundaries were expanded in 1918. A much-needed new rail station was added, built originally as a Union Station then renamed the Pennsylvania Station a decade later. These and more remade the city, but the most significant changes were amongst the people themselves. There were many prominent persons and personalities making their unique contributions to the fabric of the city in the 19-teens. With too many to mention them all, these are just eight of interest:

- Budding ragtime pianist, Eubie Blake was the son of a Baltimore longshoreman. Blake began his musical career at the Goldfield Hotel, owned by boxer Joe Gans. As his popularity grew, he and partner Noble Sissle were "discovered", subsequently moving to New York as their careers took off.

- A visitor of some repute, evangelist Billy Sunday came to town in 1916, with his usual temporary wooden tabernacle erected along Greenmount Avenue, with streetcar service at the door. In his spellbinding speaking style, he preached to one million Baltimoreans during his two months in residence.

- James Kernan was an impresario, hosting major acts and stars at his Maryland Theater attached to the Kernan Hotel, a part of his "million-dollar enterprise" along with the nearby Academy Theater. His donations and legacy to a children's hospital led to the facility named after him: the Kernan Hospital. The hospital later became part of the University of Maryland Hospital System.

- The African American men's business community opened the Arch Social Club, a place where business could be conducted and friendships made. This fraternal and business organization added opportunities as well as cohesiveness for the minority community.

- Etta and Clarabell Cone had been collecting art for well over a decade on their European adventures. They bought what they liked, and what they liked became highly collectible. Their home was a showcase for their purchases, which later were donated to become the foundation of the Baltimore Museum of Art.

- Isaac Emerson started a personal building binge in 1911, first the Emerson Hotel, then in 1912 constructing his Emerson Drug Company headquarters and Bromo-Seltzer factory. In the same year, he built the Emersonian Apartments, blocking the lake view from the 1895 Emersonian Mansions, the home of his recently divorced wife.

- George Herman Ruth was a discovery of Jack Dunn, owner of the minor league Baltimore Orioles. Dunn frequently recruited younger, less expensive players, with George Ruth one of them. On meeting the nineteen-year-old Ruth, his team-mates began calling him "Jack's latest babe". The nickname stuck: he was forever Babe Ruth.

In 1918, the city had nearly tripled in size, from 30 square miles to almost 90. Most of the land annexed came from Baltimore County, a jurisdiction largely dominated by rural interests. That rural dominance created a sense in the suburban districts that they were not receiving the government services and assistance to which they were entitled, which in turn led them to petition for annexation to the more responsive city. A great deal of political maneuvering, rewriting of legislation, and interpretation by groups such as the Greater Baltimore League accompanied this controversial annexation. Some wanted the city services; others were opposed to the costs associated with those services. Tax incentives were offered to affected residents. Politicians offered to trade votes. The longstanding majority of the Democratic Party in government was even weakened as the issues sharply divided the delegates. In the end, annexation was completed, but nearly everyone agreed that the era of annexation in Maryland had come to an end, later formalized in 1948 by an amendment to the Maryland Constitution.

Always up for a celebration, Baltimore would not be denied a chance to celebrate the centennial of the writing of "The Star-Spangled Banner". Plans were drawn for a seven-day Centennial Celebration to be held in early September 1914, one hundred years after Francis Scott Key wrote the words destined to become the official National Anthem in 1931. Key, a prisoner aboard a British warship, witnessed the bombardment of Baltimore. Upon learning the morning after ("…by dawn's early light") that the defenders at Fort McHenry had withstood the attack, Key penned a poem celebrating the American victory on September 14, 1814. In recognition of those events, Baltimore planned a seven-day celebratory event, promoted nationwide by city officials, including a multi-city tour to meet with local officials and encourage delegations from cities such as Cleveland, Detroit, Louisville, and Birmingham. Promises of support and attendance from veterans and patriotic groups were received while local schoolteachers were urged to offer educational studies about the war and Baltimore's important role in it. Students would later be called upon to participate in a "living flag", donning red, white, or blue costumes that with strategic placement of each student would result in a "flag", complete with the fifteen stars of the era, when seen from above. The seven-day event featured a theme for each day, beginning with a Patriot's Day in Druid Hill Park where a combined choir of 5,000 voices performed. The following day, Industrial Day, marked the arrival of the ship *Constellation* and a parade of industrial workers from across the city. The more low-key Francis Scott Key and Fraternal Order days followed, with a Municipal Day featuring multiple parades. Army-Navy day included major military parades through the city, followed by Star Spangled Banner Day on Saturday, September 12 when warships docked in the Patapsco opened to visitors, a statue was dedicated to 1814 Fort McHenry Commander General George Armistead, followed by one final parade led by officials from every state. Closing the celebration in the evening were a water carnival and fireworks.

Baltimore decked the halls with flags and bunting, put the Civil War frigate *Constellation* on display, conducted these many concerts and parades, and placed for the first time a buoy marking the point in the harbor where the British ship with Key aboard stood during the bombardment of Fort McHenry. The patriotically painted, red, white, and blue buoy of the Anthem celebration began a tradition that continues. The grounds of Fort McHenry, long a property of the Federal Government, were to become a city owned park at the conclusion of the celebration. Frederick Law Olmstead developed the plan for the new parkland. Thomas Edison produced a film, *The Birth of the Star Spangled Banner*, for the 100th Anniversary, one of many such productions from the Edison Company. Francis Scott Key is portrayed in the film as he sings the anthem, which had been set to music on September 17 by his brother-in-law (the tune: "To Anacreon in Heaven", a song commissioned by a British gentlemen's amateur singing society of the 19th century.)

"A WHITE MAN'S CITY"

An election slogan of 1899, "A White Man's City" reflected a stark reality: Baltimore had a long history of segregation, both by custom and law. Housing was restricted by race, with White citizens on one side of an invisible but very real line, Black on the other. White Baltimoreans were not ready for emancipated slaves and their descendants to be fully freed: the former and formal bonds of slavery had been exchanged for Jim Crow laws, disenfranchisement, and threats of violence. *The Birth of a Nation*, described as the most reprehensible racist film ever produced by Hollywood, played to packed houses in Baltimore. From its first showing and through the following seven weeks, it set records for longevity and house receipts. *The Baltimore Afro-American* newspaper reported that the shouts of hatred heard during the film did not cease on its conclusion but continued into the streets outside Ford's Theater.

The Black community sought relief from discrimination and violence in multiple ways, most often through court proceedings. These met with mixed results, at best. Years of efforts by Black leaders had fallen on the largely deaf ears of White politicians. The city had moved in a regressive direction legalizing racially segregated housing, when outraged neighbors petitioned for a prohibition of integration after Black attorney George McMechen moved into a White community. The Baltimore City Council responded with a 1910 law that codified the residential racial division, limiting any possible future inter-racial communities. The law had to be rewritten multiple times to avoid court-imposed limitations, passed by the Council each time, until in 1917, the law was ultimately found to be unconstitutional. The end of the law was not the end to segregation, however, and segregation continued to be the reality in real estate practices. Real estate agencies, banks, and homeowners themselves created an informal conspiracy to prevent Black Baltimoreans from moving out of overcrowded districts into more spacious, healthier environments with better services.

By the time Baltimore's segregation law of 1910 was declared unconstitutional in 1917, deed restrictions had come into use. The Roland Park Company in 1912 added to property documents a section on "nuisances", prohibiting any tract or building in the community "to be occupied by any negro or person of negro extraction." Inequity in housing was deeply entrenched, and worsened over time, with Black districts overcrowded and city services minimized. It was in those overcrowded districts that unhealthy conditions allowed illness and disease to flourish, which led White leaders to justify "for health reason" continuing policies of "slum clearance". Baltimore Mayor James Preston was a strong advocate of the 1910 segregation law, but when barred from a direct approach, he created a slum clearance program for the city. He would convert the "worst infected blocks" into parks. Translated, this meant to clear away African American housing and businesses from anyplace an African American community was seen as undesirable to White citizens. By 1919, the first of these clearance projects was complete as "Preston's Folly", as it was called, replaced a Black community with St. Paul Street's Preston Gardens.

For every step forward in racial justice, there seemed to be another step, but in reverse. Often those steps were quite unequal, always with a bias toward segregation. The National Association for the Advancement of Colored People (N.A.A.C.P.), established a Baltimore chapter in 1912. The following year, President Woodrow Wilson, no friend of equality, re-segregated the federal workforce. The women's suffrage movement was gaining ground as a national movement by seeking ratification of the 19th amendment. To gain sympathy and votes from the south, the movement slowly backed away from any support of Black women. By 1912, it was apparent that White women were prepared to deny suffrage to Black women in order to gather votes for suffrage from racist legislators.

At the end of the decade of the 19-teens, the Lost Cause movement, an unapologetic rewriting of history, had installed in Baltimore several monuments and statues that offered a southern interpretation of the Civil War. The Lost Cause movement offered a justification of secession including the fantasy that slavery was of a benign nature. Accompanying this thinking, by the end of the decade there came a very visible national rebirth (1915) and in Maryland (1918) of the "Invisible Empire", the Ku Klux Klan. The K.K.K. had a history of violence and intimidation against Blacks, but in this new iteration the Klan also opposed immigrants, Jews, and Catholics. In the next decade it would add bootleggers to its hate list. Segments of the city's population were pre-disposed to support both the Lost Cause and the Ku Klux Klan. Just outside Baltimore, in 1911 King Johnson, a Black man accused of the murder of a White man, was pulled from his Brooklyn, Anne Arundel County jail cell and killed by an angry mob: a lynching with all but the rope.

WAR COMES TO AMERICA

By 1914, alliances and armaments had placed European countries on the brink of war. A dozen countries had, as it was said, "sleepwalked their way into a war", a war that no one wanted. Alliances had been drawn, an assassination ignited an uncontrollable fuse, a domino effect drew more adversaries into war until all of Europe was at arms. Even non-combatants became involved as their countries were the battlefields upon which battles were conducted. Isolationist America was resistant to direct involvement in the war, but less resistant to the profitability of supplying the materials of war to the combatants. While termed a "World War" (the "Great War" until 1940), with adversaries coming from across the world, most of the action in Baltimore's interest took place in Europe.

Baltimore had multiple connections both financial and ethnic to Europe, particularly to Germany, with about 20 percent of Baltimoreans with direct or generational ties to Germany. German was spoken fluently by one-fifth of the population, thirty churches offered German-language services, and public-schools offered German language courses. These multiple German connections created an atmosphere of suspicion among non-Germans, leading to the creation of the Baltimore Division of the American Protective League (A.P.L.), a government-authorized volunteer group that "investigated" perceived disloyalty. Though federally authorized as a nationwide organization, this was effectively a vigilante group that blossomed fully upon the entry of America into the war. Badge-carrying members conducted searches; detained individuals; or investigated perceived Bolshevists, German sympathizers, violators of rationing or hoarding regulations, and others they called "slackers" for avoiding the military draft. Some 2,500 Baltimore volunteers joined the A.P.L. and initiated hundreds of local investigations, including at least one complaint directed at ever-controversial journalist Henry Mencken. In these times, neighbors were examining and testing the loyalty of their neighbors with the full support and sponsorship of the Federal Department of Justice.

The Albert Schumacher Company was a Baltimore shipping agent with its origins in Bremen, Germany. Schumacher had come to Baltimore in 1828 and began a business shipping tobacco from Baltimore, and later becoming a member of the board of directors of the B&O Railroad. With both his Bremen and B&O connection, Schumacher and B&O President John W. Garrett were responsible for the establishment of the North German Lloyd Steamship

Company's direct service from Germany to Baltimore. Baltimore was a desirable immigration port and the new service, established in 1868, allowed thousands of central European immigrants to arrive in Baltimore by ship, passing into the city, or boarding waiting pier-side passenger cars of the B&O to move onward to points west. By the 19-teens, the Schumacher company operated from a headquarters building at Charles and German Streets, the Hansa Haus (1911), representing the local interests of the North German Lloyd. The company headquarters at Hansa Haus was more than a shipping agency, as it housed offices of the German Consul. The offices and building became a meeting point, a place where North German Lloyd passengers and other German citizens could visit to meet, converse, and enjoy the comfort of a familiar German community.

At the end of July 1914, with the great European war underway, almost ninety years of seaborne immigration to Baltimore ended. Prior to the outbreak of war, a steady stream of European immigrants had arrived first by sailing ships, then on commercially operated steamships, the vessels of the North German Lloyd Line among them. At the war's outset, the Lloyd Line ships were placed at the disposal of the German Navy, making North German Lloyd a combatant and therefore subject to attack or seizure. With the risk of internment combined with the unpredictability of German U-Boat attacks in the Atlantic, the massive movement of immigrants to Baltimore came to a halt. By 1917, North German Lloyd had watched its ships and facilities confiscated world-wide. The Baltimore immigration piers in Locust Point it had used were burned, almost assuredly an act of anti-German arson. At war's end, the entirety of the North German Lloyd fleet was confiscated by the Allies, bringing to a definitive end the era of immigration to Baltimore by sea.

Germany was acutely aware of the impact in America of its wartime activity. American public opinion early in the war was largely isolationist, with the German government reluctant to risk yielding what they perceived as a wartime advantage. German actions that antagonized the Americans were to be avoided, leading to restrictions imposed by the German Kaiser on German submarine attacks, as submarine commanders were subjected to an ever-changing set of the rules of engagement. For Germany this was a war of more than bullets and torpedoes, it was also a war of image and information. Germany bolstered its image in Baltimore when the cargo submarine *Deutschland* arrived at the port on July 10, 1916. The submarine *Deutschland* was a blockade runner, designed to slip under the British maritime blockade of Germany, a Royal Navy tactic that had effectively cut off Germany from supplies that would otherwise be arriving from points across the North Sea. The *Deutschland* was a cargo carrier, over 200 feet long, capable of surface travel at just 12 miles per hour and of moving stealthily under water when she encountered enemy vessels. She had crossed the Atlantic, travelling all but 90 miles of the journey on the surface.

The mission of the *Deutschland* to Baltimore was said to be two-fold: encouraging the good will of local citizens, many of German heritage, and conducting a bit of cargo exchange, especially products in short supply in Germany. Captain Paul Koenig had brought the *Deutschland* and her cargo of dyes and pharmaceutical preparations to a dock near Latrobe Park in South Baltimore. There was an additional motive for the Deutschland's crossing to America, however, as disruptive acts of sabotage in ports along America's Atlantic coast required German funding. It was alleged at the time (and post war investigations confirmed) that the submarine brought a sizable quantity of cash to bribe saboteurs along America's Atlantic coast. *Deutschland's* Captain Koenig had been seen in the company of Baltimorean Paul Hilken, manager of the North German Lloyd steamship company's local operations, who was also suspected of being a German agent. As guests of the city, Captain Koenig and his crew were given a generous welcome, feted at events at the Belvedere Hotel and the Germania Club hosted by Paul Hilken and attended by local dignitaries.

A week after the *Deutschland* arrived in Baltimore, a massive act of sabotage took place in Newark, New Jersey, the "Black Tom Explosion", destroying tons of war materiel, ships, rail equipment, and port facilities. A connection between the arrival of the submarine and the explosion was alleged but not confirmed, the *Deutschland* soon departing for Germany, filled with a cargo of nickel, tin, and crude rubber. In postwar testimony, an accused Hilken managed to avoid incarceration by testifying against other conspirators but admitted that he was the paymaster for acts of sabotage conducted from the attic of the North German Lloyd's company offices at German and Charles Streets. It was clear that Hilken was indeed a spy, and that the *Deutschland*'s visit had not been one of good will.

On April 6, 1917, America broke off the restrictions of neutrality and entered the Great War, in the words of President Wilson "to make the world safe for democracy". The president who had for so long resisted war and won re-election on his promise to "keep us out of war", yielded to the inevitable: American public opinion had changed in the face of new, unrestricted German submarine warfare, leading to the death of Americans at sea, and reports of German atrocities occurring in Europe. Baltimore and Maryland were militarized with the opening of several major area army facilities including Camp Meade, created from farmland south of the city and quickly becoming a major training and departure point for soldiers heading to the war in Europe. Within the city limits, Army General Hospital Number Two on the grounds of Fort McHenry began operating in 1917 as a 3,000-bed receiving and later surgical facility for war wounded. A year later, in 1918 Camp Holabird opened along Colgate Creek as a 96-acre vehicle and testing ground for the Army, as well as a training facility for mechanics and drivers. The military installation at Fort Howard in Southeast Baltimore County, sited at the entrance to Baltimore's harbor, had its military complement doubled, but with good fortune, the artillery there was never fired in anger.

Thousands of Baltimoreans and Marylanders joined the fight, over 62,000 of them, many certainly Baltimoreans of German ancestry with some speaking fluent German. The city's large population of German Americans remained loyal Americans, ignoring calls to align their sympathies with their former homeland. A German language Lutheran church in downtown Baltimore makes evident how clearly German Americans remained loyal to their new, chosen country. When the United States entered the war, Zion Lutheran Church halted their relief work on behalf of German war widows. The pastor of the church, Reverend Julius Hoffmann, reminded the congregation of their loyalty oath to America, their new homeland. Church members supported the war through war bond drives and with members joining the military. Four church members were among the nearly 2,000 Marylanders killed in the war. The congregation's loyalty was affirmed, the exception doubtless being church member Paul Hilken.

The reality of war greeted the newly arrived and enthusiastic American troops. To the strains of "Over There" they sailed across the Atlantic, part of an American Expeditionary Force. Pershing was their leader; they had prepared and were ready to fight. Battle lines were drawn, trenches dug, and the American troops joined the battle.

One of those troops was Baltimorean George Redwood, fresh from Harvard and military training, assigned the task of eavesdropping on German soldiers. His fluency in German sealed his fate. At Cantigny, France, he crawled forward to the German lines to listen, but returned when he was wounded in the shoulder. The wound was dressed, and Redwood chose to return to duty. Advancing again, he was shot a second time, this time more seriously, receiving a wound to his jaw. Still, after treatment he returned to the front lines, pursuing his assignment yet a third time. He never returned. As he advanced across "no man's land", he was struck by an artillery shell and was killed. George Redwood died a hero, the first Maryland officer to die in the war, May 29, 1918. Redwood Street in downtown Baltimore was named after him, replacing German Street.

Another very different soldier's story occurred at the very end of the war, that of Henry Gunther. On November 11, 1918, Baltimorean Henry Gunther, 23 years old, was determined to redeem himself. A military infraction, complaining of miserable conditions in a letter home, had left the former Sergeant reduced in rank to Private, a situation Gunther sought to reverse with some last-minute heroics. It was an open secret that the war was set to end in an armistice that day, the 11th month on the 11th day at the 11th hour. Just before the armistice was to take place Gunther, determined to prove his loyalty and worthiness, left the American lines and started a charge against a German machine gun emplacement. The Germans called to him to stop, to go back, but he kept attacking and thus was shot and killed one minute before the war ended, 10:59 am, November 11, 1918. His was another pointless casualty in an endlessly bloody, sad war.

A HOME FRONT ENEMY

While the shooting war appeared to gather everyone's attention, another enemy was beginning a stealthier attack on people worldwide. This enemy was an influenza, highly contagious and frequently fatal, called the Spanish Flu. The strain of influenza was not of Spanish origin, but the high incidence and casualty rates in Spain had earned the influenza its name. Analysis by epidemiologists indicate that the Spanish influenza may have originated in the over-crowded military facilities of Fort Riley, Kansas, travelling to Europe with the embarking troops, with a subsequent U.S. domestic spread of the epidemic travelling back across the Atlantic with returning soldiers. This was a highly communicable disease, a fast-moving but short-lived epidemic, confined almost completely to the single year of 1918. The world-wide result of the epidemic was the death of an estimated 50 million people.

As late as mid-September 1918, the influenza has not yet arrived in Baltimore. Baltimore City Health Commissioner John Blake, aware of the flu epidemic elsewhere, indicated he had no anxiety about the situation in Baltimore, that the city residents had contracted no such illnesses. A few days later, September 24, a handful of flu cases were reported at Camp Meade, the U.S. Army base just twenty miles south of Baltimore. Illness spread quickly amongst the troops, so that by the first days of October, Camp Meade reported 1,900 cases. The military hospital at Fort McHenry soon reported 300 cases. The military quickly initiated countermeasures: quarantining those affected, ordering everyone to wear masks, and mandating that all the people on the bases should maintain a distance from one another. Participation at the U.S. military bases was compulsory.

In Baltimore, influenza cases began to be reported. The Health Department's Dr. Blake incorrectly advised on September 26 that the illness was the same influenza that had been circulating and successfully treated for years. It was workers at the region's military installations who began bringing the Spanish Influenza home with them: the first ten proven cases in the city were brought to family and friends from military installations. By October 4, there were 745 reported cases with 13 deaths, and Camp Meade had by then reported an alarming 34 deaths. Dr. Blake was given carte blanche by Mayor Preston to take measures to halt the spread of the disease, but he was reluctant to take extreme measures, asking only for small changes such as asking trolley drivers to assure good ventilation in their cars and asking residents to use handkerchiefs when sneezing or coughing. His fear was that forcing closures would do greater harm than the influenza itself. The number of cases continued to climb. On October 6, hospitals reported they were at capacity, unable to accept more patients. The telephone company reported 25 percent of its staff were ill; United Railways reported 300 sick streetcar drivers. City schools were closed by the School Board on October 8, over the objections of Dr. Blake; on October 9, Blake capitulated to overwhelming pressure, ordering a prohibition on large gatherings and theaters to be closed. The next day, retail stores were ordered to operate on limited hours. Poolrooms and churches were next, ordered closed October 11. Saloons remained open, due to the purported "medicinal" value of their products. By October 12, Blake limited the hours of bars and saloons, also mandating dentists wear gauze masks when treating patients. Slowly the increased restrictions had the desired effect, as the epidemic began to ease, but the consequences of the virus were enormous: coffins were in short supply and many poor families could not afford a funeral. The mayor provided a burial fund to alleviate that problem, had fifty city water supply and highways workers dig graves, and permitted burial without the customary embalming.

By the end of November, two months after its arrival, the flu epidemic was mysteriously gone from Baltimore as quickly as it had arrived. Over 10 percent of Baltimore's residents had contracted the flu, more than 75,000 cases. The Health Department compiled the results: over 5,000 citizens of the city had died. Nationwide, multiple waves of the illness passed through the population over several months. It was ultimately estimated that 675,000 Americans had died from this home-front battle with the Spanish Flu, almost six times the number of American soldiers who had died in the preceding European war.

A TROUBLED CLOSE

At the end of the 19-teens, times should have been good: the wartime economy had been a financial boon to the country and to Baltimore, the bloody, stalemated war had ended, the soldiers in Europe were heading home to friends and families, and a flu epidemic that took many lives had disappeared almost as quickly and mysteriously as it had arrived. However, the financial underpinnings of the economy soon encountered a disruption. While consumers, retailers, and manufacturers had anticipated a post-war economic boom, quite the opposite occurred. In the early months of 1919, prices began to rise, inflation appeared in every segment of the economy, an unusually strong dose of it, raising prices substantially across the entire economy. The annualized inflation rate approached 18 percent. Consumers balked. Spending could wait, as a "buyers' strike" caused sales to plummet as the recession of 1920-21 began.

Over-extended suppliers, who had borrowed to fund an inventory buildup for the expected post-war boom in purchasing were stuck, as there were few buyers for the products they had created, and they faced demands for repayment of those borrowed funds. It would take the "Roaring 20s" to fix these economic woes.

CHAPTER THREE:
ROARING TWENTIES

The 1920s

THE "WAR TO END ALL WARS" had come to an end. A Spanish influenza had come and gone. The catch phrase of the presidential election of 1920 was "a return to normalcy". The election proved to be a nationwide landslide for candidate Warren Harding. Harding was acknowledged as a mediocre candidate, but his "return to normalcy" campaign, combined with a series of disruptive events (a Wall Street bombing, race-based riots, violent labor strikes) led to a public interested in change, thus carrying him to the nomination and presidency. Harding was progressive in office, pushing an anti-segregation agenda, asking Congress for a federal anti-lynching law, and representing steady and stable leadership in a world that was showing evidence of quite the opposite in many foreign lands. Unfortunately for Harding, he brought with him as advisors a poor selection of friends who would use and betray him. Since he died in office just two and one-half years after his inauguration, his presidency was brief and marred by corruption and scandal, attributed to his all-too-trusting nature and an apparent inability to manage the presidential tasks at hand. His long history of sexual peccadillos would later become public, further damaging his image. The State of Maryland, long a Democratic Party stronghold, had shifted toward the Republican Harding, rejecting the Democratic candidate, Governor James Cox of Ohio. In 1920, the Maryland vote was a clear Republican victory for Harding, as he took 55 percent of the votes cast. Nationally, Harding won with 63 percent.

THE START OF A NEW ERA

The younger generation had carried the physical burden of the Great War. With the usual desire of youth to move forward in new directions, Harding's "return to normalcy" represented a less than satisfactory future. The question they asked: wasn't it "normalcy" that had created the blood bath of the Great War? A return to normalcy simply wasn't enough. There were many who seemed ready to be freed from the rigidity of the late-Edwardian era, and others would join them. The trials of war-time had created heightened expectations. The youthful returning soldiers had seen something of the world. Their attitudes and worldview had been radically changed by the experience. Soldiers had come home with more than a hope, but with a real need for a changed world, far from the horrors of wartime. Surely Baltimore in the 1920s would bring to fruition the many hopes and dreams of a population ready to move forward into a new era. These citizens would soon realize how much their city, their attitudes, and the times they lived in would change in the coming decade.

The expectations of the new decade, "normal" or not, would for some have to wait. In Baltimore, the city park at Fort McHenry was converted to a temporary hospital home for returning wounded veterans. It was U.S. Army General

Hospital Number Two, in temporary buildings on the grounds of the Fort, serving the needs of 20,000 returning veterans between the years 1917 to 1923. Those admitted might be amputees learning to become mobile again, shell shock victims needing peaceful convalescent care, veterans blinded by poisonous gas receiving job training, or those who had sustained grievous disfigurement awaiting surgery. Patients might spend as little as two weeks or as long as two years in the care of medical and rehabilitation personnel. Lives were saved or remade in this 100-building, 3,000-bed hospital. Nurse Emily Raine Williams said it best, "It was we who had to re-create, out of the wreckage of war, clean, whole and useful men."

A total of 1,752 Marylanders lost their lives in the Great War. In their memory the city and state planned for central Baltimore a monumental building, a War Memorial. A shared design and fiscal effort of the state and city, the ceremonial groundbreaking was attended by Great War hero Marshal of France Ferdinand Foch (November 1921). Construction began of a what would become a 1,000-seat auditorium facing the square block plaza in front of Baltimore's 1875 City Hall. As construction continued, the building's cornerstone was placed by state, city, and federal officials in 1923. The War Memorial in its final iteration was a neo-classical building with columns and broad steps to the front, flanked by seahorse statuettes representing the "Might of America crossing the seas to aid our allies." Inside, the walls were inscribed with the names of Maryland's war dead, and at one end hung a massive mural, *A Sacrifice to Patriotism*, created by Baltimore artist R. McGill Mackall. The dedication of the War Memorial in April 1925, just under seven years after the war had ended, was one additional step for the city and its residents to place the war years behind them.

AMENDING TIMES

The seventy-year long fight for women's suffrage had concluded when most women in the U.S. were guaranteed the right to vote with the ratification of the 19th Amendment in 1920. The women's rights movement had its beginnings at the Seneca Falls (NY) Convention of 1848. Six scattered western states had previously granted women's right to vote and surprisingly, in 1908 the little Eastern Shore village of Still Pond, Maryland, granted the franchise to female taxpayers, where three women promptly went to the polls. Just two years earlier the National American Women Suffrage Association had met in convention at the Lyric Theater in Baltimore, where Susan B. Anthony delivered her last speech while suffering from pneumonia. She died at home just weeks later.

The ratification of the 19th Amendment to the U. S. Constitution made women's right to vote a nation-wide policy. The amendment did not, however, enfranchise women of color, women of Asian or Hispanic heritage, or Native American women, the last of whom were not made citizens until 1924. Poll taxes and literacy tests continued to be used to limit access to the ballot, male or female, with some women discouraged from voting through direct intimidation. Seeking favorable opinion and catering to women's electoral interests, Congress enacted a first-ever federally funded social welfare program for women and children's healthcare. The 1920 election results immediately denied an anticipated (and feared) "women's voting bloc": women voters cast their ballots as individually as did men. Support for the act lagged once a women's voting bloc did not materialize, and the program's funding was allowed to expire.

On January 16, 1920, cities and towns nationwide went dry. With the passage of the 18th Amendment to the U.S. Constitution a year earlier, the manufacture, transport and sale of alcoholic beverages had been prohibited, save a few medical and religious exceptions. In Baltimore, beer had been a part of the city's culture almost since its beginning. Breweries and taverns abounded from the 1780s until their forced, sudden demise in 1920. Baltimore breweries that closed included National, Gunther, and Globe. Frederick Bauernshmidt, brewer of American Beer, continued to operate his brewery on Gay Street, offering a low alcohol "near beer", a product that was almost universally unpopular. Bauernshmidt soon halted all production, putting the brewery into hibernation. The Monumental Brewery wasn't so fortunate as it closed in 1920, never to reopen. Jobs were lost, the workers terminated. One of the legal exemptions to prohibition, alcohol for medical use, grew beyond any expectation, driven largely by prescriptions written by accommodating doctors. Hundreds of clubs and taverns were shuttered, though some found ways to remain open, often by offering liquor for sale illegally behind closed doors, a password required to enter. The desire of teetotalers for almost one hundred years, the "Noble Experiment" to end all alcohol abuse, would not fare well in Maryland where many openly opposed the law, others supported it in public but violated it in private, and the state's leadership took a defiant stand in opposition.

The elected leaders of the Free State, under the leadership of Governor Albert Ritchie, were openly opposed to prohibition. While all the other states enacted their own prohibition laws modeled on the Federal Volstead Act, Maryland resisted, refusing to enact a law to create a state-based prohibition enforcement mechanism. Ritchie, Governor of Maryland for the entire decade of the 1920s, held opinions and took actions that were without question influenced by the Sage of Baltimore, Henry L. Mencken. Mencken, writer, editor, and publisher, wrote in opposition to prohibition, striking a sympathetic note with Governor Ritchie. Ritchie, his eye on a presidential run in the upcoming 1932 election, had become a nationally recognized figure as he rode a wave of anti-prohibition sentiment. Throughout the nation, the enforcement of prohibition laws was mostly in the hands of local authorities enforcing local laws, but in Maryland, where there was no state prohibition law, enforcement was largely left in the hands of a very limited number of federal agents, perhaps 300 nationwide. When those agents attempted to enforce the law, they were met with local citizen resistance: crowds bullied them, even physically attacked them, and one agent in the Locust Point area of the city quickly departed after being struck in the head with a jar of mayonnaise. Ritchie furthered the state's prohibition resistance by ordering the Maryland State Police to ignore liquor violations, including illegal importing, so long as the perpetrators paid their taxes.

The decade of the 1920s became the era of the bootlegger and the speakeasy. Baltimore entered the 1920s "dry", but the reality of "dry" in Maryland was an illusion. Citizens found ways to ignore the law, as changes in laws governing alcohol consumption did not change consumer demand. As taverns were sold or closed, some joined an underground industry that required ingenuity and stealth to provide alcoholic beverages to thirsty citizens. As taverns closed, in their place "speakeasies" opened, named from an admonition to speak softly when mentioning the establishment. These were unmarked establishments, many with a following of locals who knew where to go, how to identify as a friend, and knew the password that would permit entry through, typically, a green painted door. Some were openly "above ground" clubs serving alcohol only when the managers were certain that the clients in the room offered no prohibition enforcement risk. In the Owl Bar in the Belvedere Hotel, the decorative owl blinked its eyes as an all-clear signal that it was safe to imbibe. Baltimore's "Gin Belt", a midtown area roughly bounded by Charles, Howard, Monument, and Biddle Streets, hosted a dozen or more speakeasies, many run by former tavern owners. At Howard and Chase Streets, drug store owner Joe Hildebrand operated his soda fountain, marble counter and all, dispensing whiskey through his soda spigots. Nearby were the Silver Slipper, the Pig and Whistle (access through a narrow alley), and further north on Charles Street the speakeasy of Bill Schnapp, selling locally and delivering to the cadets at a military academy in Virginia. Speakeasies seemed to be available to most anyone who knew where to look, asked the right questions, or had the right friends. The flow of alcohol continued to such an extent that Baltimore's arrest rate for public drunkenness rose once prohibition was underway, with the lure of indulging in the forbidden seeming to increase the number of Baltimoreans who drank, and how much. Operating a speakeasy slowly fell out of favor just at the end of the prohibition years when the federal Jones Law, known as the "five and ten law", was passed, making speakeasy operation a federal offense with penalties of a $5000 fine and/or 10 years behind bars.

Bootlegging thrived with the illegal manufacture, distribution, and sale of intoxicants. Everyone it seemed had become an outlaw. There were other more damaging, unintended consequences that followed from the bootlegging process. Homemade liquor had become a source of intoxicants, but the liquor produced was often poisonous, containing toxic levels of methanol, a by-product of the distilling process. Consuming even modest levels could cause blindness, while excess levels would bring about both drunkenness and death. Less-discriminating imbibers drank alcohol in many of its potentially lethal forms. But intoxicants were very much in demand, leading some businesses previously associated with the liquor business, such as Baltimore's Joseph Kavanagh Company, makers of distilling and brewing fixtures, to begin bootlegging. The shop had always maintained a "demonstration still" for client inspection, but now they put it to work, producing a rye whiskey that was safe for consumption. A distributor was found for their liquor, allowing the shop and its employees to financially survive the era of prohibition.

Maryland was the "wettest" of the states, declared a 1925 *Colliers Magazine* article. In addition to the local bootlegging trade, importing of alcoholic beverages became routine with liquor distilled outside the United States smuggled ashore at locations such as Ocean City, Maryland. The Chesapeake Bay became a thoroughfare for those who imported liquor, those who manned the boats termed "rum-runners". Liquor, wine, and champagne imports, often of the finest quality, arrived from Scotland, France, and Canada in the dark coves and marshes along the shores of the Bay. Law enforcement allowed importers' motorboats to operate as if they were unseen, unimpeded in their deliveries. Local police were disinterested at best with federal enforcement spread entirely too thin to make an impact on this liquor importing and distribution business.

AROUND THE CITY

By 1920, Baltimore's population reached 730,000 persons. An influx of workers seeking war time jobs in the prior decade had increased the city's population by 170,000. Accommodating this population was an enormous challenge, with food and housing shortages. The housing shortage demanded an immediate response; the Baltimore row house was the solution. These practical and affordable houses had been a Baltimore staple since the city's inception. While most cities built a few hundred rowhomes, Baltimore built them by the thousands. Estimates of the total number of row homes built over the centuries vary, but there is no doubt that between the years 1910 and 1930 at least 50,000 were built.

By the twentieth century, Baltimore's row houses were varied in style, size, and amenities, with more elaborate designs adding full basements, porches, even rear-facing garages. The sizes and styles of row-houses varied widely, depending upon the time they were built, but all shared one common feature: they were constructed with a brick exterior. Brick was used to comply with a 1799 city ordinance demanding masonry construction, in the hope of fire-proofing Baltimore. At the front of many of these row houses were attached Baltimore's iconic white marble steps, chosen for their beauty, durability, and local availability, made by Baltimore workers with stone from Baltimore County quarries. The houses could incorporate either a bowed or a flat front, might be of simple or grand design, reflecting styles including Italianate, Federal, or Renaissance. They might come with two or three levels, from the simplest "alley house" of just four rooms facing a back street or alleyway, to more elaborate three-level versions incorporating ten or more rooms.

Regardless of age, Baltimore row houses provided affordable houses for many generations of Baltimoreans. But Baltimore's housing was much in need of modernization by the 20th century. Early versions of Baltimore houses had neither bath nor toilet facilities: most water service arrived in Baltimore in the 1880s, with sewer service only appearing in the first decades of the 20th century. Electrification was at first an expensive luxury, but demand for service slowly grew until by the 1930s, most houses in the city were connected. Prior to the 20th century, simple Edison light bulbs with a limited service-life, might cost a household a major percentage of a day's pay, so it is no surprise that homeowners continued with gas lighting, adopting electrical service only as it became affordable. Modernization of the city's many existing homes often meant installing electrical service alongside improved plumbing.

James Keelty, an Irish immigrant stonemason, came to Baltimore around 1900. He began building a few homes along centrally located Calvert Street, then moved on to other locations across the city. By the 1920s, Keelty had devised a new style of row home that eliminated one of the biggest drawbacks of interior rooms, the lack of a window. He designed the Daylight Colonial, a row home that was wider than earlier construction with the rear most room a bit narrower than other rooms, thus creating a rear facing exterior wall in a center room. A window was added to that rear facing surface, thus making it possible to have a window in each room of the house. Skylights were often provided, especially in interior halls. Keelty preferred to build and sell houses with large well ventilated front porches with an upper floor bay window set above the porch roof.

Edward Gallagher began his building career in 1888 in the Canton area, east of the center city. Experience gained building homes there led him to establish a company that constructed sturdy rowhomes throughout the region, promoting them as "lifetime homes". He moved on to home building on Preston Street, Eutaw Place and by 1920, in the east side Sinclair neighborhood, building houses specifically for employees of the heavy industry which had grown in that area. In the 1920s, he began a new neighborhood, Ednor Gardens, named for his two sons, Ed and Norman, constructing rowhomes in several designs, many with decorative rock blasted from the site, sun porches, and the modern convenience of a garage, as more and more homeowners were acquiring automobiles. Ultimately, Gallagher built about 12,000 homes in the Ednor Gardens community through the 1920s and 1930s.

Home ownership had always been prized in Baltimore. To reduce the acquisition cost of a house, a local system of ground rents was created: purchasers could buy the house without buying the ground on which it was built. The ground was rented to the homeowner on a permanent basis, the homeowner usually making a monthly payment to the owner of the ground under his or her house. This scheme made a house with a ground rent more affordable, as even a modest saving was none-the-less helpful in making home ownership accessible. For a large portion of the population, prospective buyers could usually obtain financing through any of multiple local sources, including banks, local building and loan associations, and immigrant-operated financial services. For many Baltimoreans, home ownership and with it a path to generational wealth was blocked, as it was often unavailable to Black families. Segregation defined where Baltimoreans might live and there were no exceptions. Banks refused loans to those who might otherwise qualify for home ownership while homeowners refused to sell their homes in de facto White neighborhoods to Black citizens.

Faced with these barriers, an undaunted Black community created its own vibrant living, shopping, and entertainment space in Baltimore. It truly was a city within the city, centered along a two-mile stretch of Pennsylvania Avenue, slicing through the city diagonally to the Northwest, originating just north of the downtown shopping district. By 1920, 90 percent of the Black population of Baltimore lived in the area known as "The Avenue". The community hosted most everything needed by its residents: shops, churches, schools, milliners, newspapers, barbers, restaurants, mortuaries, and the Provident Hospital, a teaching hospital for Black doctors and nurses. Provident had opened in 1894 offering improved access to important health care services to the Black community.

"The Avenue" was Baltimore's version of New York's Harlem, truly a place for African Americans to survive and thrive. Top entertainment from the "Chitlin' Circuit", a national collection of venues accepting Black entertainers, was regularly seen at the 1300-plus capacity Douglas Theater, renamed in 1925 the Royal Theater. Jazz singer Ethel Waters appeared nearby at the segregated New Lincoln Theater, where Whites and Blacks sat on opposite sides of the center aisle. Talent on these vaudeville stages varied widely, with headliners appearing only occasionally. More often the bill was filled with local comedy acts such as Hooten and Hooten, George and Ida Hooten, who toured with a 1926 tabloid musical show, *Miss Calico*, or shared the stage with Miss Darrel, whose Oriental Dance, a contemporary euphemism for a belly dance, was described in one account as "supple with a serpentine grace." An important film, *The Scar of Shame*, shown at the Royal beginning April 15, 1929, was a feature-length melodrama of eight-reels, uniquely featuring a Black cast appearing in a story of the lives of Black citizens.

FASHION, FADS, AND FUN

The 1920s are rightfully legendary for the many lifestyle changes of the decade. These times were all about throwing off the conventions and restrictions of the Victorian and Edwardian eras, offering an opportunity for many, particularly those coming of age, to celebrate new post-war beginnings and embrace frivolous pursuits. This was the generation that was leading the change, the young people born after 1895, who had fought the Great War or awaited their return, those with little stake in a "return to normalcy" as the presidential campaign of Warren Harding proposed. Instead, many of their generation chose to cast off the past. Fashions were changing, free spirits were unleashed, inhibitions often lost and with thanks to prohibition, the now forbidden elixir of alcohol fueling changes in expectations and behaviors. There was indeed an overarching desire to enjoy the moment, one another, and the diversions of the times, driven by a recognition that the war had denied the future to many of their peers. For those who had survived, their time was now.

The music of the decade was certainly in the forefront of the cultural and social changes occurring. The Jazz Age was unfolding and in Baltimore that meant nightclubs, musicians, and moving to the latest dance crazes. This was the era of the Charleston, the Lindy Hop, and the Black Bottom. A local dance craze was the more sedate "Baltimore", which slowly gave way to the Fox Trot. The new music was heard beyond the clubs and ballrooms, and was for the first time played on the latest invention, the radio. Mechanical devices such as piano rolls and the newly invented Victrola widened the possibilities for music in the home. Baltimoreans heard live the big bands of Paul Whiteman, the raspy sounds of Louis Armstrong, and the ragtime and jazz of Jelly Roll Morton. Count Basie, Billie Holiday, and Duke Ellington were regular visitors to the city, playing to full houses, performing locally many times each year. Bessie Smith, the "Empress of the Blues", sang at the Royal Theater, prompting an *Afro-American* newspaper reporter after seeing one of her performances in 1926 to write, "She (has not) forgotten her struggles before she became famous." Smith, a woman who knew poverty and discrimination, was an entertainer of enormous appetites, one who enchanted her audiences with heart-felt, soulful blues full of life experiences, such as "Nobody Knows You When You're Down and Out", or "Back Water Blues", the latter a song telling the story of the tragic Mississippi River Floods of 1927.

Women's fashion was perhaps the most visible expression of a new era. The modest hour-glass styles of the Edwardian Gibson Girl gave way to straight lines, short hems, and bright colors. Waistlines dropped and when hems rose, a demand for new styles of hosiery and undergarments was created. Shoulders and backs were revealed, some said scandalously, and the long hair of earlier years was lopped off: the "bob" was in. By measurement, the Edwardian fabric count was fifteen yards of cloth covering a lady; the youthful flappers, a term of varying antecedents but always referring to young women of the era, were clad in one-third as much fabric. Some women wore functional jewelry: large shoe buckles that contained make-up, relieving a woman heading for the dance floor of a burdensome purse. Others wore necklaces with an adornment in which was stored the wearer's supply of cocaine, illegal as of 1914 but the drug of choice for some of this generation. Those bright colored garments made room for a new style in black: after silent film star Clara Bow created and wore a "little black dress" in the 1927 film, *It*, soon every woman wanted one. Black, a color previously seen only in mourning apparel, became overnight both sophisticated and practical, with versions for daytime and evening.

Following a war in which aircraft first appeared and flying "aces" attained hero status, almost anything to do with airplanes held a special fascination for the public. Barnstorming, stunt flyers, and wing walkers abounded, with Baltimore aviation adding an international flavor when the world-famous, world-wide Schneider Cup races were held at suburban Baltimore's Bayshore Park, October 26, 1925. Perfect weather greeted a crowd of 5,000 who watched Army Reserve officer Lt. James Doolittle pilot his seaplane aircraft to victory using a technique he had devised: diving the plane during turns allowing his aircraft to reach a record-breaking average speed of 232 miles per hour. From the east side's Bayshore park start-finish line, the route of flight took the racers east over the Chesapeake Bay, thence south toward Anne Arundel County and back to the starting line, a triangular course of 30 miles. The racers flew seven times around covering 210 miles. Doolittle outraced four other contestants, two other American military officers and one each from Italy and Great Britain.

For Baltimoreans it was a decade of frivolous fads, perhaps the most unique being pole-sitting, a pursuit in which the Baltimore region seemed to have taken a leadership role. Participating in pole sitting was simple: erect a flagpole with a modest platform atop, then climb the pole and take up residence on the platform for as long personal endurance permitted. Locally, a pole sitting champion was crowned when fourteen-year-old William Ruppert sat atop an eighteen-foot pole at his Dundalk home for twenty-three days. He surpassed Aloysius "Shipwreck" Kelly's record previously set at Carlin's Amusement Park in Baltimore. At age 13 Kelly had run away to sea from his home in Hell's Kitchen, New York City. A sailor in the U.S. Navy during World War One, he was now a gadabout seeking fun and opportunity where he might find it. The "shipwreck" portion of his name may have been more imagination than fact, but he had previously been employed as a steelworker, a high diver, and a movie double, performing stunts too dangerous for the stars. Pole sitting was a rather sedate occupation for him. After hearing of Ruppert's accomplishment, Kelly returned to Carlin's Park, reclaiming his pole sitting title, going on to longer and longer stints on high, until his last in 1952, when he returned to the ground only after suffering two heart attacks.

Baltimore had its share of dance marathons, "corn and callus carnivals" as these endurance contests were known. A deceptively simple competition: grab your partner, enter a contest, and proceed to dance together longer than the other couples on the dance floor. Cash prizes were awarded to winners while the event was underway, admission-paying spectators provided tips as incentive to the competing couples. Couples would dance, keep moving, take a brief intermission, eat a quick meal, and get back to the dance floor. In April 1923, a contest at John Carlin's Amusement Park was ended by police after the eight remaining couples on the dance floor had been at it for fifty-four hours. Contests elsewhere would reach into the hundreds of hours.

A new game arrived in Baltimore in 1922, described as something "for the leisure classes", the game of mahjong. Local members of the hard-working Chinese community had never heard of it, but one local laundry worker, Ling Po, advised a *Baltimore Sun* investigating reporter to find a young man to ask, "You find schoolboy. Johnny Hopkins maybe". Details soon followed: it was described as a game with Chinese origins, but the rules had been modified to suit American tastes. "I teach the American way" said one young schoolboy. "It is well for Americans to play the game their way." Mahjong is a game of skill for four players, using 136 domino-like tiles with numbers and symbols, some circles, some bamboo, with special tiles for wind and dragon. Exchanges take place until one player has a "set". Mahjong clubs were formed across the city, replacing bridge as their pass time. Masked and costumed players appropriated Chinese culture, playing the game in rooms decorated with luxurious fabrics and lanterns. The game's popularity was linked intrinsically with exotic and cross-racial tension, exploring the boundaries of participation in the styles of another culture.

In 1929 the city celebrated the 200th anniversary of its founding. Celebrations marking the occasion were held over four days in September, including the arrival of a Navy flotilla, led by the battleship New York, and several Army units which encamped in Druid Hill Park. Fraternal groups paraded through the city on September 7, five days before the official start of the anniversary. On the September 12 the City Hall tower bell was rung 200 times to begin the formal festivities. A speech by Mayor William F. Broening was followed with the release of 500 homing pigeons carrying invitations to dignitaries in other cities. A military parade was a premier attraction of the first day with an estimated 200,000 Baltimoreans watching as it wound its way through the city. In the evening, a reenactment of the assault on Fort McHenry was conducted using fireworks to simulate the bombardment. Spectators lining the shores numbered 100,000. The finale of the celebration was held on Sunday, September 14 with another parade through the city, ending before an audience of 5,000 gathered in the wooden stands of the Venable Stadium on 33rd Street. The parade was interrupted by a late afternoon thunderstorm, leaving both the public and the marchers in disarray. Mayor Broening ordered the final third of the parade to be repeated a week later.

THE GARMENT TRADE

When immigrants arrived in Baltimore in the middle of 19th century, they brought their talents, training, and trades. There was work for all, regardless of talents, but many of the new arrivals were skilled persons who first worked in the shops of others, later establishing businesses of their own in their own specialty. Shipbuilders, stonemasons, silversmiths, and more were joined by others who were makers of clothing, the trade of tailoring. Responding to a strong consumer demand for apparel in the thriving seaport of Baltimore, modest tailor shops were established. These small businesses grew in capacity with the invention by Elias Howe of the first sewing machine (1848) which united the capabilities of many earlier single-function machines. The sewing machine allowed the tailoring trade to reach higher production levels and to serve more clients, their businesses growing to new levels. With the start of the Civil War, the Union Army engaged Baltimore's tailors in the task of supplying uniforms. This became the perfect opportunity for local tailors to learn the process and techniques necessary to manufacture men's clothing in large quantities, using data from soldiers to devise standard men's clothing sizes. With the end of hostilities, demand for military uniforms quickly abated but many of these war time tailors opted to remain in the men's clothing manufacturing business. They adapted the uniform production techniques they had learned to the commercial market, soon developing ready-to-wear men's clothing, ultimately making Baltimore the nationwide leader in manufacturing men's apparel. By the 1880s, the city's dominance was notable: if it was a man's garment and it was made with a needle, it likely was made in Baltimore. The modest shops of 1860 had grown into flourishing downtown factories producing all manner of men's clothing and furnishings. By the 1920s, the Baltimore's men's apparel business became even more dominant, with men's apparel shipped first to the rural south, then nation-wide, and eventually sending lighter summer-weight goods overseas to Cuba and South America. Beyond clothing, the city had also quietly become the umbrella capital of the nation, with as many as 3,000 made every day to meet a new, burgeoning demand. Virtually all these needle operations were about outfitting men: the tailors of the Civil War era had focused on men's apparel, and so they remained. In Baltimore's era as a major garment-making center, it was an industry serving mostly men, in which women's clothing manufacturing accounted for less than 20 percent of the Baltimore's sewing industry output.

Baltimore's early dominance in these trades resulted from a fortuitous alignment of circumstance. The city's Mid-Atlantic geographic location had made a difference: Baltimore was near to the textile mills of New England, the cotton of the deep South, and was located on a deep-water port easing the costs of importing and exporting. By virtue of the continuing arrival of immigrants, the necessary labor force to sustain and grow industry in Baltimore was available. While many of those arriving held the skills to perform only the most basic sewing tasks, among them were many skilled tailors, fabric cutters, and talented seamstresses. By 1920, there were 27,000 workers employed in Baltimore's west side garment district.

Baltimore held a large marketing advantage as it focused on marketing to the states and cities of the southeast United States. Baltimore had many of the attributes of a Southern city, though better described as an industrial Southern city: able to project a Southern image, inspiring faith and trust in their clients, offering Southern clients the sense they were dealing with business owners who were culturally much like themselves. By the early 20th century, Baltimore's garment manufacturing became a major industry, standing alongside the business of the Port and the several shipyards lining the shores of the Patapsco. Good times lay ahead, but to get to them, the garment trades would have to endure a bump in the road.

In the years immediately after the Great War, optimism was in the air. There existed an almost universal anticipation that with the soldiers heading home, the national "return to normalcy", business would surely mean price stability and a resumption of consumer demand. This optimism was in error, as the post-war years saw a major economic recession by 1920, bringing first inflation, then high interest rates and finally, and worst of all, price deflation. Wholesalers and retailers were stuck with products that it seemed no one was willing to purchase, at least not for the asking price. In Baltimore the biggest victim of these economic hard times was the garment industry. Garment makers had increased their inventory for an expected post-war boom, many financing the production of that inventory through loans to purchase material and fund their payrolls. When consumers balked at post-war prices, garment makers were suddenly inventory-rich but cash-poor, making payment of their loans challenging at best, impossible at the worst. The most expedient remedy for the garment makers was to reduce prices to attract cash and buyers. This strategy should have worked, but the wary consumer balked yet again, leading to another round of price reductions. Inflation had become deflation, the worst of all worlds for the businessman, a period when the price today would surely be lower tomorrow, leaving consumers on the side-lines awaiting not just a lower price, but an irresistible price. In a major turnabout, garment makers ran previously unheard-of sales from the factory floor, selling off their inventory while eliminating retailers from the transaction, maximizing factory income. Others employed an unheard-of strategy: they began nationwide advertising of their goods to stimulate sales. The repeating cycle of inflation, buyer strike, and price deflation drove some producers into bankruptcy, with all of them feeling the economic squeeze. An unhealthy financial cycle slowly resolved itself over the first years of the 1920s. The economy was restored to an equilibrium by mid-1922, with minimal external interventions, or as James Grant named it in his book of the same title, this was *The Recession That Cured Itself*.

Sweatshops were an unfortunate part of Baltimore's garment industry. Sweatshops were typically small, poorly maintained, unsanitary, overheated workplaces that employed workers at poverty wages. The sweatshops existed because factory owners sought to reduce the cost of labor and thus the cost of goods by sending factory work to east side sweatshops, a cost reduction technique that was hard to resist. Baltimore's government had intervened periodically to reduce the number of these sweatshops with their unhealthy working conditions, but they would reemerge in greater numbers through the 1920s. However, the production system that included sending work to lower cost sweat shop workplaces was not without consequence; backlash from the factory workers eventually was felt. For the factory workers, sending work they felt was theirs to perform to sweatshops meant that every cut, every seam, every button sewn in a sweat shop took work away from the full-time, unionized factory employees. Inevitably labor actions led by union leaders, did occur.

One conflict became known as a "scissors war", as feuding workers used the tool of the trade as weapons. A conflict broke out between fabric cutters from different unions, beginning on the Sonneborn Clothing Company factory floor, and soon spilled out into the streets, where it was put down by police. Management, caught in between, made peace with the conflicting unions, but so long as work was sent to the sweatshops, labor peace would likely be hard to maintain. The United Garment Workers and the Amalgamated Clothing Workers, the two unions involved, struggled to resolve problems, and preserve for their members hard-earned gains in working conditions, wage rates, and equity in employee treatment. At the same time, management logically worked to preserve the very existence of their businesses, though multiple labor actions including worker strikes left some factories in tenuous financial straits. Some factories closed, while others left the city entirely, seeking new locations in more business-friendly rural environments. As economic conditions improved through the 1920s, much of the workplace tension was relieved through the application of monetary reward: higher take home wages for workers, and profits for factory owner. The majority of Baltimore's needle trades businesses would survive into the next decade and beyond.

In 1881, Jacob Epstein created a behemoth of a company, a wholesale mail order supplier of goods to retailers across the mid- and deep South. He was inspired to create a company, the Baltimore Bargain House, after travelling the back roads of rural America, offering goods to retailers in regions more remote than was attractive for higher-volume suppliers. Epstein immigrated from Lithuania as a teenager, first to New York, then to Baltimore, where he started his mail-order wholesale operation. The Baltimore Bargain House offered multiple material and clothing lines, from kitchenware to ladies' dresses, from hardware and tools to fishing tackle, from bicycles to furniture. Mail orders, shipped by express, included soft goods, clothing, and accessories made in Baltimore. The company's sales reached over $20 million in 1921, the 2023 equivalent of nearly $700,000,000. The company was later renamed American Wholesale Corporation to reflect its broader marketing, becoming the fourth largest wholesaler in the country. Its 1,600 employees operated first from 10 North Howard Street, then after 1911 from a larger headquarters and warehouse building at the corner of Baltimore and Liberty Streets. Epstein provided mail order service to retailers and hosted an annual "buyer week" in Baltimore, an event that filled the city with hundreds of travelling business owners anxious to examine first-hand the latest in new goods and products. For those unable to attend "buyer week", goods were displayed in mail order catalogs, displaying the products available through the company's mail order service, including attached sample fabric swatches for the garments available for purchase and resale.

MODERN TRANSPORT

Airplanes had captured a lot of imaginations and pointed the way to the future, but flying in this era was beset with weather delays, mechanical problems, and flight accident risks. Aircraft exteriors were still covered, at least in part, by fabric. The engines were noisy and underpowered, making aircraft slow while flying at the turbulence-prone lower altitudes. It is no surprise then that most transportation in the 1920s was solidly rooted on the ground. For the average traveler, the 1920s were all about rails and railroads.

The Baltimore and Ohio (B&O), the Pennsylvania and several other smaller lines converged in Baltimore to meet passenger and shipping needs. Passengers had multiple options to reach destinations near and far, with trains on the hometown B&O taking travelers to Pittsburgh, Chicago, Saint Louis, and connecting to other cities beyond. Service was generally reliable on the railroads, each one competing for their share of cargo and passenger service. Local service by the Maryland and Pennsylvania, the Western Maryland, or electrified service on the Washington, Baltimore, and Annapolis was available on convenient, often hourly schedules. Main line service to New York and points west was offered from multiple city stations by the competing B&O and Pennsylvania. One long distance train, the Capitol Limited, was initiated in 1923 by the B&O Railroad offering first class luxury service. It faced formidable competition for travel to the mid-west from both the Pennsylvania and New York Central Railroads. The B&O train offered on-board services for the eighteen-hour overnight trip, catering to the business traveler with secretarial service, on-board barbers, and manicurists. The ornate, chandelier and leaded-glass decorated dining car offered fine Chesapeake Bay fare, an attraction unto itself. Overnight travelers on the train could dine, sleep, and arrive refreshed at their destination, ready early the next day for business or an on-going connection. Reacting to the competitive advantage this and similar B&O trains offered, the Pennsylvania Railroad reduced the B&O advantage when in 1926, they terminated permission for the Capitol Limited and other B&O trains to access the Hudson River tunnels, owned by the Pennsylvania. Thereafter, all the B&O trains to and from New York City would terminate there, forcing New York bound passengers to disembark in New Jersey. Their final few miles would be a ferry across the Hudson River, then on-board buses that took them and their baggage to one of several stops in Manhattan.

The hometown Baltimore and Ohio Railroad had become truly competitive with other railroads across their thirteen-state route system, with its owners and stock-holders enjoying profitable years throughout the 1920s. By mid-decade, jobs had become more stable and for retirees, pensions more robust. In the words of B&O President Daniel Willard: "The year of 1926 just ended has been one of the most satisfactory in the history of the Baltimore and Ohio Company. Business has been good, employment on the whole has been steady, and we all have much to feel thankful for." Even those employees of the B&O who had survived recession downsizing, when the B&O between 1920 and 1921 had dropped 13,000 employees to a total of 59,000 system wide, knew that there were no universal good times nor security as post-war railroad labor force downsizing had impacted so many. The first to be released were usually the African American workers who by custom, union rules, bias, and even federal labor and railroad work rules had already found limited employment opportunities. Now some of the jobs they relied upon were gone. African American rail unions had been established but spent much of their energy defending Black workers from an endless onslaught of workplace bias. At a Pennsylvania Railroad employment labor hearing, testimony revealed that Black workers were paid at 60 percent the rate of Whites, despite "…performing exactly the same duties". Such was the state of labor and race relations on the rails in the 1920s.

But in 1927, to celebrate its healthy financial, employment and competitive position, the B&O railroad hosted a 100th Anniversary event, "The Fair of the Iron Horse". Built on a 25-acre parcel of land in nearby Halethorpe, just southwest of Baltimore, was a grandstand for 12,000, fronted with a rail-line that would be used to display the "century of progress" of American transportation. Nearby was the 500-foot-long Hall of Transportation, filled with railroad tools, equipment, and memorabilia from its own and other donating railroads; visitor support facilities; and an adjacent temporary rail station to allow arrival by train from the downtown Baltimore rail stations. A collection of railroad artifacts had been previously collected for the B&O's exhibit at the 1893 Chicago World's Fair, and was then displayed in Halethorpe in the Hall of Transportation. Twenty-five years later that same collection would become the foundation of the B&O Railroad Museum in Baltimore. The anniversary celebration was held in September and attended by well over a million visitors, its popularity so great that the program was extended another unscheduled week into October.

In the 1920s, America's highway system had improved. Nationwide, there were 7.5 million automobiles in 1920, with 100,000 of them in Maryland, and numbers continued growing. The owners of these automobiles took up a demand heard since the days of horses and buggies, a call to improve the roads. Improvements to a road in the 19-teens and 1920s didn't necessarily mean pavement: gravel covered, graded, even elevated roads with adjacent drainage ditches met the standard of the times. In Maryland, crushed oyster shells often replaced gravel as an improved surface. Yielding to the continuing public pressure, Maryland initiated a statewide road improvement program, with a special emphasis on replacing the 19th century's narrow wooden bridges. Federal aid was soon offered to build or improve both the long-distance highways across the country or to construct local roads. There were 250 long-distance highways carrying names like the Lincoln Highway, New York to San Francisco, or the Evergreen Highway, Portland, Oregon, to El Paso, Texas.

These highways were named, not numbered, and each was uniquely if not consistently marked to the state's own peculiar standard. Many 1920s roads were adopted by local groups, marked with small, sometimes none-too-durable signage, or with blazes carved into roadside trees. Travelling these roads meant combining a sharp eye for signage and the advice of locals when in need of more reliable direction. Maps were often out of date, incorrect, or confusing at best, relying often on changeable landmarks for direction; worse, many were suggestions only, so travelers never knew for certain if they were correct. Directions might say "Jog left, then right near the bank, continue ahead", but the road might have been straightened, the bank building might have been demolished, and the "ahead" direction pure guesswork for the driver. Named highways in Baltimore began with the National Old Trails Road, a highway that with enough care, caution, and luck would lead the traveler westward to Los Angeles. This confusion was to end when a 1926 federal financing program came with a mandate for states to adopt a nationwide numbering system for "U.S. Routes". If a road utilized federal aid, it was a candidate for a U.S. route number. Route numbers were systematically assigned, with even-numbered route numbers given to east-west highways, while north-south routes were assigned odd numbers, the numbers clearly displayed in a standardized size and format. Baltimore gained several routes, including a prominent and early U.S. Route One, Maine to Florida, bisecting the city by followed locally named streets and boulevards.

Better roads meant reliable motor trucking services. The upgraded, developing highway system slowly began to reduce the stranglehold monopoly of the railroads on cargo transport. The change was slow to arrive, beginning with local transport, then extending over longer distances as highway travel evolved. Luxurious first-class passenger service was the high-profile image builder of the railroad companies, but its financial backbone was the freight and cargo business. To facilitate the movement of cargo from road to rail, the Pennsylvania Railroad had created a local cargo handling company 30 years earlier, with Baltimore's 1893 Terminal Transportation Company offering high quality, convenient service to the railroad's customers. A teamster operation, Terminal employed horses and wagons to collect local freight from shippers, transport it to the railroad's Baltimore warehouse, then load it onto railcars for transport to a destination city. By the early 20th century, these horses and wagons had yielded to trucks, creating a modern version of the railroad's 19th century cargo feeder system. But the versatility and flexibility of truck transport over improving roadways did not go unnoticed by many shippers. By the 1920s, Maryland enjoyed an independent highway truck transport system that was becoming the mode of choice for regional and many intermediate distance shippers. Many of these companies were able to offer speedier customized delivery service, specific to the cargo handled: grocery commodities by companies like Bozel Transport, or household goods moved by a modernized teamster operation like Davidson Transfer, soon one of several such service providers. The highways had become a viable alternative and competitor to rails.

The United Railways Company was Baltimore's urban transport operator, supplying public transport in the form of street railways. Formed in 1899, United Railways was created through the merger of multiple smaller local operators into an integrated trolley system. Transfers between lines became commonplace with no duplicative fares. The company operated its own coal powered electricity generating station on Pratt Street along Baltimore's waterfront, maintained service with 1,300 electrically powered streetcars, all of them moving along a 400-mile track system. In 1915, the company created a subsidiary, the Baltimore Coach Company, which operated motor buses to supplement the streetcar service.

In the 1920s, United Railways encountered issues which would plague urban transit operations for the entire 20th century, and would eventually undermine the company's finances. The problem was as simple as it was intractable. Baltimore had grown substantially, tripling in land area with an annexation in 1918. The city's immediate region had also grown well beyond its physical borders as suburbanization increased. With this growth, providing service demanded a significant increase in the miles of trackage and the number of streetcars, thus raising the company's fixed costs. The streetcars and their passengers now travelled longer distances through heavier traffic on a journey interrupted by frequent corner stops, increasing travel time. Worse yet, an alternative to the streetcar had arrived, the automobile: personal, direct, private, on-demand, and usually faster than the streetcar. Streetcar ridership and fare revenue declined as former riders chose automobiles. The company was financially squeezed: its fixed costs remained while the fare box reflected a loss of revenue. In a compensating move, the company raised fares. The remaining riders resisted the fare increase, with more of them turning to the automobile. This vicious cycle was repeated with each fare increase, and though United Railways survived until the Great Depression, the economic woes, increased unemployment, with even lower revenues of hard times compounded already existing problems. The company would declare bankruptcy in 1935.

AVIATION

A new, formal airfield was needed for Baltimore, with the Flying Club of Maryland searching for a suitable location. While several primitive airfields were in use in the region, most were hardly more than flat, unimproved spaces, not suitable for the larger aircraft coming into use after World War One. One site under consideration was a large area of open land southeast of the city, adjacent to the community of Dundalk. The property was owned at the time by Bethlehem Steel Corporation, but good fortune smiled upon the airfield seekers, as the plant manager was a flight enthusiast who granted permission to use the property as a flying field, to be named the Dundalk Flying Field. The Club smoothed the field, created landing strips, erected a few modest buildings, and an official Baltimore Airport was created. As the field was about to be formally opened, a young Army flyer was doing some stunt flying in tailspins when his aircraft structure failed. He crashed and was killed. The field was renamed Logan Field, in honor of the deceased pilot, Lt. Patrick Logan.

Logan Field quickly grew becoming a full-service airport operating three runways paved with turf and cinders, and facilities including four military style canvas hangars for storage and maintenance. Other modest buildings for mail handling and passenger convenience were soon constructed. The new air unit of the Maryland National Guard established headquarters there in 1921, soon after the formal airfield opened. By 1929, passenger service to New York,

Atlantic City, and southward to Miami had begun. The scheduled passenger service to New York was a mere $25 each way ($441 in 2023 dollars). Airshows above the field were a steady attraction, featuring both new American aircraft designs and German, French and British World War biplanes. The Flying Club catered to an aviation hungry populace by hosting flying demonstrations and races that provided Baltimoreans the opportunity to watch as aircraft spun and then recovered from spirals, and aircraft passengers performed parachute jumps. In a test of a pilot's wartime skill, re-enactments of Great War exploits became favorites of an enthusiastic public. The field hosted aviation royalty when Charles Lindbergh and Amelia Earhart each set their aircraft down at Logan. By the end of the decade, despite the improvements, Logan Field's runways were inadequate for the larger, heavier aircraft that had been developed, thus its life as an airport would soon come to an end. Logan offered an important ten years to local aviation, but a new airport on the nearby harbor front, Baltimore Municipal Airport, was well under construction before the decade of the 1920s ended.

By 1929, a new locally based aircraft factory, the Berliner-Joyce Company was prominent in aviation events. As well as dignitaries, several already famous aviators thrilled spectators with their maneuvers, including Lt. Al Williams and his original "outside barrel roll". The acrobatics began with a climb, then a circular dive with the pilot on the outside of the circumference of the circle. The company opened but closed in short order, leaving behind a factory building and a few aviation artifacts, including a wind tunnel that would become an industry necessity. With the Great Depression, commercial aircraft orders disappeared, forcing the company to shift to military customers. Multiple reorganizations followed before the company was purchased and moved to California.

The most important aviation event of the decade attracted little in the way of public fanfare at the time, but it would turn out to be the most significant. Glenn Martin was an aviation pioneer, most recently building aircraft in a factory in Cleveland, Ohio. Seeking larger property, one where his factory could be near an airport as well as adjacent ice-free water for seaplane use, he determined that his company would move to Baltimore. He and his company were courted by Baltimore City officials, seeking to add his new operation to the emerging aviation center in Dundalk. They seemed to have tried too hard, and Martin, a very private man, was offended by what he considered pressure tactics, consequently shifting his search to Baltimore County. Through successful extended negotiations, Martin quietly acquired the almost 1,300 acres needed for his operations, with his factory opening in 1928. In May 1929, the Navy ordered 25 biplane flying boats, soon adding 5 more to the order in June, and starting the factory operations on a solid footing. From that small beginning, the Martin operation would have a profound impact on aviation and the future of Baltimore.

RADIO ARRIVES

Baltimore radio began almost as soon as there was broadcasting, offering listener friendly radio to entertain. Guglielmo Marconi had sent messages across the ocean years before (1901) but the messages were just dots and dashes, the Morse Code created years before for the telegraph. Morse dots and dashes were adequate for commercial use, especially to reach ships at sea, but held little to no appeal to the casual listener. The Marconi Company established radio operators on board ships that permitted regular and routine as well as emergency communication. The Marconi system met the commercial needs, but voice and music transmission appealing to the general population was impossible until Reginald Fessenden perfected it in 1906. Improvements to Marconi's and Fessenden's contributions were made, and while the Great War limited application, by the early 1920s broadcasting and radio were ready to revolutionize communication. Early radio stations and sets had difficulty broadcasting and sorting out competing signals from stations broadcasting on the same or similar frequencies (stations on the dial), as they were interfering with one another. Stations even shared broadcast frequencies, agreeing to broadcast only during allocated time periods. By 1927, a more mature radio industry emerged as federal regulations began the process of assigning specific frequencies for broadcasting.

In these early radio days of the 1920s, radio signals would fade in and out for no immediately explicable reason. Researchers examined the problem but were unable to determine the cause. Dead spots appeared, areas where the radio signals didn't arrive. Investigations were called for. A *Baltimore Sun* news account from March 1923 named Baltimore as "the deadest spot in the country." Local scientist C. Warfield Keefer in 1927 linked radio's fading signal problem to the "earth's currents", mentioning the impact of sunspots, magnetic storms and in a great leap of overstatement, electrified trolley lines. The quality of the broadcast sound was also in question. In the first years of broadcasting, several hundred stations came on the air, many with marginal equipment including poor quality microphones. Perhaps there should be quality over quantity suggested one listener. In its infancy, broadcast radio had great potential but would have to overcome many technical challenges to meet it.

Baltimore went on the air in November 1921, though not many people owned radios. Local radio began when Calman Zamoiski, the son of a local electrical equipment distributor, began broadcasting from a bedroom in his home near Druid Hill Park. Like many youth of the time, the creation and possibilities of radio were of intense interest. Zamoiski soon moved to larger quarters in a nearby unused stable. Seeking a more formal standing, Calman's father's company, the Joseph M. Zamoiski Company became the licensee of a new radio station with call letters WKC, and thus became the first formal radio broadcaster in Maryland. The enterprise was short lived, with young Zamoiski's WKC broadcasting for just 20 months, March 1922 until November 1923.

From these small beginnings, the few but growing number of citizens who owned radios were treated to local programming such as sermons, concerts, and educational talks. On the air was a new station, WCAO, March 1922, followed by WFBR whose owners, the Maryland's 5th Regiment, began broadcasting from their local armory. Here then was the **W**orld's **F**irst **B**roadcasting **R**egiment, a promotion minded station cleverly broadcasting news updates from an airplane circling above the city. Station WCBM began broadcasting from the Chateau Hotel at North Avenue and Charles Street, with much of its programming originating from the nearby First Baptist Church. This connection to the church and its religious content was so heavy that the station became informally known as the station **W**here **C**hrist **B**lesses the **M**ultitudes. When local station WBAL, owned by the Consolidated Gas and Electric Company, began broadcasting concern was voiced by its competitors that WBAL's more powerful signal would drown out other stations, but the station went on the air in 1925 with promises that this would not occur. Here then was the solution to those so-called dead spots discussed in earlier years, areas where reception was limited: follow WBAL's lead and construct more powerful transmitters. WBAL broadcast the evangelical message of G.E. Lowman, a local businessman turned clergyman, who quickly developed a nationwide, then a world-wide following. WBAL continued its nationwide contribution when in 1937 the station's new announcer, Garrison Morfitt, a local McDonough School graduate, went on to national radio and then television celebrity, changing his name to Garry Moore.

Perhaps the greatest contribution of radio was the way it linked the nation by sharing broadcasts of news, sports, and entertainment through the creation of radio networks, groups of stations that simultaneously broadcast shared programming. Radio networks, with stations linked by the long-distance lines of the Bell Telephone System, had first appeared in 1926 when the "Red Network" appeared, so named as the original map showing the 19 member cities was drawn with the connecting lines in red ink. Baltimore's first network link was the "Blue Network" when WBAL radio joined that group in 1927. Competing station WCAO joined yet another group, the "UBS" network, which became the Columbia (C.B.S.) system. Radio networks became the means for listeners to access wider-ranging, even star-studded on-air entertainment. From their homes, listeners could access events such as baseball's World Series, October 1922, or Charles Lindberg's return to America after his trans-Atlantic flight, broadcast live in 1927. The Dodge Victory Hour, named for the automobile company's new model, the Dodge Victory, used 12,000 miles of telephone connection wire to join 47 radio stations, including WBAL. A nationwide network variety show, the Victory Hour, was hosted by Will Rogers in San Francisco, introducing songs by Al Jolson singing from New Orleans, alternating with musical numbers by Paul Whiteman's orchestra from New York. Thirty-five million Americans tuned in to this 1928 shared experience.

Radio had linked the country, quickly moving from novelty to an essential during the decade of the 1920s. Early earphone-equipped crystal sets were replaced by table-top, even wood-encased floor model radios. The sales of radio sets across the nation doubled, then doubled again. The 1930 Federal Census, specifically asking about radio ownership as well as enumerating the population, reported that millions had joined the radio audience: 40 percent of America's households now owned a radio. Baltimore and America were quickly becoming dependent on the wonders of radio.

A DECADE OF INDUSTRIAL GROWTH

Baltimore emerged from the "Great War" as an industrial center, well exceeding the 19th century years of growth during the Industrial Revolution. It was now a city of factories, smokestacks, ships, and steel, of factory workers and those who made it possible for them to work. The decade of the 1920s would transform the city and its industrial base once again: more than a mere industrial city, Baltimore would become an industrial giant. Across the city, thousands of products would be created, from leather shoes to sugar cookies, from canned goods to canvas, all in a concentration of factories, workshops, and stores, accompanied by a vast number of small sales, service, and supply providers. These large and small operations were mostly concentrated along the banks of the Patapsco River and in the neighborhoods of Canton, Locust Point, Hampden, and to the south, Curtis Bay. Workers lived in homes nearby, many becoming the second, third, or even later generations of family members living and working in the same neighborhood. Across the city were a half dozen paint factories, industrial casting makers, printing plants, iron works, copper smelters and coppersmiths, fertilizer producers, canners of oysters and vegetables, and a belt railroad with tracks seemingly connecting every pier, factory, and main line railroad. Nearby in the Jones Falls Valley duck cloth makers were supplying the nation with tents, tarpaulins, and backpacks. The riverfront with its wooden piers and warehouses imported ores of copper and iron, coffee, bananas, produce, and more, while exports of steel, canned goods, clothing, or machine produced goods went in the opposite direction. A network of ships, railcars, and motor trucks, all in motion, became the pulse of the city, with the river channels, the roads, and the rails the arteries of Baltimore's commerce.

The Port of Baltimore had in the 1920s become second only to New York as the largest port by volume on the Atlantic Coast. There were months when as many as 500 ships called on Baltimore, docking along the 45 miles of Patapsco River banks, inlets, and coves. In the center of the city, the piers often accommodated seafood or vegetable sales, with retailers selling from ship to consumer at waterside along Pratt Street. The Port of Baltimore offered intercontinental steamship service and almost as importantly, a connecting system of regional and local steamers calling on cities and towns throughout the region, with Annapolis, Chestertown, even Norfolk and Richmond only a steamship voyage away. Downstream, the steel mill at Sparrow's Point had a steady stream of ships laden with iron ore arriving and ships filled with steel products departing. Iron rich ore, a cargo originating from Cuba and South America, was destined to become steel, while newly fabricated steel products departed destined for ports as far as Hawaii. Standard Oil had built and operated a major refinery in the Canton area, a ship load of crude oil arriving almost daily, gasoline or kerosene departing as often. It was this energetic port that gave Baltimore a major competitive advantage over many other industrial centers, offering businesses a location second-to-none with year-round ice-free saltwater access connected by multiple rail lines to an inland population of customers.

City boosters of the 1920s were overwhelming in their predictions for Baltimore's future prosperity, with many envisioning a future skyline of skyscrapers rivaling those being built in New York City. The city had two towers from a prior decade, each reaching about 300 feet above the ground, but plans were underway for a true skyscraper, one that would tower over the city, at over 500 feet tall. Not everyone was pleased by this high-rise prospect. Commenting on the possibility of local skyscrapers and a perceived competition with New York, H.L. Mencken stated in his typical acerbic style: "…there never was any need of them here…Wasting millions on them is a kind of confession that Baltimore is inferior to New York…" He went on to say that a true Baltimorean is one who "…lives in Baltimore because he prefers Baltimore. One of its greatest charms, in his eyes, is that it is not New York."

Objections by Mencken and others aside, the city got its first true skyscraper in 1929 with the completion of the Baltimore Trust Company building on Light Street. Baltimore Trust was at the time the largest banking company south of the Mason-Dixon Line. The building was a 34-story tall, Art Deco styled, brick-faced office tower, a structure that achieved grace and beauty with its proportional lines and horizontal setbacks. The building's marble floored lobby had decorative panels on its walls commemorating the Great Baltimore Fire. The building was erected for the consolidation of the bank's operations, but it was a consolidation that never took place: Baltimore Trust was one of the first bankruptcy victims of the Great Depression. With the bank's failure, the building became a highly visible local symbol of the nationwide collapse of the banking industry, the industry that led the country down into the depths of economic hard times. The three-million-dollar building (fifty-three million in 2023 dollars) was a product of the 1920s, a downtown tower built on expectations of a bright economic future. But it was instead occupied in the 1930s by the New Deal's Federal Public Works Administration, a 1933 relief agency positioned to provide jobs for the citizens of Baltimore and Maryland.

Baltimore had built a thriving diversified industrial economy that saw it through the 1920s. Confidence in the future of the city and the region grew through the 1920s as more and more businesses selected Baltimore for their new factories and operations, with each year seeing the addition of a major industrial or commercial business. Company after company chose Baltimore and its energetic port as a new site for their operations, the harbor a vital factor in their selection, as many were reliant upon convenient, cost-effective import and export. Combined with the high rate of home ownership proudly achieved by residents, Baltimore would ultimately be better positioned than many similar communities to survive the coming hard times of the 1930s.

In 1920, German meatpackers William Schluderberg and Thomas Kurdle joined forces, and a little piece of Baltimore history was created: Esskay Meats. The Schluderberg and Kurdle families had been butchers in Baltimore since the 19th century. Combining their businesses would take advantage of Kurdle's large customer network while using the superior 1919 facilities of the Schluderberg operation. The two men created a company that would provide meats and jobs for Baltimoreans for the next 70 years. A disadvantage for the early years soon arose when Esskay's new processing plant was built on the east side of the city, whereas livestock typically arrived on the city's west side rail lines. This inconvenience would necessitate occasional cattle drives from the arrival tracks to the plant's livestock pens, proceeding directly through the center of the city.

McCormick and Company had been founded in 1889 by Willoughby McCormick. He began his company in the basement of his home at 33 Hanover Street, moving several times until in 1896, the company relocated to 44 South Charles Street, adding a spice mill building nearby at 21 East Lombard Street. Both addresses were in the path of and destroyed in the Great Baltimore Fire of 1904. The company and its records were completely burned out, forcing a move to temporary quarters until 1921 when operations could be consolidated at a new building at 414 Light Street. McCormick operated for a half century from their new nine-story factory, grinding spices that filled the downtown air with exotic aromas. Processing, warehousing, manufacturing, packaging, and shipping were all contained in this central Baltimore facility.

The American Sugar Company built a major sugar refinery on the waterfront in the Locust Point section of South Baltimore in 1922. With the opening of this new facility, Baltimore restarted the sugar refining business that had been lost in the economic upheaval of the Panic of 1873. The Panic was a major economic downturn that led directly to a national unemployment rate of 14 percent and the bankruptcy and loss of Baltimore's several sugar-importing and refining businesses. With the opening of the new American Sugar refinery, the sugar business had returned to Baltimore. The new plant opened in a waterfront location with bulk sugar shipments from the Caribbean, Central America, and Florida regularly arriving by ship, the cargo unloaded directly into the new factory where it was refined, packaged, and shipped. On site rail service was provided, with motor trucks later added to transport to the market-place the many variations of the sugar product: granulated, powdered, liquid, and more.

Generations of Baltimoreans knew the name Stieff Silver. It was in 1924 that Gideon Stieff, son of company founder Charles Stieff, built a new manufacturing facility on hilltop land purchased in the Hampden area of Baltimore. Stieff and his future wife, Claire, were said to be picnicking in Druid Hill Park and noticed a sylvan area adjacent to the isolated mill village of Hampden. They were attracted to the location not only for its pristine appearance, but also realized that the unfolding automobile age would allow showroom customers to visit and purchase products away from the company's existing modest downtown retail location. Stieff had already recognized the importance of convenient access in the coming automobile age. He adopted a retail strategy of making products priced and targeted for the expanding middle class, a strategy that proved highly successful, making it necessary to expand the new factory in 1929 to meet increased consumer demand.

The mail order retailer Montgomery Ward came to Baltimore in 1925. While Jacob Epstein had in earlier years created the Baltimore Bargain House, a gigantic mail-order wholesale merchandise emporium in downtown Baltimore, Montgomery Ward was searching for something different. The company sought a unique site, one with direct rail access while being near to what they called "breathing space", with green undeveloped area adjacent to it or nearby. Baltimore was able to offer just such a site: at Monroe Street and Washington Boulevard, a large vacant plot was available along a B&O rail line with the city's 117-acre Carroll Park directly across Monroe Street. The company constructed a mail order retail catalog warehouse of 1.2 million square feet, eight stories high with an executive penthouse atop and a retail store on the lower two levels. The mail order and retail store provided employment for 1,500 Baltimoreans.

Glenn L. Martin was an Iowa native who had relocated and built his first homemade airplane in his backyard in Los Angeles. He was a major aeronautical pioneer, partnering with the Wright brothers and others. His aircraft manufacturing life took him to St. Louis, Cleveland, and finally Baltimore. He was encouraged to locate his factory near the Dundalk area, but opted to purchase just under 1,300 acres in Middle River, 12 miles east of the center of the city. Two hundred of those acres were used to build an aircraft factory, at the time the most modern in the world; the remainder was set aside to create an adjacent airport. The property was sited along an estuary of the Chesapeake Bay, large enough for runways to operate newly constructed aircraft to depart, while also allowing the sea planes built in the factory immediate access to ice-free water.

The Procter and Gamble Company was by the 1920s a world-wide consumer products phenomenon. Growing from a small partnership operation formed ninety years earlier, the Cincinnati-based company constructed a new harborside Baltimore manufacturing plant in 1929. Procter and Gamble's decision to build in Baltimore was based in part on the city's location, a dependable labor market, and access to raw materials. The Procter and Gamble factory was constructed at a cost of $5,000,000 ($88,000,000 in 2023 dollars) on a ten-acre plot at Locust Point, included multiple interconnected buildings, each dedicated to a particular product line, with the overall goal to expand the company's production of soap products including Ivory Snow. With a large meat packing industry in the city, the plant had a supply of fats and oils available close at hand while exotic oils from Asia could be brought to the plant by ships transiting the Panama Canal. Access to the port was a major factor for Procter and Gamble in selecting Baltimore as their new manufacturing location.

The Western Electric Company, the manufacturing division of the Bell Telephone System, opened in Baltimore in 1929, building a waterfront complex of buildings on the 125-acre site of the former "Coney Island of the South", Riverview amusement park. Telephone equipment and long-distance cable were in great demand by the mid-1920s, making necessary a company expansion of its manufacturing capacity by adding this southeast Baltimore factory. The site precisely met the company's criteria for site selection, including size, access to rail and water transportation, fair tax assessments, and the pro-business, favorable political climate offered by Baltimore's leaders. Harbor-front bulkheads were added to the waterfront property, with ship channels dredged to permit large vessels to call on the factory. Construction of the several buildings that made up the manufacturing complex continued through the year; creating a cable plant covering 7.5 acres and an insulated wire plant with another 6.4 acres soon under roof.

These businesses were certainly not alone in choosing to locate in Baltimore but represented some of the largest new operations at the time. Among the many other companies growing, expanding, or building in Baltimore in the decade included Lever Brothers, a soap product maker occupying a factory on Holabird Avenue; a major Coca Cola Bottling plant in the central part of the city; and a more modest headquarters for the Globe Poster Printing Company, a business destined to print popular show card posters for the next 90 years. These businesses didn't have the job density of many other new operations but offered modern plants and factories with employment opportunities that were long term Baltimore industries.

MAKING STEEL: SPARROW'S POINT

Steel had become ascendent as the building material of choice early in the 20th century. Ships were built with it, steel bridges spanned rivers, machine tools made of steel reshaped more steel for tools and utensils, and steel auto frames and bodies replaced those of less durable materials. Steel would soon help builders reach to the sky with the construction of office towers of immense height. A single steel mill in the Baltimore region was repeatedly expanded over time to provide steel in varying shapes, sizes and functionality. Steel was modern, steel was the future, and Baltimore had become a major steel supplier.

Southeast of the city, the Maryland Steel Company constructed a mill in the late 19th century on the Sparrow's Point Peninsula. The growth-oriented Bethlehem Steel Company bought the mill in 1916, company President Charles Schwab stating: "We contemplate here the largest steel plant in the United States." Expansion was well underway by the 1920s, with spending on new development reaching $85 million dollars (in 2023 dollars, $1.2 billion.) The expansion readied the steel mill for the future: land was filled to add acreage, ship channels were dredged for efficient importing of iron ore, more Bessemer and open-hearth furnaces were constructed to increase steelmaking capacity, existing product buildings like the rail mill were modernized and repaired, additional tin mills for flat steel were brought online, and new and more specialty product buildings were constructed.

An early 1920s client for Sparrow's Point steel mill was Dole Pineapple. James Dole had a plan: he would grow pineapple on his plantations in Hawaii, then process and pack them in cans, shipping the finished food product to the mainland for purchase by consumers. He made a visit to Baltimore at a time when the city was a pineapple canning center, giving him an opportunity to visit the steel mill at Sparrow's Point. He would have observed at the mill the heating of iron ore, coal, and limestone in Bessemer furnaces to make pig iron, the iron subsequently converted to steel, then rolled flat until it met the desired thickness of thin sheet steel. The quality of the steel made at Sparrow's Point was sufficiently high that Dole became a Sparrow's Point customer: the steel was shipped westward through the Panama Canal, journeying almost 7,000 miles to Honolulu, where Dole used it to make cans. His company then filled the cans with fresh pineapple, processed the product, and sent the finished canned pineapple back across the Pacific. No doubt some of those cans made their way to Baltimore, perhaps to the modest corner grocery stores of the J.W. Crook company.

A chain reaction in Sparrow's Point sheet steel soon began: more customers, more cans, more products. Sparrow's Point began making tin plate for Baltimore's Continental Can Company and their client, the Campbell's Soup Company. In 1923 alone, Campbell's ordered and purchased 500 million cans, the majority made from Sparrow's

Point steel. Other uses soon emerged: wooden car bodies were obsolete by the early 1920s, replaced by steel. Flat sheet steel, thicker than that used for can making, was stamped into auto fenders, doors, and car bodies. By 1926, steel bars were being stretched into new shapes, becoming rods and wire which then became bridge cables, spikes, staples, pipe, rods, springs and more. Wire became nails, some of them galvanized. Thousands more Baltimoreans became steel mill workers, populating the company town of Sparrow's Point, as well as nearby Dundalk and Turner Station, then further afield Highlandtown in east Baltimore, where the United Railways Number 26 streetcar, known as the Red Rocket, would transport the workers to their jobs at the mill.

The Bethlehem Steel Sparrow's Point operation was more than steel production, as adjacent to the mill was a ship building yard. The shipyard had opened in conjunction with the mill in the late 1880s, becoming a beehive of activity prior to and during the Great War. The Sparrow's Point shipyard built 10 tanker ships in 1918 alone. In 1921, Bethlehem Steel acquired yet another yard, this one along the newly constructed Key Highway. The ship building facility of what had been the Skinner Shipyards in Locust Point became a part of the Bethlehem Steel Shipbuilding Division. The Locust Point yard was converted to repair work while the Sparrow's Point yard delivered 61 new ship hulls: cargo, oil tankers, even passenger vessels, during the 1920s. The yard produced literally dozens of car floats, ferries used by railroads to transport rail cars across bodies of water, some for local use by the Baltimore and Ohio to move railcars across the Patapsco River. Employment at the yards during World War One was about 12,000 workers, but 1920s prosperity increased that number to 18,000. Baltimore was never a one-industry town, evident in its long history of food packing, garment making and more, but in a city where much of the population, the workers, and their families relied on just one employer, Bethlehem Steel, as the key to their future, it had become very close.

AN ENERGETIC CITY

In Baltimore, the decade offered seemingly a multitude of exciting events in so many fields of endeavor, one can only imagine the constant "head turning" the average Baltimorean experienced to keep up with change. Women had become flappers and voters. Industry grew, new factories and jobs seemed to arrive every year. Henry Mencken became the Sage of Baltimore, ruling the local literary roost. Culture was accessible, a Baltimore Museum of Art and a Baltimore Symphony both arrived. Films were new and then suddenly they talked. Automobiles modernized transportation while radios joined telephones to modernize communication. The city and the times were changing.

Credit. A consumer revolution arrived, as momentous and long-lasting as any change in the decade. Until the 1920s, purchases were generally paid in full at the point of sale. In the 1920s, installment buying plans gained acceptance, allowing consumers to purchase items previously out of their financial reach. Costly items had become affordable as they could be acquired by making periodic partial payments. Sears Roebuck and Company, who sold goods to one third of the country's population, and J.C. Penney, which had expanded to 1,000 stores, both led the way. Buying on credit had begun. Credit purchasing drove the decade's consumer-based prosperity. That some things should not be bought on credit, like corporate stocks, would not be apparent until late in 1929.

Sports. The 1920s was a decade of amazing sports. Horseracing's Preakness Stakes at the Pimlico Racecourse was won in 1920 by what many have described at the greatest racing horse ever: Man O'War. A horse for the ages, many said. Man O' War's 1920 race record was winning all 11 of the 11 races in which he was entered. Edward Sparrows, columnist for *The Baltimore Evening Sun* wrote of him in 1920, "nothing like him has ever been seen in action". The Baltimore area hosted another horse race, perhaps the most difficult of the nation's steeplechase horse races, the Maryland Hunt Cup. The four-mile race over twenty-two timber fences found a permanent home in the Worthington Valley just north of the city in 1922. In baseball, the International League Baltimore Orioles had become a baseball phenomenon: by 1924 the team had won five straight pennants. In the 1922 season, a young left-hander and future Baseball Hall of Fame member named Lefty Grove compiled a record of 27 wins, 10 losses, striking out 330 batters along the way. The 1924 team again played with a lineup that included Grove, and added 21-year-old Dick Porter, a future International League Hall of Famer, who hit for a 0.363 average. Grove, often described as the greatest left-handed pitcher ever, and Porter, a farm boy from Princess Anne, Maryland, who went on to a successful eleven-season major league career, each contributed to an Orioles 1920s baseball dynasty.

Rocketry. Perhaps the decade's most impractical oddity, in a decade of eclectic oddities, was the work of three young men from Hampden who assembled a gasoline powered rocket ship. Robert Condit, a recent Polytechnic High School grad, with friends Harry and Sterling Uhler, three science minded lads, planned to launch a rocket ship. Angle iron, canvas, an air compressor, gasoline for propellant, and steel pipes for rocket tubes were assembled, a total investment of $5,000. As Harry Uhler later said of the destination: "...we wanted to go to Venus. Mars was too far, and we figured the moon was a burned-out planet and not worth seeing." Caught up in the optimism of the times, Lindbergh had just crossed the Atlantic, and anything seemed possible, so the young men were perfectly serious. Communication was not deemed necessary: "We didn't bother setting up any sort of a radio hook-up, figuring that Condit would tell us all about it when he got back". A test flight was attempted. The 25-foot-tall bullet shaped rocket went about 100 feet. No one was fatally injured although Condit did break both his legs. Some egos were doubtless bruised. The "Rocket to Venus" didn't get there.

Vaudeville. Baltimore was a regular stop on the vaudeville circuit providing entertainment featuring a variety of entertainers on a single bill: magicians followed by singers, acrobats, and the inevitable comedians. There were literally dozens of entertainment venues across the city, including the west side Hippodrome Theater, which seated 2,300, and in the center of the African American community, the Royal Theater "On the Avenue." Entertainment for the family could be found at many locations, including James Kernan's Maryland Theater on Franklin Street, adjacent to the Kernan Hotel. More than any other local venue, Kernan brought major star power to the city: Eddie Cantor, Will Rogers, Al Jolson, and Charlie Chaplin all appeared at the Maryland. Each of these venues alternated between local and nationally known entertainment and increasingly, motion pictures. For much of the decade, the silent feature was the regular fare until "talkies" began to appear. At their peak through the 1920s, most theaters offered multiple live and film shows daily with 30,000 Baltimoreans patronizing them each week.

The Movies. Motion picture theater-going was not limited to the center city, major movie house, prominent among them the Stanley, Lowes, Palace, and Empire. These were joined by others providing the latest in film, so movie-goers could attend one of the many smaller community-based auditoriums that dotted the city. Many appeared in the early 1920s first as silent motion picture houses, later offering "talkies". The first acknowledged motion picture with sound, *The Jazz Singer* starring Al Jolson, was shown at the Metropolitan Theater on North Avenue, January 8, 1928. The motion picture moved on to the Cluster Theater in Fell's Point, an early adopter of both sound films and air conditioning. The grand edifices of the center city were not copied in these outer reaches of the city, although the

Forest Theater on Garrison Boulevard featured an elaborate brick facade that attracted attention. Once inside, it was a pure utilitarian lobby that greeted the theatergoer: a vending machine offered a choice of candy for a nickel; further inside seven hundred seats were ready for patrons to watch second-run features like Mabel Norman appearing in *Jinx*, featured on the screen in January 1920. The Forest anchored a strip of stores: an Arundel Ice Cream shop, a Reads Drug Store, a shoe repair shop, a delicatessen. There was, in the southwest corner of the city, the Columbia Theater located on Washington Boulevard, which held its grand opening November 13, 1921. It too ran second-tier features, perhaps accompanied by the latest installment of the serial *The Green Archer*, a silent motion picture series featuring a plucky female investigator, a reclusive millionaire, and a kidnapped damsel. Near Patterson Park, the Grand Theater had a unique green-fronted marquee rising above its stainless-steel box office. The theater was modernized and remodeled in 1926 to permit the showing of motion pictures. The site of the Harlem Park Theater was originally a church on Gilmor Street, but after two fires damaged the property, the most severe in 1924, the property was sold and on it was built a 1,500-seat theater in Spanish style. The Harlem Park catered to a Black audience, becoming known as the "best illuminated building in Baltimore" with an elaborate array of exterior light bulbs.

Amusement Parks. Baltimore offered a great deal of outdoor entertainment. By the 1920s, electricity was an increasingly common amenity with "electric parks" becoming all the rage. With roller coasters, carousels, and other amusements, as well as picnic grounds and often live entertainment, these venues were the perfect choice for family or couples' outings in the warmer months of the year. Bay Shore Park, a Chesapeake Bay waterfront resort of 30 acres was owned by the United Railways Company to boost weekend trolley ridership. Riverside Park, whose land was used later in the decade to build a Western Electric factory offered an across the water view of Baltimore's new flying fields in Dundalk. Gwynn Oak Park in Northwest Baltimore was a chaste version of some parks, no alcohol permitted. Carlin's Park, owned by John Carlin, featured amusements, dancing, swimming, and in the winter, ice skating. Carlin seemed always to have a new attraction ready to draw patrons, from roller coasters and dance marathons to fireworks and freckles contests. Carlin's brought Rudolph Valentino to town in 1923, and 5,000 screaming women showed up there. In 1924, he displayed an elephant, Mary Ann, for the amusement of visitors. But facing winter's reduced revenues and Mary Ann's high feed bills, Carlin sought to donate the animal to the Baltimore Zoo. They declined the offer, whereupon mayoral candidate Howard Jackson took up the animal's cause, encouraging school children to collect pennies for Mary Ann. Now a political elephant, she found new lodging at the Baltimore Zoo as soon as Jackson became Baltimore's mayor.

RACIAL REALITIES AND REACTION

Baltimore was not a universally hospitable place to live, as many citizens were excluded from much of the city's pleasures, amenities, and opportunities. Racial segregation ruled the times. The Black community was effectively confined to specific districts of the city, including the near Northwest district along Pennsylvania Avenue. As previously mentioned, the "City Within a City" was a segregated, largely independent community of minority businesses and workers supporting a community of their peers. But this community was disadvantaged in ways well beyond housing.

A population living in congested quarters inevitably was subject to illness and epidemic in numbers beyond the wider community incidence. Tuberculosis, an airborne infectious disease of the lungs, caused a 10 to 12 percent higher rate along the "Avenue" corridor. It and other such epidemics and disease rates were often cited by city officials as dangerously unhealthy communities. The city's frequent solution to the health problem was to raze the entire community, displacing the residents into a new living environment. It was rather like squeezing an inflated balloon, with pressure applied to one area leading to a bubble in another. The squeezing, the razing of a community, merely moved the overcrowding problem, though it could not alleviate it.

By the prevailing rules of segregation, schools were to be separate but equal. This pipe dream of a plan never bore fruit, as noted in the United States Supreme Court landmark 1954 decision desegregating schools, where the principle was simply stated: separate could never truly be equal. That was certainly true in 1920s Baltimore, where even the treatment of the teachers themselves violated Maryland state law. The law was specific in calling for teachers of both White and Black students to be compensated equally, but that parity was neither achieved nor enforced. The compensation of the teachers of Black students proved to be significantly less than that of their counterparts instructing White students. When considering this teacher inequity in the classrooms, the age of the school buildings, and the availability of supplies, it was clear the reality for Black students was to be at a disadvantage.

For many years prior to the 1920s, Maryland had been perceived as a moderate place, politically siding sometimes with Democrats, at other times with Republicans. The state had a reputation as one of the more tolerant of the states, with Baltimore perhaps leading the way. But a Maryland measured by the standards of the Ku Klux Klan had become "un-American". An organization founded in racial intolerance, the Klan strengthened in 1920s Baltimore, finding disfavor with other issues of the times:

- Bootleggers were said to violate the sanctity of the family by encouraging drunkenness;

- Catholics residing in Maryland provoked the Klan's ire by their mere existence;

- Catholic political activism gave even greater offense;

- Gambling, especially on horse races, upset the moral;

- Elkton Maryland defied the sanctity of marriage offering "no questions asked" marriages;

- Teenagers were un-American, using new slang words parents couldn't understand;

- Youth danced the Charleston and used automobiles for "immoral" purposes.

The Klan, first organized in the post-Civil War years, had lain dormant organizationally for dozens of years. Maryland's Jim Crow laws seemed to have replaced the overt actions of the Klan and those sympathetic to it. A test of local sympathies was a small K.K.K. parade in Baltimore in 1922. Then voices threatening violence were heard, directed at Black men held in jail for "offenses" against White citizens, especially White women. In August 1924, Carroll Gibson was moved to the Baltimore City Jail to avoid threats by White mobs in Talbot County, Maryland, against Gibson, who was Black. Nine years later, George Armwood was moved in the same manner, for the same reasons, though only temporarily: he was returned to Talbot County after Baltimore authorities received assurances of Armwood's safety while held in custody. Talbot County officials providing those safety assurances failed to control local passions, and soon after Armwood was lynched at the hands of a White mob.

A Kleagle, the term applied to a local chapter of the Klan, appeared in the Baltimore community of Hampden (Kleagle #57) in the early 1920s. Statewide, Klan membership was likely 25,000, about 1.5 percent of the state's population, with half of those among the state Klan hierarchy. Klan claims of broad support from Marylanders were proven incorrect in the 1926 Gubernatorial election, when voters chose Governor Albert Ritchie, an outspoken opponent of the Klan, over a Klan supported candidate. Ritchie had been re-elected by the largest plurality in the history of the state to that time. The people had spoken.

THE END OF THE RIDE

For the citizens of Baltimore, the 1920s had started slowly, with a post-war economic recession, accelerating into what is fairly described as the "Roaring Twenties". Roar they did: high times at parties, new lifestyles with a new morality, liquor flowing (albeit illegally), drug use (also illegal), music loud and inviting, and while some looked on with dismay, clubs, theaters, and speakeasies became community cultural centers. The citizens who could took the ride of a lifetime in experiencing all that the 1920s had to offer.

In October 1929, a declining stock market set in motion a series of economic events and attendant social changes that became known throughout the 1930's as the Great Depression. Suddenly all that had been for the 1920s a new normal, a new routine, a new lifestyle, was ending. Over-extended buyers in the "can't-lose" stock market who had bought stocks on credit with money they didn't have, commenced a series of failures that collapsed the economy. Stocks fell, buyers were asked to fulfill their purchase commitments, and with that beyond their means, the economic system began to unravel. Loans that had been made to facilitate stock purchases were called in, to no avail. Unable to collect funds that had been loaned, banks found themselves cashless and unable to meet the withdrawal demands of their depositors. The banks failed. Depositors lost their savings. The money used to buy, sell, build, loan or even gift was gone. Bankruptcy entered everyone's vocabulary. The Great Depression was underway.

January 1, 1930, was a mild day in Baltimore, with moderate winter temperatures, but this was perhaps the only thing encouraging about the new decade. Baltimore residents, now numbering over 800,000, had grown accustomed to the good times of the 1920s, but the early 1930s would be unfriendly to Baltimore, its citizens, and its businesses, so very unlike the decade that had just preceded. As the decade of the 1930s began, there soon began a long period of wishing for better days. Unknown to anyone at the time, reaching those better days would require a long wait. The 1920s and their prosperity were gone, and the grand ride was over.

CHAPTER FOUR:
A DECADE OF UNCERTAINTY

The 1930s

THE 1930S WERE A DECADE of uncertainty: as the decade opened, much about the future was uncertain in the minds of many Baltimoreans. First their jobs, then their savings, had disappeared. Where would tomorrow's meal come from: a bread line? a charity? By mid-decade, the future was slightly more assured, as a halting economic recovery slowly reached the population. New protective social safety nets began to have an impact on people's lives. In Baltimore, an economic recovery meant new jobs in new businesses at the city's new General Motors plant, or a return to jobs in recovering operations, such as the steel mill at Sparrow's Point. Uncertainty of a different type continued at decade's end when war drums in Europe and Asia began sounding. The possibility of a return to war for America, for Baltimoreans, with all the distress, dislocation, and dilemma that came with war, created perhaps the greatest uncertainty of all. The challenges of the 1930s changed Baltimore, changed America, in profound ways. Through it all, Baltimore's citizens endured the uncertainty, some participated in an evolving labor movement, and others watched as some unique local personalities emerged. This was also a decade of entertainers, entrepreneurs, and an emerging civil rights movement. Those things plus a bit of Baltimore miscellany make the story of Baltimore in the 1930s an unexpectedly energetic one.

The economic story of 1930s, the biggest story of the decade, began far away, away from the center city department stores of Hutzler's and Hochschild's, from the shipyards of Sparrow's Point, or from the row houses of Highlandtown. The story might be said to begin with overextended banks and the stock exchanges in New York. But to be more accurate, it began across America with citizens borrowing cash, money they couldn't back up with collateral such as property, to invest in an overheated stock market. You couldn't lose — until you did. Early stock market losses set off an economic chain reaction that was the Great Depression. One couldn't sell those declining-value stocks fast enough. Good fortune smiled on Baltimore with its high rates of home ownership and diverse industries cushioning many of the worst of the decade's economic blows. The economic decline came accompanied by its inevitable partner, high unemployment, and even many of the city's formerly wealthy suddenly found themselves impoverished, with bread lines forming to feed a starving population.

Leading Baltimore's decline was the banking industry. Banks failed and with those failures, depositors had lost their savings. Those savings had been loaned to others, many of whom purchased rising stocks. When stock prices plummeted, the borrowers were caught owing more than their stocks were worth, and were unable to repay their debts. In the absence of re-payments, banks were unable to meet the cash withdraw demands of their depositors. These depositor "runs" on limited cash available toppled the banks, then the banking system. On February 23, 1933, Governor Ritchie took action to block further damage as banks couldn't meet withdrawal demands. He declared a

Maryland "bank holiday", pausing depositor withdrawals from banks across the state. Ritchie went so far as to authorize bank depositor scrip – promissory notes – to partially satisfy customer demands. Weeks later, a similar Federal Bank Holiday was established.

Public apprehension over bank stability focused on two highly visible local bank failures. The Baltimore Trust Company was the largest financial institution in Maryland, representing an early 20th century consolidation of four institutions: National Exchange Bank, Atlantic Trust Company, National Union Bank of Maryland, and Century Trust Company. Baltimore Trust boasted of their 95,000 depositors and holdings of eighty-million dollars in assets. By 1929 the company had opened its new headquarters building at 10 Light Street in downtown Baltimore. But a collapsing economy, with asset values precipitously declining, put the bank into a fatal downward spiral, leading it to close its doors in September 1931. The bank's new headquarters building sat vacant for years, partially occupied later by a few government agencies. By the late 1930s some depositors managed to recover some of their financial losses through bankruptcy proceedings.

The failure of the popular Park Bank added personal tragedy to financial loss. The bank's officers appear to have relied upon stock investments' continuing rise in value, depending upon those rising values to help them undertake some risky and allegedly illegal investment activity. A significant portion of the bank's loan portfolio was termed "insider trading", loans made by the board to themselves, to chase the rising values in stocks. In June of 1932, with public distrust of banks at an all-time high, a bank board member committed suicide. His death was widely reported, thus turning a general distrust of banks into a specific depositor "run" at Park Bank. Typically, lines formed with many depositors seeking their funds at the same time. To quell depositor fears, the bank obtained as much cash as they could gather, putting it on display in the closed and locked lobby. It wasn't enough. By August, the once popular bank was out of cash; the loans made to the board members were uncollectible; the Park Bank was insolvent. An investigation led to the arrest of both the bank's board chairman and president, each accused of bank fraud. Before the trial of the executives ended, the board chairman had also committed suicide. The bank president was convicted and sent to prison.

Bank holidays mitigated depositor panic, and the creation in 1933 of a Federal Deposit Insurance Corporation (F.D.I.C.) program guaranteeing most deposits did the rest. These were highly visible signs to the citizenry that a new administration in Washington, D.C., had recognized and responded to the crisis. Not everyone was made whole, but these steps allowed stability to return to the banking system. By mid-March, many of the less impacted banks had reopened. In all, across the nation 9,000 banks had failed, taking the savings of their depositors with them. The bank crisis soon became yesterday's news, dimmed by a new reality, as America's industrial output dropped by half and the Baltimore unemployment rate was rising.

SHATTERED LIVES

To the dismay of everyone, the nation's economy continued its early 1930s decline; the heady times of the 1920s had become a distant memory. Jobs became scarce in Baltimore, where by 1933 the unemployment rate for the city reached 20 percent. Baltimore was doing well in comparison to many parts of the nation, if a 20 percent unemployment rate could ever be considered better: the unemployment elsewhere peaked that year at 25 percent. Bread-winners had become bread-line standees. Businesses made cutbacks: the steel mill at Sparrow's Point cut workers from the payroll, then cut the work hours of those remaining. At the depth of the decline, only a few thousand very part-time workers manned the steel furnaces.

The federal government appeared to be frozen in a state of inaction. President Herbert Hoover denied any need for direct relief, proclaiming that to do so would injure Americans' industriousness. His attempts to fuel the economy by offering business subsidies were misguided and unproductive. Under Hoover, public morale declined further as citizens saw only a bleak future, one beset with a barrage of bad news: bank failures, lost savings, unemployment lines, and a proliferation of soup kitchens. It would be three long years until a late 1932 election and an early 1933 inauguration of the new presidential administration of Franklin Roosevelt began to offer hope. A patchwork of local relief efforts had arisen, with help coming from diverse quarters. Baltimore City government agencies created programs that should have helped but were derailed by program leadership who tended to see a cheat and idler behind every application for aid. Applicants who had recently migrated to the city in the hope of aid were encouraged to "move on". Charitable organizations stepped up their efforts, but theirs was stop-gap effort at best. Some Baltimoreans flexed their organized labor muscles, hoping to find new power through group unity, but met with only marginal success. Others sought dramatic change by embracing one of many ideological alternatives: communism appealed to some, others saw fascism as a way forward. These pathways would in the end prove to be unsatisfactory or unacceptable. It was to be a "New Deal" from a new president that responded best to the needs of the citizenry.

LABOR REACTS

The economic hard times of the 1930s led to a challenging environment between business and labor. With declines in business levels brought on by the depression, managers in many operations inevitably reduced product output and staffing: workers lost their jobs. Employees had historically been using organized labor action as a strategy to improve their circumstances, but now collective actions would be forced to move into a protective mode to assure that employers conducted furloughs or perhaps reduced wages in an equitable manner. In Baltimore, longshoremen, truck drivers, garment workers, auto-workers, and meat packers each would do their time on the picket lines during the 1930s.

Strike actions in Baltimore were more complicated than similar actions in other cities with local strikers facing "The Baltimore Plan". The Baltimore Plan was an anti-strike, anti-labor series of multiple sequential steps, often supported by local government initiatives. If workers went on strike, in anticipation of picket line confrontations, police were pre-emptively summoned by company officials to stand guard over company property, arrest some strikers, and assure access for replacement workers. This significant and reliable level of government sponsored employer protection meant that employers could depend on Baltimore's political and police powers to be available and exercised on their behalf, making a successful labor action all the more difficult in the city. Employers could hire replacement workers, strike breakers, that were guaranteed police protection as they crossed union picket lines. Baltimore had a reputation for being a business-friendly community, and indeed the Baltimore Plan demonstrated that it truly was, often at the expense of its citizen employees.

The Baltimore Plan was evident in the unsuccessful labor action of the Baltimore taxi driver strike of 1935-36. Although a maritime union action, including the eviction of incumbent union leaders who could not meet the interests of their rank and file, met with some success on Baltimore's waterfront, such was not the result for local taxi drivers. Taxis in Baltimore came to a halt in 1935 when the drivers took to the picket lines to gain both higher wages and union recognition. The taxi companies retaliated by hiring replacement drivers, who were able to drive through picket lines because police equipped with the espantoon (Baltimore speak for a wooden baton) were ready for action at the taxi yard gate. In an escalation of tension, striking drivers began to sabotage the company's taxis where and when they could. The company then armed the replacement drivers. The labor action by the drivers continued, until in 1936, both parties were called into court. The presiding judge ordered the drivers back to work under the prior pay scale, rejecting any recognition of a driver's union. Such was the nature of labor strife in Baltimore in the mid 1930s.

LOCAL RELIEF

The Great Depression had hit Baltimore hard: citizens were hungry, and in need of jobs, housing, and health services. With the leadership of Mayor Howard Jackson, local relief programs were placed under the oversight of the Baltimore Economic Relief Commission (B.E.R.C.) B.E.R.C. was a private-public partnership headed by business leaders supervising social work activities, but this mismatch of skills, tasking business decision-makers with solving social problems, led the agencies activity away from much needed relief. People who had migrated to the city in an unsuccessful search for jobs found B.E.R.C. to be hostile to their requests for relief. They were defined as "vagrants", denied relief measures, and pushed to "move on" away from the city. There was an underlying racial undertone to much of what the city did, or did not do to help. The Great Migration of Black Americans had been underway since before the Depression, bringing many of the rural poor from the south to northern cities, including Baltimore. Suspicion was directed at those most in need of help, and city government appeared more interested in denying benefits to migrants, terming them "cheats and chiselers" than in extending the help needed. The local B.E.R.C. programs did aid some Baltimoreans, but these local efforts became secondary as a wide array of better-funded, more well-managed Federal New Deal initiatives gained footholds in the community.

If B.E.R.C. relief efforts were graded, theirs was at best a "C-" effort. Conversely, the health department in Baltimore would receive an "A+" for improving the lot of a Baltimore community in need. The city's health department, the oldest in the nation, began aggressive programs addressing communicable diseases, including smallpox and diphtheria, accompanied by an extensive pre-natal intervention effort. Supported by the health professionals at the Johns Hopkins Hospital, citizen hygiene was improved, and disease rates declined. The Babies Milk Fund Association offered home visiting nurses, assuring proper nutrition for infants; in the decade of the 1930s, infant mortality was reduced by one-third.

Lead poisoning was another health problem of the era in need of a solution, arising from an unexpected source. Many automobile batteries of the 1920s and 1930s consisted of lead plates spaced to allow acid poured as a liquid between them, all encased in a wooden box. When the battery failed, the lead- and acid-saturated wooden battery cases were simply discarded, making them available for scavenging. The battery wood became a significant health concern when the hard times of the depression made the recovered scavenged wood an attractive fuel for home heating.

When burned, the lead-saturated wood released vapors, so that residents were breathing the lead laden, poisonous air. Baltimore health officials reacted by controlling battery case disposal, making them unavailable to citizens as an alternative fuel. Lead poisoning rates dropped.

POLITICAL ALTERNATIVES

Some Baltimoreans searched for political alternatives to what was an unresponsive, seemingly paralyzed Hoover Administration. The Communist Party held appeal for some with its lure of worker equality shored by reports of its success in the Soviet Union. Party leadership quickly adopted positions designed to make it even more attractive, pointing out the failure of capitalism impacting Americans, with special attention paid to the needs of the minority community, and a strong position favoring civil rights. The local *Afro-American* newspaper stopped well short of advocacy, but did remark, "The Communist Party seems to be the only party going our way." Alliances with the labor movement seemed to be a natural next step, but despite their efforts, the party gained little traction in conservative Baltimore. Communist rallies were hosted, but in its best year, 1934, those events failed to attract more than a thousand citizens.

Some Americans found fascism to be an approach to current economic conditions that offered them hope, order, and perhaps a path to recovery. Many Baltimoreans, as much as 20 percent, were of German ancestry, some fluent in German, and historically supportive of Germany and all things German. In the 1930s, Germany had chosen fascism to drive its own economic recovery. The glorified German post World War One economic recovery was well known. Less understood was that the economic miracle touted by Germany and her supporters was unsustainable, as it had been made possible only by militaristic aggression and abusive practices against a selection of their citizens. These aspects of German recovery were well disguised or hidden, certainly not discussed by those who supported this German brand of fascism. In a move to create favorable opinion and publicity, the German battle cruiser *Emden* visited the Port in 1936, docking at the Recreation Pier at Fell's Point. Ceremonial visits by local dignitaries were soon followed by ship tours for thousands of local visitors. In 1937, a German American Day at the Gwynn Oak Amusement Park attracted a record-breaking crowd of 23,000. Those who saw the truth and understood the reality of the many tumultuous events in Germany led local opposition to the pro-German rallies with counter-protests in the streets, the two sides often separated by cordons of police. German style fascism was a stronger contender than communism as a political alternative, but it was likewise found to be no true solution for Baltimore's economic woes.

A NEW DEAL

The new 1933 administration of President Franklin D. Roosevelt offered a New Deal, a collection of policies, executive orders, and laws designed to lead to citizen relief and economic recovery. The New Deal was designed to put money into citizens' pockets, thence into circulation, while offering savings protections through the Federal Deposit Insurance Corporation. Farm policy changes were made to help embattled farmers cope with hard times. The newly-created National Industrial Recovery Administration, with its "Blue Eagle" symbol and "We Do Our Part" slogan, offered highly visible signs that participation in the recovery was universal. The business community's initial positive reception to the N.I.R.A. turned more negative as the agency began adding labor-friendly provisions to its policies: collective bargaining mandates, workplace safety standards, and an expanded minimum wage eligibility. Resistance to the N.I.R.A. solidified through legal action. Passing through the courts, the United States Supreme Court found the N.I.R.A. was an over-zealous delegation of Congressional authority to Roosevelt's Executive Branch. On May 27, 1935, many of its provisions were declared unconstitutional, a day the New Dealers called "Black Monday". Angered by the rulings of the "nine old men" on the court, Roosevelt threatened to change the voting balance on the court by adding six new justices, effectively "packing" the court. The president's court reform legislation eventually died in Congress, but not before several existing justices began to vote in favor of many of the New Deal's provisions. The Roosevelt administration then offered a replacement legislative package that was larger in scope than previous efforts, and it was passed by the Congress. The new legislation created and included among its programs the Social Security program and a robust National Labor Relations program. It was known as the Second New Deal, implemented in 1935.

Much of conservative, anti-union Baltimore was a hostile environment for programs like those of the New Deal. The political leadership of the city was resistant to relief programs, maintaining the opinion that the solution to the unemployment problem was one for the citizens themselves to solve. Mayor Broening began his Beautify Baltimore program, asking citizens to hire the unemployed for household work and to hire children to search their neighborhoods for repair work. Heavy promotion of Broening's "Beautify" plan included inserting flyers into telephone company monthly telephone bills, ignoring the fact that many in the city had long ago, as a cost saving measure, disconnected their telephones and therefore didn't receive a telephone bill. Broening lost the next election, but the new mayor, Howard Jackson, was no improvement. The new mayor continued his drumbeat of attacking relief programs, terming recipients as persons "on the dole." Religious and community groups worked to fill the gaps for many poverty-stricken Baltimoreans, but it was federal, not local or charitable, programming that made a true impact on Baltimore and her citizens.

Virtually no aspect of the economy was left untouched by the programs of the New Deal. For immediate impact by creating the jobs that workers needed, nothing exceeded the activities of the Works Progress Administration (W.P.A.). The Works Progress Administration became for many the popular and public face of the New Deal. Created by an Executive Order in 1935, the program placed millions of workers into paying jobs, building lasting infrastructure. Thousands of public buildings plus hundreds of schools and post offices were constructed, remodeled, or repaired nationwide. The W.P.A. made many visible contributions to the Baltimore region, with a new Eastern High School on 24 acres at Venable Park on 33rd Street opening in February 1938. New Baltimore area post offices were constructed in Catonsville, Dundalk, Towson, Bel Air, and Ellicott City. Interior mural decoration in many of the new buildings was added by W.P.A. artists employed in Federal Project Number One, a program employing writers, artists, actors, and musicians in projects or programs though out the country. Under the auspices of the W.P.A.'s Project Number One, bookbinders at the Enoch Pratt Library were put to work rehabilitating portions of the library's collection. The W.P.A. built new or paved existing roads, 600,000 miles of them nationwide. In Baltimore, highways and bridges were constructed. The Hilton Street parkway crossed the Gwynn's Falls valley and a 400-foot-long span crossed east to west over the Jones Falls Valley at 29th Street, both opening in 1939. Rehabilitation programs included the highly visible landscaped and park-like Preston Gardens in downtown Baltimore and improvements at The Patapsco Valley Park, Maryland's first state park. The Patapsco site was one of earliest New Deal programs, work accomplished by the 1933 Civilian Conservation Corps (C.C.C.), an environmentally sensitive program that built eight hundred new parks across the country, complete with trails, shelters, and millions of newly planted trees. In Maryland alone, the C.C.C. put 30,000 unemployed, and presumably most-at-risk young men to work at twenty or more "camps" during its nine years of operation.

By the mid-1930s, the programs of the New Deal with most impact were those that included job initiatives. Jobs would get money into circulation, an essential first step to heal the wounded economy. Bank holidays, the establishment of F.D.I.C., federal support of credit unions, Fair Labor Standards legislation, even money for book binding and public art, each took their place in the New Deal's array of recovery initiatives. The most enduring New Deal program was support of senior citizen financial security, the creation of the Social Security program. By providing for the long-term welfare of retirees, it joined the New Deal's federal intervention, as breathtaking in scope as it was successful in defining a path to economic recovery.

OPPORTUNITY AND OPTIMISM

Living through the Great Depression, some Baltimoreans found opportunities beyond those being created by governmental intervention. Entrepreneurs found new pathways for personal and economic success. Talented people found a way forward. Four stories here are of Baltimoreans who defied the odds, inventing, innovating, putting themselves forward, building a future by finding then meeting the opportunities they were presented, or in some cases, created for themselves.

Gustav Brunn fled persecution in his native Germany, arriving with his family in Baltimore in 1938. A spice merchant before he fled Germany, it was natural for him to seek work in the local spice industry. McCormick and Company put him to work, the perfect employer to utilize his experience and skills. But Brunn lasted on the job just two days, his lack of English language skills complicating his employment. From adversity came inspiration, however. Taking the advice of other immigrants, Brunn opened his own business on Baltimore's Market Place, The Baltimore Spice Company, blending and selling spices according to recipes from his homeland. It wasn't long before he responded to the local specialty of cooking crab, developing his own special spice blend. The blend was perfected by 1940, with a name that came later: an associate suggested changing the original name, "Delicious", to a name familiar to Baltimoreans. He named it "Old Bay" after the name of a local steamship company. His former employer apparently sought to duplicate the blend, so Brunn named nine additional spices to the original four, expanding the list of ingredients printed on the container. The nine were in trace amounts, so tiny even Brunn himself said, "We ourselves couldn't have duplicated (it)". By the time of his retirement in 1985, the Old Bay recipe and name were sold, not once but twice, ultimately to the rival company he couldn't work for so many years before: McCormick and Company. Brunn had made his way in a time of economic upheaval.

Harry and Lena Tulkoff traveled from New York to Baltimore in the mid-1920s. The couple settled into a store front at 1103 East Lombard Street where they operated several food related businesses, selling Jersey Ice Cream, the brand they had sold in their New York store, plus hot dogs and Coca Cola, all sold from push-carts. The Tulkoff's began to focus on produce sales, moving to larger quarters a block away, becoming the "New York Fruit Company". As a business owner dealing in produce, Harry was approached with an offer to purchase a large supply of horseradish root that the original buyer had decided not to purchase. Harry bought the entire supply, carefully managed it for preservation, and by the mid 1930s, the New York Fruit Company had a new focus: prepared horseradish. The product when properly prepared and spiced eliminated an unpopular household task for the local housewife– grinding and preparing horseradish. Demand for the Tulkoff product grew, and other produce lines and businesses were dropped. The path from New York Produce to Tulkoff's horseradish had been established. In the 1930s, even amid a depression, Harry and Lena Tulkoff proved that commerce and new business could still grow and ultimately prosper.

Cab Calloway came to Baltimore at age eleven. From a home in the Druid Hill neighborhood, young Cabell Calloway III spent entirely too much time on the streets of the city for his mother to ignore. Frustrated that her talented son was heading in the wrong direction, Cab found himself enrolled at the Downingtown (Pennsylvania) Industrial and Agricultural School, an institution which was effectively a reform school. The hope was that he would find a new direction. On his return to Baltimore in 1922, he found an interest in music, and began singing lessons. Over more parental objections, he started performing in night clubs, that avocation tempered only by his talent as a basketball player for Frederick Douglas High School in Baltimore. Declining an offer from the Harlem Globetrotters, Calloway had by 1930 been performing in Chicago and New York, attracting the attention of Louis Armstrong and Thomas "Fats" Waller, then joining a group known as the Missourians. The Missourians were soon renamed Cab Calloway and his Orchestra. By sheer tenacity, natural ability honed through perseverance, and a shrewd business sense, a talented 23-year-old kid from Baltimore was leading the house band at the Cotton Club in Harlem, routinely appearing on radio programs, and earning $50,000 a year ($960,000 in 2023 dollars). He recorded "Minnie the Moocher" and "Saint James Infirmary" in 1931, becoming the "Hi De Ho Man" of the entertainment world.

Myles and Betty Katz took a chance in 1932, at the very worst of times in the Great Depression, when they bought a small chain of failing restaurants and renamed them, White Coffee Pot Restaurants. Their initial purchase grew to over thirty locations throughout the region, all with a simple slogan, "Good food at fair prices". The stores were brightly lit affairs, a counter and a series of booths, a jukebox usually alive with music, waitresses dressed in white, with fast service ideal for the working man or woman. Locations were open twenty-four hours a day, seven days a week. One location in the southern reaches of the city, in the small south Baltimore neighborhood of Brooklyn, attracted workers from many nearby factories including General Refractories and Harbison Walker, both makers of bricks to line the steel-making furnaces at the Sparrow's Point Steel Mill. Often joining them were trainmen from the Baltimore and Ohio Railroad. The promise of good food, fast service, and modest prices drew them to the White Coffee Pot's Brooklyn location, just one block south of the railroad tracks, nearby where they had parked their train, its engine idling during the crew's dinner hour. The chain changed hands in 1956 but continued operating in the same manner, local and friendly, with a steady and regular clientele. A success story begun by the Katzes, pleased employees and customers until the lights were turned off sixty-plus years later.

A GRADUAL HEALING

By the middle of the 1930s, commerce in the Baltimore area was clearly in a gradual economic recovery. Consumer confidence was improving, shuttered stores were re-opening, and new businesses were being created. The cycle of a downward economic spiral, a lack of consumer spending, leading to employee layoffs, leading to even less spending, had been broken. The trend of Baltimore's gradual recovery was also being seen in nationwide data. Disappointing skeptics, the economic turnabout strongly coincides with the stimulus created by the New Deal. National data showed that measures of all economic activity had stopped declining and were by 1935 beginning to grow. Each year through the remainder of the decade, from 1935 forward, Baltimore was adding jobs and experiencing increased economic activity.

In October 1934, General Motors representatives and Baltimore Mayor Jackson broke ground for a new multi-million-dollar Chevrolet manufacturing plant. Building a factory capable of producing 80,000 vehicles per year during an economic crisis, when many couldn't afford food, was certainly a complete act of faith in the future. The plant, located in the southeast portion of the city, was designed as a two-story facility, with auto bodies made on the plant's upper level and the automobile chassis on the lower. The body and chassis were mated as the vehicle assembly operations continued, the body descending from second floor to first, there joined together, and then continuing along the assembly line to be completed. Fewer than six months had elapsed from factory ground-breaking to the beginning of vehicle manufacturing, with many of the 2,500 factory assembly line employees drawn from the roster of the construction workers who had built the new facility. Upon its opening, the new factory had effectively converted the 2,500 original construction jobs to 2,500 newly created, permanent, full-time positions.

Vincent Bendix, whose company was a manufacturer of Bendix Air Brakes and other automotive components, by the 1930s had taken a personal interest in two modern technologies, electronic devices and aeronautical engineering. He acquired several companies in each of those industries, merging them in 1936 into a new entity known as Bendix Radio. The company would produce aircraft electronics, starting with radio for communications, then aircraft direction finders and radio compasses. At the outset, Bendix chose to locate his company near the research and development center of the Naval Research Laboratory (N.R.L.) in Washington, D.C. The Washington, D.C., area did not adequately meet his needs for operating a manufacturing facility, leading him to search for an alternative. He found Baltimore a more suitable site, close enough to stay in touch with the trends and discoveries of the N.R.L. while offering a more adequate manufacturing labor supply. Bendix opened a Baltimore plant on Fort Avenue near Fort McHenry in 1937, supplying a very welcome 500 new jobs to local workers. The company thrived in its new local headquarters from its opening, later expanding into over seven thousand jobs, held mostly by women, during World War Two.

In 1938, a major manufacturer, Westinghouse Electric Company, opened a new plant along the Washington Boulevard in Southwest Baltimore. This new operation merged the 250 employees working in two existing Westinghouse company operations: one in Pennsylvania, the other in Massachusetts. The plant was built specifically so Westinghouse could focus on electronics, its location desirably placed near the contracts emanating from Washington, D.C. The Baltimore facility, a large structure constructed of wood (as steel building components were in short supply during a pre-war military buildup) specialized in two military applications: modern electrically controlled torpedoes and cutting-edge development of radar. Radar sets such as those built in Baltimore were of the top-secret SCR-270 model that had been installed on the island of Oahu, in Hawaii. The system detected an incoming Japanese attack on December 7, 1941, but skeptical leaders ignored the radar warnings. Employees numbered into the thousands as Westinghouse Baltimore operations grew with the manufacture of radar, then with development of other military applications.

Lever Brothers was a manufacturer of soaps and cleansers that was formed in the late 19th century England. By the late 1930s, the company expanded from a single plant in Massachusetts with a 1938 purchase of the Hecker Brothers soap factory on Holabird Avenue in east Baltimore, where Lever hired 1,000 Baltimoreans to operate the plant. Hecker Brothers was the maker of Gold Dust and Silver Dust Soap powders, popular laundry powders that Lever Brothers had sought the right to market and manufacture in conjunction with the purchase of the factory. These Gold and Silver soap powders faded in the face of strong competition after World War Two, with the factory switching to the manufacture of several of the company's other products, including Rinso soap powder, Lux and Dove soap bars, and Swan and Wisk detergents.

SPECIAL TIMES, SPECIAL PEOPLE

The 1930s found Baltimore filled with interesting, important, and noteworthy personalities, many with local roots, others as visitors to the city. It was an eclectic group, encompassing a wide array of interests and accomplishments, including literary, sports, political, and entertainment figures. From journalists to trumpeters, from artists to immigrant angels, they offer to us interesting stories to be told, something for everyone. Looking beyond the hardship of the Depression and the hopes of the New Deal, here are the stories of a few of those personalities of 1930s Baltimore.

Scott and Zelda. Among the many prominent visitors to the city, none were more well-known than Scott and Zelda Fitzgerald. A couple who had spent the prior decade on the move, they spent much of the 1930s in Baltimore, settling in for a time of recovery for each of them. Henry Mencken urged them to come to Baltimore to obtain treatment for Zelda's mental illness at the Phipps Clinic at Johns Hopkins. Taking up residence in a Victorian cottage, La Paix, in Towson, they found a quieter life in Baltimore to recover, he from chronic alcoholism, she from schizophrenia. He wrote as best he could, but from a state of alcoholic depression he described writing "with a feeling of utter hopelessness" while Zelda shared her time between La Paix and treatment at Hopkins. The couple were very much A-List celebrities in Baltimore, spending time at luncheons, house, or dinner parties and attending motion pictures. But their illnesses overtook them, and Zelda inadvertently set fire to the La Paix house, losing them their lease, while Scott's alcoholism grew worse. In the end they each drifted on, he met death in California in 1940, she in North Carolina in 1948.

Entertainers. Baltimore hosted several visiting jazz musician visitors in the era. Some were native sons who had made good, bandleader Cab Calloway and drummer William "Chick" Webb among them. A gifted pianist by the name of Thomas "Fats" Waller sent his *Ain't Misbehavin'* show to Baltimore in 1930, where it included the "Connie's Hot Chocolates" revue. The original show spent much of 1929 on Broadway and by 1930, the show headed out in a touring company, arriving in Baltimore in late January, just as the Great Depression was gaining momentum. The hit show played James Kernan's Maryland Theater, located on Franklin Street, a venue for many visiting showmen and entertainers of the time.

In 1931, trumpeter Louis Armstrong made a strong impression when he arrived accompanied by bags of coal for the needy. Scheduled to appear at the Royal Theater, he made an offer that anyone who bought show tickets in advance would receive a free a bag of coal as a gift. This offer of home heat or coal stove fuel arrived in a time of great need. Armstrong prioritized the gifting of the coal to women raising families, with no mention of buying a ticket to his show, in a simple act of generosity.

Henry Mencken had become prominent well before the 1930s began. A Baltimore native, he had started as a newspaperman, gradually gaining prominence in the 19-teens, especially with his strong anti-prohibition advocacy. Mencken had written, opined, editorialized, and registered his thoughts on a variety of topics for some twenty years. His 1925 coverage of the Scopes Monkey Trial in Tennessee was exceptional, certainly the high point in his newspaper career, and helped make his reputation for excellence. His writings, both editorial and literary, earned him the title: "The Sage of Baltimore". Mencken married Sara Haardt in 1930, apparently surprising everyone, calling it the result of following a hunch, saying "This seemed to be a superb one". Sadly, Haardt was in poor health and died in 1935.

He managed and edited the prestigious magazines, *The Smart Set*, leaving it in 1924 when he and drama critic George Nathan founded *The American Mercury*. From his home on Hollins Street in Baltimore, Mencken travelled on a regular basis to New York City to serve as editor and publisher of one, then the other publication. Mencken, using the *American Mercury* magazine, determined that the magazine would be "elegantly irreverent", featuring writers of the era including among many others, Scott Fitzgerald. Mencken retired from the magazine in 1933.

The 1930s however proved to be the start of his reputational unravelling, at least in the minds and hearts of Baltimore's "Man in the Street". The decade began well enough with his popular and constant written and verbal assault on the failed policy of prohibition. Mencken then turned his attention to the New Deal and its popular policies. He wrote and spoke vociferously in opposition to the New Deal as a handout to those unable to make it on their own. It seemed the more he said, the worse his reception. In the 1930s, his acerbic style was very much out of step with the woes of the Great Depression, leading him to pivot to writing about happier times, producing stories like "Happy Days", "Newspaper Days", and "Heathen Days", published in the *New Yorker* magazine. The effect of these stories was to restore his reputation as a great man of letters, but by decade's end, Mencken had fallen out of favor, his unrelenting negative opinions of the times and the people proving costly to his reputation, and losing him the editorial platform at *The Baltimore Sun* newspaper.

Lillie May Carroll Jackson made history in the 1930s. Her mantra of "God helps those who help themselves" was never more evident than when she, assisted by her daughter Juanita, initiated her 1931 "Buy Where You Can Work" program. That program's message was a simple but effective one: the Black community should shop only at stores where a Black worker could be employed. This effort was directed at Black unemployment, which was often double the unemployment rate of Whites. The "Buy Where You Can Work" program harnessed the economic power of the minority community, causing businessmen to hire Black workers to maintain customers while moving toward a modest amount of equality in civil rights. She headed the Baltimore branch of the National Association for the Advancement of Colored People (N.A.A.C.P.) starting in 1935, a position she would hold for 35 years, thus presiding over the powerful civil rights organization through many of the battles and accomplishments of the 1950s and 1960s. Baltimore's branch of the N.A.A.C.P. became one of the largest such affiliates in the nation, numbering over 17,000 members. Jackson's accomplishments were many, from leading boycotts to organizing classes to prepare her community to take civil service examinations, to mentoring legal leaders like Thurgood Marshall. Dr. Jackson was at the forefront of the protests that surrounded the abuses of the times directed at African Americans, from bias in hiring, unfair labor practices, educational inequality, to terrorizing behaviors directed at individuals, including the 1933 lynching of an accused but untried George Armwood, reportedly Maryland's last lynching victim. Anti-lynching activism and protests followed the murder of Armwood, the Baltimore branch of the N.A.A.C.P. was re-invigorated, while Maryland Governor Ritchie's political career came to an end with his mishandling of the Armwood matter. The result was the movement of the national, but not the state, anti-lynching legislation a bit closer to approval in Congress.

Julia Friedenwald Strauss met one of the decade's most serious problems heroically and head-on. As the new German Nazi regime raised the level of persecution of its Jewish population, the situation for Jews there became impossible to tolerate. Emigration was one solution to the plight of many with America, across an ocean and far away, a prized destination. But America's doors were barely open. American xenophobia had been on powerful display since the early 1920s and a crisis in Europe was not about to alter in any meaningful way the refugee limits imposed by the U.S. Congress.

To gain entry and obtain a necessary but very scarce entry visa, a refugee needed to file an affidavit of financial support and name a specific individual as an American sponsor. Connecting potential refugees to sponsors was the second problem in this process, the first was finding sponsors at all. That is where Julia Strauss made her mark. Her work with the Baltimore branch of the National Council of Jewish Women mobilized her community into first, identifying sponsors for refugees, then completing the paperwork necessary, and finally, once a visa was granted, assisting the newly arrived immigrants in acclimating to their new life situation. The refugees were further assisted by other agencies such as the Hebrew Immigrant Aid Society and a specially formed group, the Refugee Adjustment Committee. The work of Julia Strauss and the cooperation of her many sponsoring persons made Baltimore a home for 3,000 Jewish refugees during the 1930s.

Theodore Roosevelt McKeldin was a self-made man. A true Baltimorean, he graduated from local high school Baltimore City College in their evening program while working full time in a bank. His education continued in evening law school at the University of Maryland while continuing full time daytime employment. He entered the political arena as Baltimore Mayor William Broening's assistant, regularly appearing statewide throughout the 1930s as the mayor's representative. He became well-known as a speaker for Rotary Clubs, Conventions, and church groups on issues as diverse as the unemployment problem, the future of Baltimore aviation, and the quality of Maryland's dairy products. McKeldin was elected in 1934 at age 34 as president of Baltimore's Junior Association of Commerce and in that period, he created the Baltimore-based charity, Santa Claus Anonymous. The organization's goal was simply to "give a child a Christmas". Thousands of Baltimore children received gifts and gift certificates, a few dollars perhaps, at a time when gift giving was impossible for many families during that Depression Era. He was urged to run for mayor and did so, unsuccessfully, in 1939. A gifted and memorable orator, his star continued to ascend and he was elected in 1943 as a Republican mayor in a heavily Democratic city. In the 1950s he served two terms as governor of Maryland. He later returned to run for mayor of the city in 1964 and was elected to a single four-year term, overseeing the initial steps of Baltimore's Inner Harbor redevelopment.

Elizabeth Barger was a Baltimore housewife turned sports superstar. In the mid 1930s, a young woman walked into Seidel's Bowling Center on Belair Road. She didn't know it then, but she would become the best female duckpin bowler ever! At the time Barger began bowling, there were about 200,000 duckpin bowlers in the country, a number that has steadily declined over the years. The game is alleged to have been invented in Baltimore by none other than baseball greats John McGraw and Wilbert Robinson, but a closer check reveals the game had actually been played in New England for at least a dozen years before the 1900 date claimed by Baltimore bowlers. Mary Elizabeth "Toots" Barger became a champion at a game that Baltimore adored, bowling with half-size pins, where a single score of 120 was a major accomplishment. In 1947, Barger bowled to an average of 119. Newspapers printed accounts of her exploits and scores and she won competitions year and after year, becoming a true Baltimore champion in a sport that had found a home in only a dozen east coast states.

Isaac Emerson had been a Baltimore personality for several decades before the 1930s began. His Emerson Drug Company began making Bromo-Seltzer in 1888, a successful antacid formulation to relieve pain from headache, heartburn, upset stomach, or indigestion. Emerson was also responsible for a number of Baltimore landmarks including the Emerson Tower, the Emerson Hotel (razed in 1971), and the Emersonian Apartments. The Emerson Tower was the headquarters of his Emerson Drug Company. The building featured a six-story manufacturing facility abutting on two sides the iconic 15-story Emerson Tower, built in 1912. The tower was of Romanesque design, recalling a similar tower Emerson observed during a visit to Florence, Italy. It was in the 1930s that the Emerson Tower lost its memorable top. Architect Joseph Sperry had placed a rotating 51-foot, 20-ton blue Bromo-Seltzer replica bottle as a crown for the Emerson Tower, its illumination said to have guided ships into the Port of Baltimore. The bottle display proved to be too weighty for the building to support, which led to its removal, and by 1936 the blue bottle was just a memory.

John Carlin was an amusement park entrepreneur without peer in Baltimore. His Carlin's Park was promoted as "Baltimore's Million Dollar Playground", open year-round offering "clean fun for the entire family". By the 1930s, the park expanded from a dance hall to include amusement park rides (two roller coasters, a swing ride, a carousel, and others) and a one-thousand-foot-long swimming pool surrounded by a sandy beach, each open in the summer. In the winter, ignoring the seasonal closing of most amusement parks, an indoor Iceland Ice Rink offered public ice skating, shows featuring figure skaters, and for a time, a home for the Baltimore Orioles of the Eastern Amateur Ice Hockey League. Never without a creative idea, Carlin hosted live bands at all-night dance parties as well as entertainers, operas, vaudeville acts, and shows. "Shipwreck Kelly" (Aloysius Anthony Kelly, 1893-1952) came to Carlin's to establish a world record for the latest fad, flagpole sitting. Carlin's sponsored dance marathons for several years, contests with rules that required contestant couples to stay in motion for extended periods of time, and the last couple standing awarded a monetary prize. One of Carlin's 1930 dance marathons, termed a World Championship, lasted four months, with over 3,100 hours of dancing. Spectators would come to watch and encourage their favorite couples, occasionally tossing "tips" to the participants as additional incentive. Around the clock, the dancers shuffled on, often one asleep in the arms of the other, with diminishing length rest breaks as the contest continued. Hilda and Chris Schindle outlasted all the other couples to win the event and the prizes in December 1930. An amusement park of Carlin's size and scope was not without its difficulties. Almost everything was built of wood, and inspectors would routinely close buildings for fire code violations, until in September 1937, a ten-alarm fire burned much of the park to the ground. Carlin rebuilt, hosting a twentieth anniversary celebration the following summer.

Leo Kanner uncovered a major human trafficking scandal in the 1930s. The Rosewood Center was the State of Maryland's "Home for the Feeble Minded", offering custodial care to unfortunates who were mentally challenged. Kanner, who did early studies on autism and developed a testing protocol named after him, noticed that some of the patients at Rosewood were being released into the care and custody of wealthy Baltimore families. A single attorney, Harry Wolf, was serving writs of *habeas corpus* on behalf of young mostly female patients. Wolf would argue vigorously in court that the patient should be released; after achieving the desired release of the now former patients, he allegedly had them "adopted" by families who would set them to household chores and work. The result was that the released patients had effectively become slaves for the rest of their lives to the chosen families and households. When Wolf's scheme was uncovered, the attorney had 26 similar cases pending before the court, with 166 prior cases having been heard by the court prior to Kanner's 1933 Rosewood discovery. Kanner later located many of the victims when he learned they had gone to reside with "society ladies" who promised a loving home after paying Wolf (or other attorneys) to deliver a resident of their choosing. Some later even expressed dissatisfaction, complaining their maids seemed slow or stupid. Kanner later told his colleagues. "This discovery, however, did not deter them from ordering another girl from the lawyer…" once they had discarded the prior one.

Ogden Nash arrived in Baltimore in 1934, moving his family from New York to a home in the Guilford section of the city. Nash was a writer of poetry, but not of the epic or sonnet type, as his offered witty observations of the times, events, and human nature. Nash became a Baltimorean soon after he wed Baltimore native Frances Leonard. Nash wrote hundreds of short, lighthearted poems, published in more than twenty books, most of them originally written in cursive on yellow pads of paper. A meticulous man, when he found he had written a word that was a poor choice, he would not scratch it out, instead he would carefully erase and search for another. He travelled from Baltimore to his writing and speaking engagements by train, as he hated to fly. He thought the airplane an unhappy invention, writing at one point of the Wright Brothers "as two Wrights who made a wrong". When asked which of his quips he would be most remembered for, his response was to offer one of his earliest poems (1922), inspired by his self-described "unregenerate youth". The seven-word poem? "Candy is dandy, but liquor is quicker".

DIVERSION AND DISCOVERY

A new president and a New Deal slowly boosted morale and by the mid-1930s hope replaced despair for many if not most of Baltimore. Diversion from the cares of the day was available in an unusual potpourri of interesting, even fascinating events. Baltimore in the 1930s was a city of many possibilities.

One way to take one's mind off the hard times, to find a smile, some joy, even happiness was to divert one's attention. Some would term it escapism, to find a happier, if imaginary place or circumstance. The motion picture industry took up the escapist challenge, beginning an era of entertainment that would immerse audiences in another time, another place, or a fantasy world. Audiences became visitors to Skull Island to meet King Kong, sharing Fay Wray's travails atop the new Empire State Building. For a nickel, the world of bread lines and bad news was far behind, audiences vicariously joining a Busby Berkeley revue, with a hundred chorus girls costumed in dollar coin pendants singing, "We're in The Money". Ruby Keeler and Dick Powell seemed to be the perfect antidote to dreary days and times, if only for 97 minutes, as they joined together to star in *Gold Diggers of 1933*. For pure fantasy, few motion picture stars of the era could offer their audiences more hope and love than Shirley Temple. Beginning in the early 1930s with such films as *Bright Eyes* (1934) and *Curly Top* (1935), Temple made twenty additional films before the decade came to an end. The seven-year-old was everyone's favorite little leading lady, sharing dilemmas and then providing solutions to problems. Judging by their success rate, these and more like them met the public need for escape.

Fantasy sometimes does come true. It did for two young Baltimore boys, Ted Jones and Henry Grob, in the summer of 1934. The youngsters decided to bury their accumulated savings in the basement of an unoccupied Baltimore house. Given the loss of savings endured by so many in recent bank failures, perhaps burying the money was, at the time, a perfectly reasonable decision. Digging a hole for the burial of their treasury, they struck a metal box. Someone with the same idea of burying a treasure seemed to have been there before them. The box they discovered was found to contain gold coins, worth $200,000 in today's dollars. The boys were on the cusp of great wealth. In the 1930s, it was illegal for individuals to own monetary gold, so they turned the treasure over to the police. What followed were investigations, claims of ownership by many (all ultimately ruled bogus by the courts), and lawsuits. In the end, the two boys were awarded shares of the treasure, with the court ruling they could not access the awards until they achieved adulthood. Ted received his share, but in the absence of modern medical care, Henry sadly never would, as he died from pneumonia before his eighteenth birthday.

For the family that made Hendler's Ice Cream, 1932 was a year to remember. Hendler's Ice Cream had been made in Baltimore by Lionel Hendler since 1905. His flavors, the quality of the product, and a distribution network of 400 stores made Hendler's the local ice cream brand of choice. His success attracted a series of unsuccessful criminals and extortionists until finally in 1932, his son Albert was kidnapped by three men who planned to hold him for ransom. Albert was evasive in his answers to questioning, even when threatened with a gun, to the point where the kidnappers began to doubt the likelihood of obtaining a ransom. Threats were replaced by cooler heads, so the kidnappers decided to release him. He was driven to the south end of the Hanover Street bridge where the kidnappers dropped him off, returning one of the three dollars they had taken from him so he would have cab fare home. Albert chose to not report the kidnapping to his family nor the police, and so the episode should have ended there, but the disappointed kidnappers made a second try. They sent a threatening extortion note demanding $7,000. The police were then put on the case, a decoy package was mailed to an address in New York, an arrest was made, the trio were ultimately sent to prison.

HOT TIMES, LITERALLY

Inevitably, there were "hot times" in the city during the decade, whether in music, in baseball, or in police work. But one particularly hot time affected everyone: unparalleled weather.

This was the era of hot shows, of the "big bands" and their unique musical stylings, full orchestras playing the latest songs, making the hits, led by bandleaders who became stars themselves. The west side Hippodrome Theater was one of the more prominent venues for these bands, and in keeping with the times, while the audience was segregated, musicians of all races were welcome to play there. Among the 1930s bands playing the "Hipp" were three of the biggest names of the era: Glenn Miller, Benny Goodman, and Guy Lombardo. Notable at the time also was the Harry James orchestra, led by James but inspired and initially funded by Benny Goodman. James and his orchestra played the Hippodrome in late June 1939 accompanied by a male soloist making his debut with the band, a relatively unknown singer by the name of Frank Sinatra. Sinatra had rejected the stage name of "Frankie Velvet", and soon moved on to other bands and other locations, but his "big time" start occurred in 1930s Baltimore.

In the 1930s, hot times were in the sports world in an era when every sports fan's eyes were on the national pastime, the game of baseball. In this decade, Baltimore was not among the select few cities with a major-league franchise. Major league play in Baltimore had ended in 1902 and would not return until 1954. The city did have a minor-league Baltimore Orioles team, of the International League, playing teams both domestic and international from Canada to Cuba. In the 1920s, these minor-league Orioles had been a true powerhouse team, but the 1930s offered fewer bright spots for the fans. The success rate of their red-hot slugging first baseman, Joe Hauser, made headlines in the sports pages of two dailies, *The Baltimore Sun* and *The Baltimore News*. Hauser was with the team for an impressive two years, having come down to them from the major-league Cleveland Indians. In those two Orioles seasons, Hauser had a very hot bat, and became a home run king, hitting 63 home runs in his 1930 season, while batting over .300. The minor league Minneapolis Millers bought his contract for the 1932 season, whereupon Hauser departed Baltimore.

The 1930's hot times in Baltimore were more than singers and batters. In at least one case, the hot times mimicked the gangster movies of the era. The formula for escapist crime-gangster-police motion picture always included a car chase scene, with getaway cars pursued by police cars. In the movies, cars careened around curves, often with passengers in each vehicle firing guns wildly at one another. In real life Baltimore, there was such a car chase and while it wasn't quite as dramatic as those in the cinema, unlike those in motion pictures this chase was in real life with real risks to life and limb. In June of 1938, Patrolman Robert Rice spotted a speeding car on Hanover Street on the city's south side. With his partner out of the patrol car on foot patrol, Rice elected to pursue the speeding motorist in a hot pursuit. Rounding a curve near the Hanover Street Bridge, Rice's patrol car spun and crashed sideways into the bridge. The entire right side of the car was caved in, injuring Rice, and crushing the car exactly where Rice's partner would have been sitting.

And the hot times continued in Baltimore, literally throughout the summer of 1936. This was the decade of the Dust Bowl in the Midwest when the 1930s offered not only the Great Depression, but an unrelenting drought accompanied with excessive summer heat. The Midwest Dust Bowl was a climatic nightmare, driving farmers into bankruptcy, when crops failed year and after year until the money for new seed for another season was gone. With no prospects for crops and no money to pay the mortgage on their property, an estimated 2.5 million farm family members were forced off their land. The arid conditions worsened when a hot dry wind arrived, turning the rich topsoil to dust, which then was carried away on the wind. That midwestern dust had blown eastward, coating all in its path, beyond the Atlantic coastline and even coating ships at sea. For Baltimore, the huge heat bubble that had covered the Midwest slowly migrated eastward, raising local temperatures everywhere along its path. By July 10, 1936, the temperature in Baltimore joined other cities on the East Coast to set a local all-time-record high of 107 degrees. These 1930s were the hottest temperatures (to date) ever recorded in Maryland.

ENDURED, ENDING, AND EXPECTATIONS

Unique events, economic crises, and banking chaos, all led to unprecedented interventions by local and national government. In their wake there emerged a new expectation for Americans, for their government and for themselves. Most importantly, people's faith in the future, their morale, had been buoyed by the New Deal. Business and industry in Baltimore and most other places were recovering. Jobs were becoming available; bread lines and soup kitchens became fewer and fewer. The New Deal money injected into the economy was soon followed by money flowing from commerce. The uncertainty that marked the early years of the 30s was ending, but slowly being replaced by the sound of war drums from across the seas. In 1917, America had gone to war. Now, a mere twenty years later, those same European war drums were sounding loudly again, the same forces seemed to be gathering toward an unpleasant certainty. China was already embattled and aflame. Spain was in the midst of a Civil War. Even with the hope that a policy of isolation might keep America out of yet another war, neutrality was becoming untenable.

America was a country with a divided opinion as new European and Asian wars grew in intensity. Baltimore was especially conflicted, as its population of German descendants remained a potent minority in the city. Thousands of German immigrants had arrived after the Great War, joining the 50,000 second and even greater numbers of third generation German Americans already in residence. Henry Mencken, the Sage of Baltimore, spoke openly about this German heritage conflict, saying "My grandfather made a mistake when he moved to America, and I have always lived in the wrong country." Neutrality for some continued to be a guiding principle, yet by 1939 hostilities seemed unavoidable. National leadership began war time preparations, with many of those preparations directly impacting Baltimore and Baltimoreans. A new United States Maritime Commission made plans to open new shipyards and build five-hundred new cargo vessels. One of the new shipyards would be located on land in the Fairfield section at the southernmost reaches of the city, from which its first ship would be launched in September 1941. The steel mill at Sparrow's Point, across the harbor and within sight of the new shipyard, would certainly be asked to supply the steel for those and more ships.

In Middle River, Maryland, the aircraft factory of Glenn L. Martin was limping along with a few small military orders and even fewer orders for commercial aircraft. The company had been bankrupted early in the Depression, emerging as a financially weak entity after receiving a government loan, and by early 1939 the company was employing just 3,600 Baltimoreans. But overseas, Germany was threatening to bomb European capitals, and the French military was taking the threat seriously, quickly seeking to enlarge their own air force with more aircraft. A visit by French aviation personnel to Martin's modern but mostly empty factory led to contracts to build 115, then another 100 aircraft to defend France. The Glenn L. Martin company suddenly become a significant military aircraft supplier, that first contract alone exceeding the company's entire previous year's sales by 50 percent. In July 1939, the United States Army Air Corps placed an order for 385 of a new model aircraft, to become known as the B-26. The Glenn L. Martin Company had effectively gone to war. By December 1939 over 12,000 production workers were building aircraft around the clock.

Preparing for war was not without opposition. Baltimore was host to both pro- and anti-German meetings and protests. The city was said to be home for four separate German "Bund" cells. Bunds were anti-Semitic, anti-Communist, pro-Nazi organizations opposing any anti-German activity in America. A nationwide isolationist group, the

America First Committee, founded in 1940 by a few Yale University students, opposed any involvement in foreign wars with prominent American and committee member Charles Lindbergh a very visible spokesperson opposing American entry in any conflict. Lindberg had visited Germany, first in 1936, at the behest of the U.S. State Department, subsequently making more visits to Nazi Germany at the invitation of the German government. In Baltimore, "no foreign wars" presentations were periodically held. In October, just 6 weeks before the Pearl Harbor attack, the America First Committee sponsored Father James Gillis, editor of the *Catholic World*, who rallied an audience of 1,800 at the Lyric Theater. His presentation was on the topic, "America Can't Police the World", a popular iteration of the era's anti-war movement. On December 8, 1941, the day after the Pearl Harbor attack, the America First Committee was overwhelmed with member resignations, including that of Lindberg.

CLOSING A DECADE

The decade of the 1930s would test the endurance of all, even for Baltimore, a city whose citizens knew how to endure hard times. The 1930s were a prolonged time of uncertainty in many ways, for it was a decade in three distinct parts, beginning with an already-in-progress economic crisis of epic proportions, followed by recovery, then preparation for an impending war. Years of hard times were first, 1930-1933, with jobs, money, and prospects, each threatened or gone. Confidence in the future was lost, uncertainty even over the source of one's next meal ruled the times. Three years after the economic collapse of late 1929, the country elected new leadership offering new ideas. Times took a turn for the better, 1934-1936. A promised recovery began to take hold and by mid-decade, after some legal jousting over the Constitutionality of some programs, relief and jobs had arrived. The economy was mostly healed, the unemployment rate was continually declining, and money was in many more pockets. At the end of the 1930s-decade, attention was appropriately turning to international affairs and the prospect of war. In the last years of the decade, from 1937 to 1939 the prospect of war from across the oceans cast a shadow over these recovering times. Optimism became uncertainty yet again. Reluctantly for some, pragmatically for many, the decade came to a close with war preparation. In the next decade, peace would become a dream, young lives would be lost, and a rigorous testing would continue for years into the future.

CHAPTER FIVE:
THE WAR YEARS AND BEYOND

The 1940s

BALTIMOREANS ENTERED THE 1940S WITH a cautious mindset of hope, tempered with fear. The hard times of the 1930s would remain in the minds of the people of Baltimore, as those living through the Great Depression had learned to expect the worst. They expressed their worry in a persistent frugality, while beginning to savor the good things that came their way. Jobs and a degree of prosperity had returned, food had become more plentiful, citizen savings were government insured, and everyday attitudes seemed generally hopeful. The political leadership that had guided them through their decade of despair was appreciated by all but the harshest critics. Franklin Roosevelt would defeat Republican Wendell Wilkie to serve a previously unheard-of third presidential term, though Wilkie's positions on the issues of the day were closer to Roosevelt's own than much of his own Republican Party.

An unsettling issue was the threat of foreign war. Through the 1930s a long, slow buildup of German militarism, in defiance of the World War One armistice, led to German annexation of regions and then entire countries. Word was filtering to the outside world of the mistreatment and systematic abuse of segments of Europe's population. The Japanese military dominated Japan, replacing an emerging democracy with a nationalistic, capitalist oligarchy with an emperor as figurehead. The country sought economic independence through conquest of neighboring lands, beginning with Manchuria in 1936. A civil war broke out in Spain, a proxy war for future opposing forces. Ethiopia was invaded. The world stood by hoping to achieve peace despite the growing indications that peace would not be possible, fruitlessly negotiating for "Peace in Our Time". By the early days of 1940s, the sounds of war, artillery, bombs, and gunfire were heard across the world. The nagging home front issue was: would America be a part of this new war?

PREPARED

By the end of 1941, the United States had been engaged in war preparation for several years. At the steel mill at Sparrow's Point, the shipyards at Fairfield, and the aircraft plant of Glenn L. Martin, production demands were already creating jobs and prosperity. The city and its citizens were going to war, figuratively at first and later, literally. The regional population swelled as job seekers arrived from points near and far. Yet a wary public, remembering the severe losses of a prior European War, was reluctant for the United States to get involved. President Franklin Roosevelt persevered in war time preparation, creating first an exchange of American warships for placement of American naval bases throughout British islands in the Caribbean, then in December 1940 expanding to a comprehensive war materiel Lend-Lease program. In a further preparatory step, a peacetime military draft was initiated, the first peacetime draft in American history. From Baltimore, the very first draftee was Joseph Howell, reporting to the draft board

November 25, 1940. By nightfall, he was on his way to Fort Meade. He was the first of 242,000 Maryland draftees. While Congress imposed limitations on the deployment of these new soldiers, this was a very public, very visible step alerting the American public that the nation's comfortable neutrality could be coming to an end.

War was not upon America yet, as many held out the hope that no war would come, but the policy of U.S. leaders was to be prepared, and so preparations began. A nationwide conversion program for factories was established by the Federal War Production Board mandating changes to current factory output. Current industrial production would be halted and replaced with new products to satisfy the nation's war time needs. Steel, ship, and airplane production was expanded, while other Baltimore producers were redirected: Continental Can Company would make military hardware, Ellicott Dredge would manufacture Liberty ship engines, and spice company McCormick and Company would produce DDT. The General Motors automobile plant was renamed Eastern Aircraft and reconfigured to produce aircraft sections for Grumman's Wildcat and Avenger airplanes. Baltimore business and citizens participated in what would become a massive upscaling of production.

Another form of preparation was also underway. Baltimoreans were becoming aware of a humanitarian tragedy unfolding in Europe. By 1940, the persecution and forced relocation of Europe's Jewish population had begun in earnest. Until mid-1941, Nazi Germany encouraged Jewish emigration. The chief obstacle to the United States as a destination for these refugees was restrictive United States immigration policies. Not all applicants could be accepted for the limited number of visas offered and a local sponsor was required to even apply. Jewish and Christian organizations reached out to sponsor and assist in refugee relocation.

The *Baltimore Sunday Sun* newspaper published a special "Extra" edition the evening of December 7, 1941, with a bold headline reading "**JAPS DECLARE WAR ON U.S.**" All the pre-war preparations would now be put to the test.

WE'RE IN THE WAR – SHIPS

No other federal agency would have more impact on Baltimore than the United States Maritime Commission with its 1936 plan to build about 500 ships at a series of new ship building yards across the country, one of them to be operated by Bethlehem Steel in Baltimore. The ships to be constructed were of a simple, standardized World War One design, the EC-1, to transport freight, with oil products to be transported in another modified design, the T-2 tanker ships. This new local yard in the southern Baltimore City community of Fairfield would ultimately build 384 EC-1 Liberty ships over the course of the war, more than at any other yard in America. By 1944, they began construction of another cargo design, the Victory ship. Altogether 94 Victory ships would be launched, including the uniquely named *Goucher Victory*, after Baltimore's Goucher College, in June 1945. Across the Patapsco River at the Bethlehem Steel Sparrow's Point shipyard, another 10,000 Baltimoreans were constructing T-2 tankers for the war effort.

These yards were both operated by Bethlehem Steel and headed up by Jack Willis, a leader who was later described by U.S. Maritime Administrator and former Congresswoman Helen Bentley as the "world's greatest shipbuilder." Willis, a veteran shipbuilding administrator who had come to Baltimore in 1914, described the World War Two assignment of building Liberty ships as something that was simply "laid in his lap." He led the efforts of 50,000 local shipbuilding personnel that effectively built a "bridge of ships" across the Atlantic. The very first Liberty ship, the *Patrick Henry*, was launched at the Fairfield Yard on September 27, 1941, several weeks before the country entered the war. There were to have been 500 Liberty ships built, each named for a famous American, but war time demands led to the construction of 2,751, so many that builders began to run out of easily recognized names. This shortage of names led to Liberty Ships with less-familiar names such as *John W. Brown*, after a labor leader, and the *A.J. Cassat*, after the seventh president of the Pennsylvania Railroad. Not all of Baltimore's shipbuilding effort occurred at a Bethlehem Steel facility, as there were other yards around the harbor doing the same or similar work, including one operated by the United States Coast Guard.

The Liberty ship was a design initiated in World War One, a slow-moving cargo vessel meant to be quickly and economically built. From keel-laying to launch could be accomplished in just 40 days, the speed of construction aided by using welded joints to replace the traditional labor-intensive riveted construction. By 1944, Fairfield production had shifted to a larger, stronger, and faster cargo vessel, the Victory ship. Just over 530 of the Victory ships were built, 94 of them in Baltimore. Fairfield was the only east coast yard selected to build them. Each Victory ship was of a more modern design, larger than the Liberty with a bit higher top speed, capable of cruising at 17 knots compared to the Liberty's typical speed of 13-14 knots. Brave men sailed these ships across the oceans to deliver war time cargo, through thousands of miles of unpredictable oceans, effectively unarmed yet facing enemy attack from the air or below the seas, only to return and repeat.

Not all these new ships had an illustrious career. While some 200 Liberty ships were lost to enemy action, the loss of 12 ships that suddenly broke in half and sank was almost as alarming. Initially, defective welding was blamed for cracks forming in welded seams. Research ultimately showed that the culprit was the steel itself: subjected to the icy waters of northern latitudes, the steel became brittle, cracks opened, and the dozen ships sank. The T-2 tankers fared better than the Liberty ships, with only a dozen lost during the war. Most were victims of enemy torpedoes, but one T-2 tanker was lost to defective welding. The *Schenectady* had just completed its sea trials in January 1943 when in the harbor at Portland, Oregon, a defective weld failed at a critical stress point. The temperatures were around freezing and the waters still, leading investigators to locate the welding failure.

Other Liberty ships suffered more dire fates. The Liberty ship *John Morgan* was built in Baltimore. On June 1, 1943, the *Morgan* set sail on her maiden voyage with a full cargo of equipment, planes, tanks, and ammunition. She sailed just 150 miles to Cape Henry, at the mouth of the Chesapeake Bay, where in a fog bank she collided with the tanker *Montana*. The brand-new *Morgan* broke in half, exploded, and sank immediately, with the loss of all sixty-seven merchant mariners on board. The *Montana*, set afire, lost a dozen crew in the collision, but was ultimately salvaged.

WE'RE IN THE WAR – STEEL

Industry in Baltimore was responsible for a good deal more than building ships. The ships were made of steel, and the steel mill at Sparrow's Point had become one of the largest such mills in the world. Sparrow's Point was a city unto itself, a workplace with every support service imaginable, with tens of thousands of workers making steel around the clock. A steelworker might be a grizzled veteran of the mill, but given the rapid pace of war time expansion, was more likely a newly hired recruit. The demands of steel making meant more hands were needed to run the furnaces, operate the coke ovens, run the production tools, deliver the ore, remove the slag, drive the cranes, trucks, and rail engines, and maintain it all. Among the workers, Black and White, young and old, a sense of cooperation, protection, and survival prevailed in a workplace filled with hazards. They were making the product that would make the tools of war.

The mill offered employment to a diverse population, including minorities, but opportunities were far from equal. The story of McCall White, one African American Bethlehem Steel worker recounted in *The Baltimore Book*, gives a more nuanced testimony to the inequity Black workers faced beyond segregated locker rooms and water fountains. White was hired in the early 1940s to work in the newly unionized steel mill, though getting hired at all presented a unique challenge. White was a high school graduate from Baltimore. He knew that he would be considered ineligible for employment at Sparrow's Point because of his education and his perceived "city sophistication". To be hired, White claimed to be a farm boy with minimal education and once hired, was assigned to pay grade number one, encompassing the mill's dirtiest jobs. This was the case with all Black workers. There were 31 more advanced and lucrative grades, but with the work rules in place at the time, seniority only counted toward promotion within the employee's current department, making advancement to more desirable positions virtually impossible for workers such as White.

BEYOND SHIPS AND STEEL

The war effort seemed all encompassing. In Baltimore, citizens toiled in multiple industries producing other, even more sophisticated products: airplanes, radios to go in them, and wiring to connect their electrical systems. It seemed that everyone was working in a business that impacted the war effort. If the work didn't directly add to war production, it supported the efforts of those that did. Three of the local war production industries, goods destined for the war effort, included the Glenn L. Martin Company, the Bendix Radio Corporation, and the Western Electric Company. These three businesses alone employed about 65,000 Baltimoreans. Beyond these companies thousands more workers were employed by hundreds of local companies, providing the supplies, tools, raw materials, and chemicals needed for war production industries. There were more supporting services that included railroad and trucking operations, a medical community that kept workers healthy, and retailers assuring that workers' personal needs were met.

Martin Aircraft built various different aircraft in several production facilities around the city, as well as at their main assembly factory just east of the city in Middle River. Glenn L. Martin had been making aircraft in Baltimore since 1928, a modest effort of mostly seaplanes operating out of his east side waterfront factory and private airport. With the advent of war, a major increase in production was demanded, requiring an increase in the workforce to 53,000 employees at its peak. Aggressive hiring accompanied by an extensive training program was needed to convert novice new hires to task experts in a matter of weeks. Martin was producing as many as 23 aircraft each week through the war years, 7,000 in total from 1940 from 1945, half of them large aircraft like the B-26 Martin Marauder. Hiring and training at Martin included minority workers, an opportunity for local African Americans to gain meaningful, well-compensated employment, and a key element in the expansion of a Black middle class in Baltimore.

Vincent Bendix had created an automotive products company, but his interest in both aviation and radio communications led him in the 1930s to the form Bendix Aviation, a company that would be responsible for many wartime products his corporation created. This new company moved from Chicago to suburban Washington, D.C., before finally settling into a factory on Fort Avenue in Baltimore. Incredibly, Bendix radios, direction finders, and navigation devices were installed in every Allied aircraft operating in the European Theater during World War Two. In a patriotic move, Bendix released the restrictions on patents his company held for the wartime products they had developed, allowing their royalty-free use by other domestic manufacturers.

The Bell Telephone System had opened a manufacturing facility in Southeast Baltimore in 1929, operated by the system's manufacturing arm, the Western Electric Company. The vast factory was to be a manufacturer of telephone wire in this era of the Bell System monopoly on telephone communication. Only the reduced demand for telephone service of the Great Depression prevented operating at peak production. Research into electrical wiring applications, coaxial cables, and long-distance communication continued at the facility and by 1940, the company had taken up the task of manufacturing wire for the military. War time production at the factory ranged from heavy application wires that would link Army field telephones to the more delicate wiring harnesses for aircraft manufacturing, each produced by teams of women at the 2.5 million square foot factory. The peak employment at the factory during the war reached 9,000 employees.

Baltimore's diverse economy proved to be a major war time industrial asset. Industrial operations were directed to produce new products, most often related to their pre-war processes or specialties. The Bartlett Hayward foundry on Scott Street switched from casting ornamental iron to casting 26-foot diameter bronze propellors to be installed on Liberty ships. In the Jones Falls Valley, Frank Schenuit converted his automobile tire factory to the production of aircraft tires. Nearby, Mount Vernon Mills created a fireproofing, mildew preventative process for military canvas applications such as tents, tarpaulins, and backpacks. Crosse and Blackwell stopped producing jellies and jams to make packaged rations.

Around the city and the region, every company and every employee seemed to find a way to apply their resources to the war effort. Contribution to the war effort was recognized by the military when war production E-Awards (for excellence) were awarded. The prestigious Army-Navy awards were given to twenty-six different Baltimore companies. Eighteen of those companies received the award several times during the war years. E-Award flags proudly flew over Baltimore factories and the E-Award collar pin decorated the clothing or uniform of many a Baltimore worker.

PEOPLE: NEW TIMES, NEW JOBS, NEW RULES

Who were these Baltimoreans who welded the ships? Made the Bethlehem steel? Riveted the Martin aircraft? Wired Bendix radios or built Westinghouse radars? Employees came from every background and from many places, but most importantly they represented a new generation of worker. When the military began enlisting and drafting eligible men, these new soldiers and sailors came from jobs in the industrial and commercial sectors of the economy. Job vacancies abounded as enlistees and draftees left their civilian employment behind. Work-places were shorthanded, labor shortages became critical, and newspaper want-ads went unanswered. It became apparent to employers that traditional sources of workers could not meet the workplace demand. Business and industry would have to be prepared to tap new sources for employees. Limiting employment opportunity by race and gender was a practice that could no longer be afforded. Women were joining the workforce and minority applicants began to receive previously unavailable job offers. Traditional employment barriers were being broken, and though there was resistance in some cases, war times created changes that could not and would not be reversed.

Before the war, the average woman was on a predictable life path. Generally, women were destined to be home-makers, with young single women preparing for work as clerks, typists, teachers, nurses, librarians, or receptionists. These were jobs defined as "women's work". Once women married, their outside-the-home working days were usually numbered, as the expectation was that they would become homemakers and mothers. High schools ran courses in "home economics", teaching young women the skills of home management. The concept of a woman picking up a rivet gun, wiring a direction-finder, or operating a city trolley car was viewed as absurd. Then came the war, and the women stepped up to become major contributors to the war effort, proving to be capable and successful, surprising everyone but themselves.

A nationwide recruiting effort was made, resulting in many new workers in Baltimore.

Meda Brindall came to Baltimore to become a welder at the Fairfield, Maryland, shipyard. With her welding partners Lula Barber and Meta Kress, this single mother proved to be a hard worker doing a hard job, seven days a week. She knew lives depended upon her: "I wasn't there to fool around. I was there for the war effort."

Mae Eckley was a riveter at the Glenn L. Martin aircraft factory. From Juniata, Pennsylvania, Mae and her work partner assembled the tail sections of B-26 Bombers. She made 97 cents per hour, paid on Fridays with cash in a small brown envelope. She and her work partner Margie rode the trolley to see shows at the Hippodrome Theater.

Niada Green worked at the Edgewood Arsenal, an Army munitions manufacturing facility east of Baltimore. At first unaware of the nature of the work, Ida admitted, "I didn't know we were going to work on ammunition". A local girl, she took the bus to Edgewood every morning, then back home to the Baltimore in the evening.

Elsie Arnold was a Garrett County, Maryland, native who came to Baltimore to help build aircraft. Elsie was recruited by the Glenn L. Martin Company and soon joined the slacks-wearing riveters, in an era when women wearing trousers was unheard of. In her later years she appreciated the opportunity, saying: "It really opened up a great deal for women."

These women workers' contributions were often made possible through childcare, housing, and recreational programs established by employers like the Glenn L. Martin Company. Affordable childcare was funded with assistance from both employers and the preparatory war time assistance legislation, the Lanham Act (of 1940). At the Martin Company's facility, regular nurse visits and check-ups enhanced the youngest children's safety and security, while overcrowding of local schools was prevented in part with additional federal funding at the nearby Victory Villa School. Female dormitories were established early, followed soon after by apartment communities like the 1943 Mars Estates and Victory Villa Gardens. Even the United States Farm Security Administration placed 1,700 temporary trailer homes nearby. More family-friendly lodging became available when multi-bedroom homes were built nearby. Recreational opportunities included the Minta Martin Girls Club (named for Glenn's mother) and a nearby church-sponsored United Service Organization (U.S.O.) club. While in-plant fraternization was restricted between the many young single female factory workers and visiting airmen on tour (who were destined to fly the aircraft being built), airmen on an evening recreational walk through any of the nearby housing communities or attending the Our Lady of Mount Carmel U.S.O. were able to bypass the formal limitations.

Not every woman worked in a factory, nor was every woman a "Rosie the Riveter", a generic term for women in the workforce doing traditionally men's jobs to contribute to the war effort. Some 350,000 women joined the military, many as medical nursing staff. Bravery Under Fire commendations were awarded to 1,600 of them, with more than 500 receiving combat decorations. One woman represents those with the secret task of decoding messages. Janice Martin was a student at Goucher College in 1943. An apt pupil, she was one of twelve recruited by the U.S. Navy to attend secret classes in cryptology while still enrolled. After graduation, she would soon become an Enigma Code breaker. She and her peers performed a life and death task: if the German U-Boat messages they decoded offered clues to enemy locations, U. S. convoys could be re-routed to avoid attack.

While the war created opportunity for women, for African American workers the jobs that could be had were a lifeline to a new, completely different future. Black citizens had long been subjected to Jim Crow laws, segregated facilities, and often unrelenting bias. Now there was a path forward, one that offered training and a move into a skilled, better-paying job. Such opportunity for minority citizens was an altogether new concept in 1940s Baltimore. A Civil Rights movement had been underway in Baltimore for some years since Lillie May Carroll Jackson opened the N.A.A.C.P. offices in the city. She and the N.A.A.C.P. were responsible for the Double V campaign – the familiar Churchillian V for victory over Nazism, combined with a second, opposite hand V, for victory over racism. But these gestures, actions and plans were offered in a society where there still existed physical threats to Black persons.

For Americans of color, the opening of these war time opportunities began with a meeting between A. Philip Randolph and President Franklin D. Roosevelt. Randolph, a union activist who had organized Black railroad sleeping car porters, and subsequently became a civil rights advocate, had threatened to call a mass march on Washington, D.C., with numbers likely to reach 100,000 participants. The purpose of the march was to demand non-discrimination in hiring. The President briefly resisted Randolph but to avoid embarrassment or problems resulting from the proposed march, on June 25, 1941, he issued an Executive Order banning discrimination in hiring in any defense industry setting. A door had been opened to minority hiring.

Thousands of citizens of color qualified for training and employment in the defense industries, offering a path to the middle class, more than simply income from a few pay checks. Segregated facilities continued to exist as did other forms of discrimination, and in Baltimore, significant barriers in housing. Employers could evade of the spirit of the law by reporting substantial numbers of Black employees, even though Black and White were often not working side-by-side. White workers might toil in one facility, while workers of color might be in a separate, remote plant. At one company, a group of White workers walked out on a "wildcat" strike, a strike typically not authorized by union officials, when a Black worker was promoted to be their supervisor. This was not an infrequent event, leading in one case to the federal government exercising its authority by taking control of a Baltimore plant.

At the newly opened Bethlehem Steel shipyard at Fairfield in Baltimore, there were no veteran shipbuilders: new hires would fill employment needs. Virtually everyone needed training, so there existed a clear opportunity for even the least experienced applicant to be hired. The yard hired minority workers, and if war-time photographs are to be believed, Black and White did in some cases work side-by-side. The final statistics at Fairfield: 46,000 workers, 14 percent of whom were minority hires, or about 6,000 minority workers gaining skilled jobs and the resulting better pay checks.

THE LIVES OF THE PEOPLE

Every Baltimorean was called upon to contribute to the war effort. Some would enlist directly to join the fight. Others would work long hours in a war industry factory. Civil defense workers, plane spotters, or community helpers were often volunteers. Home-bound citizens could plant a Victory Garden. But every Baltimorean, every American, shared one daily reality. Rationing placed limits on the availability of nearly everything useful: no nylon for stockings, as it was used for parachutes; limited gasoline for cars, as oil was reserved for aviation fuel; foods of every description, meaning more for the troops, less at home.

Personal transport received a double dose of rationing: both tires and fuel were limited. When the rubber plantations of Southeast Asia fell to Japanese invasion, access to raw rubber from the plantations there ended. With large military demands for rubber, civilian use for automobile tires was curtailed. Synthetic rubber had been perfected in Germany in the early 1930s and while a product of interest, it was available only in very limited quantities. Rationing regulations limited the number of tires a person could own: four on the ground, one in the trunk. To replace worn-out tires, owners had to "recap" the existing ones, a process of fitting new tread to the existing tire casing. Fuel was rationed as severely as tires: a modern army relies on mobility and fuel is a key to that mobility. Rationing of domestic supplies was essential, using a process that was in two parts: automobiles received a windshield sticker classifying allowable use, while the driver received a matching coupon book allowing limited fuel purchases. The average driver had an "A" sticker, an allocation of four gallons of gasoline per week. Non-essential driving was prohibited. To enforce the limitations, Maryland even sent inspectors to Ocean City, Maryland, to identify summer weekend driving violations. Car-pooling reduced personal consumption as did the use of public transit. For a few, access to a healthy black market for fuel helped most of all. Fuel rationing worked: by 1943 domestic consumption had dropped by 20 percent.

Public transit had a role in the lives of Baltimoreans for generations, but with the war effort and the strict limitations placed on personal vehicles, transit service became even more important. Since 1899, the United Railways Company had operated the street railways, streetcars, and a system of bus transport, many electrically powered, moving passengers throughout the city. The company did not fare well in the hard times of the 1930s with the advent of and competition from the automobile and the expansion of the city into more remote suburbs. These factors each played a part in United Railways declaring bankruptcy in 1935, replaced by the Baltimore Transit Company, a new operator of the same streetcars, buses, and in 1938, new trackless trolleys over a network of hundreds of miles of street routes and rails. Trackless trolleys were electrically powered, rubber-tired vehicles that took advantage of the streetcar's overhead wiring infrastructure, operating largely over routes where track maintenance or replacement was prohibitively expensive. The transit company's ridership soared in the 1940s with special service provided to workers at the large factories around the region. Cars would be waiting at factory exits for the next shift of workers to board for their homeward trip. The transit cars ran their routes full, day and night, city and suburban. The job of trolley motorman was available to female operators but was denied to African Americans. (The first Black operator was not employed until 1952.) Ridership was largely integrated.

For one Glenn L. Martin war time worker, Irene Morgan, Jim Crow laws ran squarely into her patriotic B-26 workplace efforts. Baltimorean Irene had journeyed to her parent's home in Gloucester County, Virginia, to recover from a miscarriage. On July 16, 1944, her return trip to Baltimore aboard a Greyhound Bus was interrupted when at an intermediate stop, the driver ordered Irene to vacate her seat and move to the rear of the bus. The racially integrated bus was travelling in interstate commerce. Therefore, Virginia's Jim Crow laws were not applicable, and much like Rosa Parks years later, Irene refused to change seats. The driver summoned the local sheriff, a confrontation ensued, another deputy joined the fray, and Irene was arrested. Local courts found her guilty. An appeal wound its way through the courts, and ultimately the United States Supreme Court sided with Irene Morgan.

For many, rationing was an inconvenience, but the bigger shortage was in housing. Baltimore's war time industries saw an influx of thousands of job seekers who became workers, but adequate housing was unavailable for many of them. Baltimore's housing inventory was limited given the demands of population growth in the 1920s and the lack of construction in the 1930s. Dormitories opened and were quickly filled. House trailers, even travel trailers were sought-after options. Lines formed wherever and whenever vacancies became known, or even suspected. The Sparrow's Point steel mill energized home construction activity in the nearby Dundalk area while the Glenn L. Martin Aircraft Company built the housing development known as Aero Acres, its street arrangement which if viewed from above, shaped like an airplane, the streets named after airplane parts such as Compass Road or Fuselage Avenue. Several hundred housing units were quickly built there of Cemesto, a non-rationed building product of sugar cane fiber pressed between layers of asbestos, the dangers of the latter material not yet fully understood. Barns, attics, and garages, all were pressed into service, and even bed-sharing – sleeping in shifts – was made possible for workers on alternating around-the-clock shifts.

Victory Gardens, a source of home-grown fruits and vegetables, flourished. "Feed yourself and you feed a soldier" was the often-heard slogan encouraging citizens to create, tend, and harvest their own back yard farm. Community gardens, shared garden tools, and instructional classes were available, while garden plots near the transit lines were urged as cars may not be available to transport the bounty. Plot designs using plans available from the University of Maryland Extension Service were available, but Mrs.Venia Kelar of the Service advised these urban gardeners that pressure cookers for processing the vegetables would likely not be available due to steel shortages. The gardens themselves often fell victim to a typical home garden invader as Mrs. Baker of Grantley Road discovered, saying, "So that's what been nibbling at my leaves" when she discovered about twenty rabbits "conducting their own Easter Parade" through her garden.

Many aspects of everyday life including education were impacted by war time adjustments and accommodation. With the start of classes in 1942, the University of Maryland Medical School began to compress medical school course work into continuous education, foregoing the usual semester and holiday breaks. These future doctors and nurses were already needed at military hospitals to support and tend to the needs of the wounded and injured. The medical school graduated multiple classes each year. Students were admitted every nine months, and a four-year curriculum was completed in three. Stanley Karesh, Class of '43, said it best, "[we] expect to see action in this war… we entered to learn; we go forth to serve."

Motion picture theaters enjoyed a bonanza of clients. Patriotic films, depictions of war time successes (and occasional enemy cruelty) played well to audiences. Romantic dramas were typical fare, the soldier and his girl separated by circumstance, a reflection of the times. A few of the classic titles shown in the era: *A Yank in the R.A.F.*, *Desperate Journey*, *The White Cliffs of Dover* and the classic, *Casablanca*, shown first in Baltimore at the Stanley Theater, February

1943. *The Baltimore Sun*'s review of Casablanca was enthusiastic: "Mr. Bogart, brusque and formidable in action, and unusually soft, for him, in the love scenes, has a field day in this picture, and Miss Bergman has never been lovelier or more appealing." The theaters were open for business much of the day and night, as shift workers' end times varied and they were apt to arrive at almost any hour: after a shift, after a meal, 8 am, 8 pm, midnight, or any of the hours in between. For a modest amount of money, twenty-five cents (inflation adjusted, about $5.00), one got a seat, a movie, air conditioning, and for those in a distressed accommodation situation, perhaps a nap. A few hours could be spent in the new 1,100 seat Senator Theater on York Road, a grand palace that had opened in October 1939. For just a quarter of a dollar, it was a great diversion, and a war time bargain.

Telegrams were a sure means of sending a message from one party to another. Birthdays, anniversaries, any special event, a Western Union telegram allowed far-off and sometimes nearby well-wishers to commemorate the occasion. Paid by the sender, the message zipped through the wires, was printed at the destination city or town, where a messenger carried it to the doorstep of the recipient. Receiving a telegram could signal tragedy, however, if the sender was a military representative. The wording usually began, "We regret to inform you…", the message an announcement of a loved one's fate, likely missing or dead. Almost 2,000 Baltimoreans died in the conduct of the war, 1,400 in direct battlefield action, others from non-combat conditions such as accident and illness. By October 1944, this terse notification method was altered to be a bit more humane when commanding officers of the individual began to write condolence letters to the next of kin. Baltimore families continued to make their contribution to the war effort, very often including a family member's life.

With the capitulation of Germany in May 1945, and finally, the announcement of the surrender of Japan three months later, the war was at long last over. Within hours of the August announcement of the end of War in the Pacific, 200,000 Baltimoreans flooded downtown streets in celebration. Along Baltimore Street alone, 100,000 people were cheering, singing, shouting, and dancing. The factories that had been producing war goods for years were closed for the day so their employees could join the festivities. Traffic came to a standstill. Churches filled with thankful worshippers. Harbor whistles blew, an unidentified man beat a bass drum, sailors sang "Ain't gonna study war no more", others sang "Auld Lang Syne". Police described the celebrants as well-behaved, bringing with them confetti, noise makers, flags, even cowbells. Liquor establishments had been closed upon the late afternoon peace announcement, which may in part be responsible for the crowd's overall good behavior. The police department reported just 21 persons arrested, each for what was described as a minor infraction. It was the perfect ending to a long trek through the war years. Baltimore, and America, were at peace again.

HEADING HOME

By the end of World War Two, Maryland had sent 5 percent of her citizens to war. Soldiers and support staff were spread across multiple continents and on the oceans in between, and with few exceptions, each wanted only to return home. At war's end, there were a total of over seven million American soldiers waiting overseas to be repatriated to home shores. Inevitably, the repatriation became a drawn-out logistical process with some troops designated to remain as occupation forces, others slated for early return, and all limited by available shipboard space. Complicated by the military's requirement of maintaining segregated facilities, shipboard space was further limited. Moving millions of soldiers was never going to be an easy task, even as part of the nation's fleet of cargo transport Liberty ship vessels were converted to troop transports. The massive movement of getting the troops home would take well over a year. Faced with long waits in often inhospitable surroundings, troops protested departure delays. In Manila 20,000 soldiers marched in protest. Large numbers took to the streets even in Honolulu. When the Secretary of War arrived in Guam, soldiers there burned him in effigy. "Bring Daddy Home" letters flooded Congress. President Truman was alarmed, but the protesting soldiers avoided mutiny charges with the diagnosis of General Dwight Eisenhower: "acute homesickness." In this atmosphere of unrest and delay, the soldiers continued to wait, as did their folks back home.

A much less acknowledged "heading home" reverse migration was also taking place. Maryland maintained nineteen prisoner of war (P.O.W.) camps, housing some thirteen thousand captured prisoners. Italian soldiers had been the first to arrive, followed by and soon outnumbered by captured German soldiers. These prisoners often found life in the P.O.W. camps offered them better treatment than they had received in their own army. Very few felt any need to try to escape from any of the local camps, with just one German officer shot trying to escape and a single suicide occurring the day after the German surrender. The prisoners were paid when they performed productive work on farms and in clearing forests, with the captives often finding friendships with Americans they encountered. At the end of the war, some of the P.O.W.s headed home to Europe accompanied by new American wives.

NEW ISSUES, NEW CONCERNS

As one might expect, the end of World War Two meant different things to different Baltimore citizens. Most important for many was that their sons and daughters, husbands and wives, brothers, sisters, and friends had survived the war and would soon be coming home. The state would soon see the return of 95,000 soldiers to civilian life, but not everyone was returning: the City of Baltimore alone had suffered the loss of some 2,000 lives; across the state another 2,400 Marylander lives were lost. But the end of the war counted more than just the toll in human life. Lifestyles which had been altered during the war would soon change again, as war time policies eased. It was hoped that the long-endured rationing and shortages would soon be over, that food would be in abundance, and new fashions, even nylon stockings, would be available for the ladies. The harsh reality was that many shortages continued. This time the culprit was no longer the war. Rationing shortages were replaced by post-war consumer demand exceeding the ability of the economy to return to producing civilian products. Workplace employment changed with the end of war time extended work hours, often seven-day work weeks to meet production quotas. By far, the greatest of the post-war changes would be family formation: long postponed marriages and subsequent childbearing would no longer need to be put on hold. Young people's lives could resume, there would be weddings, and soon would follow a boom in the birth rate.

A POST-WAR PROBLEM

After the war, returning soldiers expanded Baltimore's population to just under 950,000 residents (U.S. Census, 1950). The war time housing shortage had become a post-war housing shortage, with a peacetime challenge for young couples. The housing they needed had simply never been built, as war time had disrupted that industry as well. New families were being formed, further delay was not tolerable, the separation and insecurity of the war years was past, but the shortages led many to temporarily house with parents or relations. At war's end, a race to quickly build more houses began in earnest, but even that was not the final step in resolving the housing problem. Building homes was essential, but once constructed there was another obstacle to overcome. Buying a home meant financing the purchase, and financing was yet another challenge for these young marrieds with no credit experience. Soldiers on the battlefield do not build a credit history.

This post-war housing finance problem had actually been foreseen. Congress began a response to the shortages and the financial needs of returning soldiers with the creation of government backed lending programs and passage of the Veteran's Readjustment Act of 1944. This act authorized Veterans Administration (V.A.) loans, allowing new families with a returning soldier at the head to obtain a bank loan for home purchase, with the credit risk guaranteed by the United States government. The program was a godsend for many but not for all, as racial bias slipped easily into the process. White soldiers generally had few if any problems qualifying for a V.A. loan, but African American soldiers found quite the opposite was true. Federal laws, composed by racist southern legislators, made it virtually impossible for Black soldiers to use their G.I. benefits. Black soldiers could qualify for a loan, but often banks wouldn't lend the money, realtors wouldn't show the houses, and few homeowners would sell a house to an African American. Across the nation, there were entire V.A. districts, many outside locations where such resistance might have been anticipated, where entire groups of Black soldiers were denied V.A. loans, every single one.

Once a V.A. loan was procured, a home purchase could soon follow so long as the chosen home conformed to housing standards established within the V.A. loan program. Beyond overall condition, the property's plumbing, heating, construction, and other systems were all subject to a rigorous inspection and would have to be found acceptable before a loan was approved. In Baltimore, those buyers who had an interest in remaining near family and friends in the city's established neighborhoods found that older homes in city neighborhoods often were unable to meet the minimum V.A. housing standard. Many Baltimore row homes had been stripped of amenities, even plumbing, and sometimes divided into multi-person residences in response to war time housing shortages. They were not repaired. They were not rehabilitated. They received no loan assistance. Potential city home buyers would have to look elsewhere, where the outlying greener pastures of suburbs with a selection of newly constructed homes sure to meet V.A. loan standards would lure them beyond the city limits.

SUBURBS BECKON

Baltimore had long been expanding and suburbanizing away from a central core. In a city where the row house was king, with multiple iterations, styles, and sizes, growing families could often "upgrade" by simply moving to a larger row house within the city, often within close proximity of their previous home. Residents of immigrant communities in Fell's Point had years earlier headed north and west to suburbs that were within the city limits, perhaps a row house in the Bolton Hill neighborhood. The planned community of Roland Park, a bit further north, had been created some forty years earlier to offer housing with covenant deed restrictions, available to only the most well-heeled, White, non-Jewish buyers. New residential districts in Pimlico and Mount Washington offered yet more distant possibilities. Baltimore's early story of suburbanization was one of leap frogging one community over another until the expansion was sufficiently vast that even the passenger trolley company, United Railways, couldn't offer affordable service to those more distant residents. This early outward trend continued into the post-war years with many of the new suburbs growing well beyond the city limits. Baltimore and Anne Arundel Counties, adjacent and contiguous to the city, were the first jurisdictions in the region to find their "close-in" farmland growing not crops but houses immediately after the war.

It was apparent at this point that the suburbs were the future of Baltimore. The community of Rodgers Forge had begun as a close-in suburban rowhouse community with construction in the pre-war years. Straddling the city-county border, Rodgers Forge resumed building in the post-war years, offering homes that included racially restrictive deed covenants. Unlike most other suburban development, this was a more walkable community with services nearby, thus not especially automobile dependent. More typically, an automobile was essential. An early auto-dependent development with uniform design was quickly built on vacant land in Anne Arundel County and named Harundale. Here a new suburb was built contiguous to a long-established community, Glen Burnie, offering hundreds of simple, largely premanufactured homes built on concrete slabs. Their steel frames and in-floor radiant heat set them apart, as did their modest size, three or four rooms, usually 1,000 square feet at an affordable price of $6,900. Twelve hundred of these houses were built and quickly sold, but there were no nearby shops, groceries, or amenities. Harundale was not alone in developing vast numbers of houses, as post-war home building created suburban housing on the city's eastern edge, adding to existing communities such as Joppa, an 18th century village and seaport, military-oriented Aberdeen, and Havre de Grace, a community fully forty highway miles distant from the center of the city. Baltimore saw suburban growth to most points of the compass, its citizens willingly accepting longer distances from the city for more open space and larger houses. As always, it was automobile ownership and more roads that made possible this suburban lifestyle.

In 1948, a little-debated, almost unnoticed Constitutional amendment to Maryland law changed forever the fate and future of Baltimore. The general election included a ballot question that would modify the manner and procedures used by Baltimore City to annex contiguous lands of surrounding counties. The ballot question created little in the way of controversy. With no current annexation plans, there arose no organized opposition to the question's placement on the ballot. In past annexation events, the city could target areas, seek Maryland General Assembly approval, and add the real estate and residents. The city would then purchase from the county any annexed structures and facilities, such as fire equipment or public works yards. Even a post-Civil War change requiring that annexation first gain the approval of voters in the affected jurisdictions didn't stop the annexation of 35 square miles of Baltimore and Anne Arundel counties in 1918. Many in the to-be-annexed area of Baltimore County had expressed a desire to be annexed, with close-in residents viewing the county as dominated by rural interests and desiring access to services the city could provide. However, this 1948 proposed amendment established more stringent conditions for annexation. If approved, an annexation proposal would mandate a special election held only for the affected residents of the proposed annexation area. The annexation would be approved only if a majority in the proposed annex region agreed to the annexation plan. Again, in the absence of any annexation plans or organized opposition, the ballot amendment was approved. For practical purposes, this amendment froze the borders of the city and with it, the tax base. Later reporting asserted that "healthy cities grow" whereas the passage of the amendment had "converted the city from a shining jewel to a charity case."

THE MARRIAGE AND BABY BOOM

The year of the wedding was 1946. At the Basilica of the Assumption in Baltimore, America's first cathedral, there were 764 ceremonies performed, triple the number of weddings in the pre-war year of 1940. Other churches and venues saw a doubling of demand. Ceremonies became weekday affairs as reception halls were in short supply with venues like The Alcazar on Cathedral Street or the Lord Baltimore Hotel on Baltimore Street booked solidly. In a *Baltimore Sun* article Catherine Demos is quoted, "There were so many weddings going on that we got tired of going to weddings. Every time we turned around, there was a shower or a wedding." Weddings happened fast, leaving little time for planning. The returning soldier was on a schedule dictated by the military and train schedules. He and the new bride were often married within days of his return. War time engagements, often stretching over years, quickly became post-war marriages. Wedding apparel was scarce, so some brides went to the women's garment mecca of New York to acquire suitable clothing while other ceremonies were conducted with bridesmaids donning mismatched attire. White gloves were non-existent, and brides made do with alternatives in color, or not at all. In that same *Baltimore Sun* article, bride Julia Krometis reported that at her wedding, two bridesmaids wore rose colored gowns, two others wore chartreuse. In the end, despite the apparel and color problems, the couples were just as married as anyone else. Adding to the complexity, setting up housekeeping was equally or perhaps more difficult. The housing shortage continued; apartments were simply not available. More than one couple moved into and shared parental homes.

Young families were soon created. The birth rate soared to over 26 births per thousand people, increasing almost 50 percent over prior years. Measured for eighteen years starting in 1946, 76 million births were recorded nationwide. These birth statistics are not coincidental: families forming post World War Two is a measure of not only a response to long-delayed partnering, but also reflected confidence in the economic future. The 1930s and hard times of the Great Depression led many to sense it was not a time to expand family obligations. Research repeatedly has shown birth rates and economic conditions are linked, the latter causing the former to rise or decline. With a war on the heels of the Depression, the first years of the 1940s and the war on the home front meant jobs, regular paychecks, and prosperity. The economy had improved, people were optimistic, and by the mid-1940s, it was well beyond time for family formation. A baby boom was inevitably underway, with its effects felt for many of the decades that followed.

A POST-WAR DILEMMA

Women in the workforce was a war time reality. The pre-war percentages of married women working outside the home, about 10 percent, had been thoroughly disrupted with war time worker shortages. Millions of male workers had departed for military service leaving little choice for employers except to hire woman and minorities, or the work would not get done. The hiring of females in non-traditional roles due to the war time labor shortages was a first step, but casting aside prejudices also included the hiring of minority workers. During the war years, over one-third of jobs were held by people who before the advent of war would not have even been considered for the jobs they held. However, circumstances were changing once again for these groups of war time workers.

There was a post war surprise ahead for the women workers. These "Rosies" as they were called (after "Rosie the Riveter", a ubiquitous symbol of a women doing her part in the war effort) had set production records with decreased manufacturing time and improved quality. In short, they and the minority workers alongside them created a resounding success story. But both groups were seen as expendable in the face of post-war downsizing. The products of war were needed less or not at all, so some operations closed, while others were shrinking, eliminating, or reducing the number of jobs. The entire Fairfield shipyard, builder of hundreds of ships, was closed and reverted to pre-war ownership within two months of the war's end. The return of thousands upon thousands of soldiers expanding the labor pool, meant that there was suddenly a labor excess. Too many people, too few jobs.

This did not bode well for either the "Rosies", or minority workers. Regarding women workers, American attitudes were stuck in the past. An article in *The Harvard Business Review* pointed out that since Rosie's skills were no longer needed, she needed to "go home and bake cookies." For minority workers, much of America slipped comfortably into its prejudicial pre-war attitudes. Neither group would remain silent in the face of the unravelling of their wartime accomplishments and new status. But with the soldiers returning from war and looking for work, perhaps even the job they had left behind, they were the priority. These circumstances led to an expectation that the young women who had been recruited from local high schools, trained, and performing admirably, would willingly depart the workplace for education, marriage, or relocation. Women were perceived to be out of place in a factory and so layoffs targeted them first, regardless of seniority or job performance. While Civil Rights activity was a pathway to equality for minority workers, enduring that long and tortuous legal road to equality might not yield a paycheck any time soon. Jobs might not disappear altogether, but new opportunities were rare, with existing workers often shunted into work assignments at lower pay and requiring less skill.

The story was much the same at every war time production plant in the city. Glenn L. Martin Company shrunk, as there was no further need for more B-26 bombers, and even the existing ones were bordering on surplus. The company would transition to other products, including civil aviation, but there would never be a call for 50,000 aircraft builders again. People would have to leave, voluntarily in some cases, at company request in others. Bendix Radio had employed over 8,000 workers, mostly women, in a series of facilities across the city and suburbs. By war's end, all the company's operations, manufacturing, design, and development, were consolidated into a single northside area facility. The end of war time product demand prompted a relatively fast conversion to the manufacturing of automobile radios, but the number of Bendix employees would of necessity decline.

A SPY STORY

The "Baltimore Papers" became part of a cause célèbre in 1948. Baltimorean Alger Hiss, a former U. S. State Department official, was accused of espionage by Whitaker Chambers. Chambers was a Soviet defector and spy who claimed to have known Hiss in the 1930s as a Communist agent. In this emerging era of Cold War, a personal Communist connection could prove disastrous to anyone, especially those involved in government. Hiss' reputation hung in the balance, and he denied the accusation. The accusation and the denial set off a series of events that included Congressional hearings, a pumpkin patch, retyped papers mysteriously showing up in a Baltimore law office, and Hiss ultimately convicted and serving time in prison.

The late 1940s saw the end of the uneasy war time alliance between the United States and the Soviet Union. Communism had been viewed as a threat to America for decades, and Soviet Communist espionage was an obvious concern, well into the next decade. When Whitaker Chambers, a defector who was known to have been a Communist claimed to have recognized Hiss as a Communist Party member of the 1930s, a Congressional investigation was initiated. Leading a reluctant Congressional committee investigation was an outspoken anti-Communist Congressman from California, Richard Nixon. Evidence was presented to support Chambers' claims, some of which was film Chambers had hidden in a hollowed-out pumpkin on his Westminster, Maryland, farm. Documents purported to contain secrets were mailed to Hiss' attorney's office in Baltimore, becoming evidence of Hiss' Communist ties, indicating that he had spied for the Soviets. It was not clear that these "Baltimore Papers" contained actual confidential information, and even their authenticity was in doubt. Hiss testified before the investigating committee, denying the accusations, and calling the evidence against him fraudulent. In a bizarre turn of events, because of his testimony, Hiss was then accused of perjury, found guilty, and sentenced to prison. He was released after three years and spent the remainder of his life, over forty years, working to clear his name. Later post-Cold War statements issued by ex-Soviet-era military archivists affirmed that Alger Hiss had not been a spy.

THE NUCLEAR AGE

When the nuclear weapons that ended World War Two were detonated in 1945, the United States was the sole nation in possession of the secrets of this potent weapon. In the aftermath of a World War Two victory, years of sacrifice of blood and treasure had led to America feeling invincible. The full implications of the birth of the atomic age were little understood, and perhaps only those closest to the project understood the changes atomic weapons had wrought. But the sense of American invincibility was short-lived when a mere four years later the Soviet Union, aided by a German-born spy named Klaus Fuchs, had successfully detonated their own atomic bomb. The loss of America's shield of invincibility was a shock of epic proportion: suddenly, the Soviet Communists were equally as well armed as their Western opponents.

Baltimoreans offered a mixed reaction to the news. Some were doubtful: a traffic officer at Baltimore and Charles said he was too busy "with these crazy drivers" to worry about what the Russians were doing. Others were more concerned: Highland Avenue resident Lillian Myers more accurately opined "they'll be plenty of worrying". A skeptical Roland Park resident Mr. H. Van Horn thought the Russians were primitive and perhaps "they will blow themselves up." Then there was Hillary Dawn, an exotic dancer just arrived from La Jolla, California. She offered an opinion that maybe folks had better live more for the moment: "I have noticed the audiences have gotten larger." Hardest of all to digest for the man in the street were reports and opinions offered by many presumed experts. "These are not fanciful suppositions" proclaimed Air Force Major General Hugh Knerr. In 1949, soon after the first Soviet atomic bomb detonation, Knerr began listing top targets for Soviet atomic attack. In his published accounts, Baltimore and its port were near the top of the list. He described the city as a near-perfect atomic weapons target. Civil Defense officials offered maps of Baltimore with concentric circles of destruction zones superimposed. The rings described destruction: total annihilation at the center, surrounding severe damage, gradually reducing as distances from the Mount Vernon Square target increased. School children were taught to duck-and-cover; if a brilliant flash was seen, presumably this was a nuclear detonation, and they should immediately duck under their school room desks. That their desks were usually made of flammable wood, and the bomb's 2,000 degree expanding ball of fire was headed toward them, one might question the likelihood of a safe outcome for the children. But then trusted adults had to do something, and teaching children to duck-and-cover was at least something. The long-term implications of such an attack were not understood; for the average Baltimorean "nuclear fallout" and "nuclear winter" were terms that would not come into use until the next decade.

This was the beginning of a new atomic age, the infancy of the atomic age for the city, the state, and the country. It was a time when apocalyptic destruction could be contemplated. Worse, we were no longer alone in the possession of this lethal weaponry. The atomic age would factor large again in the next decade.

ABOUT THE PHOTOGRAPHS IN THIS BOOK

THE BALTIMORE MUSEUM OF INDUSTRY maintains an extensive library that includes thousands of archival photographs. The photographs in this text are sourced from that collection. Their appearance here would have been impossible without the support and cooperation of the museum's Executive Director, Anita Kassof, and the patient search efforts of Ken Jones and Maggi Marzoff, each of whom tolerated my shifting priorities, plans, and impossible requests, which they somehow managed to fulfill. My (and I hope your) thanks and appreciation to each of them. Photographic images are Copyright, The Baltimore Museum of Industry; or a part of the museum's photographic collection believed to be in the public domain.

The Holiday Street Theater, erected 1874, opposite City Hall. This masonry structure, a nickelodeon movie house, was razed around 1918.

Devastation: the aftermath of the Great Baltimore Fire, February 1904, looking east at Baltimore Street At left center stands the "fireproof" Continental Trust Company building, which survived 2000-degree temperatures and was rebuilt and reoccupied within two years.

A post-World War One parade, Baltimore and Light Streets, circa 1919.

Young "flappers" surround the latest rage, the airplane. Circa 1920.

Robert Maslin, owner of radio station WFBR, poses outside his studio, circa 1930.

Washington, Baltimore and Annapolis Railway Station, southwest corner, Howard and Lombard Streets, c. 1930.

Banana importing, direct from ship to waiting rail cars. Circa 1930.

Standard Oil of New Jersey gasoline station, Paca and Pratt Streets. Standard and its Esso brand offered competition to the hometown brand, Amoco, and its Lord Baltimore Stations. Circa 1930.

War Bond drive, encouraging investment by workers at Bethlehem Steel, Fairfield Shipyard, 1943.

Sparrow's Point Shipbuilding, 1945.

McCormick and Company headquarters, left, Light Street near Lee Street looking north. The Light Street Piers which occupied the streetscape to the right were razed in the 1950s, and northbound Light Street expanded on filled land.

Chesapeake Bay Bridge, connecting the western and eastern shores of the bay, viewed from the west bank ferry docks, in foreground. The bridge replaced cross-bay ferries in 1952, providing access to Maryland's Eastern Shore counties and the growing vacation destination, Ocean City, Maryland. Few infrastructure changes had a more profound effect on the residential and vacation habits of Baltimoreans.

Fast food, 1950s-style. Interior of a Little Tavern hamburger shop.

Baltimore Inner Harbor, prior to redevelopment, circa 1960.

Thomas D'Alesandro III. The son of three-term mayor Thomas D'Alesandro, Jr., he served as mayor for just a single term during the difficult years of the 1960s.

U.S. Bi-Centennial Celebration of Tall Ships, July, 1976. The Gorch Fock (West Germany) entering Baltimore Harbor.

CHAPTER SIX:
MODERNIZING AT MID-CENTURY

The 1950s

THE BETTER DAYS THAT MOST had hoped for arrived, and the 1950s did not disappoint them. The promise of an expanding consumer economy meant times of plenty instead of rationing, a time of jobs for the asking instead of hard times and bread lines. This would be a time of the mass production of consumer goods, the ascendency of a new device called television, and the birth of the automobile age, where an automobile would grow from optional to essential, from boxy and dull to a bright asset covered in chrome. This was the decade when the new phrase "baby-boom" was literally being born. The 1950s opened the doors to these new times, new ways of thinking, and new ways of living.

America in the 1950s would first have to cope with another war, as hostilities had broken-out on the Korean peninsula. It was said to be a "police action", a proxy battle between pro- and anti-Communist nations. The action became the leading edge of a larger conflict, a "Cold War" that was the backdrop of a continuing international competition between the Soviet Union and the United States. For Marylanders and Baltimoreans, it was more local: American soldiers headed to Asia to do battle, thousands of them from Maryland, with 527 of them killed in action.

A new Baltimore would grow out of a worn-out infrastructure neglected for too long. The hard times of the 1930s and the war years of the 1940s meant that city repairs, rehabilitation, or renewal constantly pushed into the future. Central Baltimore was worn-out: neglect had taken its toll. Unoccupied buildings lined many streets. Traffic was chaotic with adequate parking non-existent. Downtown shopping continued as ever, since a suburban alternative had yet to emerge, but that threat to a central retail district would soon arrive. Some felt the city needed to compete with the suburbs, offering spacious parking, wide streets, and new construction. "Urban renewal" was becoming another new catch phrase, and in 1950s Baltimore, there was much to renew. For many, Baltimore presented a vision of slums to be cleared, buildings to be built, and highways to be created, starting with the 1950s symbol of urban renewal, the bulldozer. In the words of renewal consultant Robert Moses (formerly of New York), when commenting on the city's older, past-prime areas, "the more of them that are wiped out, the healthier Baltimore will be in the long run." City fathers seldom disagreed. Some of Moses' thinking was accepted by the Greater Baltimore Committee (G.B.C.), a non-profit business and civic organization which often served as an advisory "think-tank". The G.B.C. had envisioned a change to the city core, proposing an urban renewal and reconstruction plan for a portion of the city center they titled "Charles Center". Heading up the urban renewal plan and a major driving force was real estate developer James Rouse.

The Charles Center plan was unveiled in 1958, offered to city fathers and the public for review. A positive reception led to a bond issue, financial support voted on and approved. The bulldozers soon went to work. Thirty-three acres of land would be cleared, saving five "grand" buildings, with the work leveling properties of varying merit, from tiny shoe repair shops to warehouses to the venerable Miller Brothers Restaurant. Fayette Street was to be bridged over and straightened, Lexington Street would be closed between Liberty and Charles Streets. A series of plazas and pedestrian overpasses would appear, and beneath it all, plenty of parking, seen as vital to compete with the suburbs. The Charles Center plan would refurbish downtown from Lombard to Saratoga Streets, Charles to Liberty Streets. New construction began just as the decade of the 1950s was ending. The 1950s design called for a showcase building, which would be Baltimore's first modern skyscraper. A competition chose architect Ludwig Mies van der Rohe's design in the International style: a very tall but simple box, lacking ornamentation, with plain horizontal bands of windows, was completed in 1962. Nearby, the Morris A. Mechanic Theater brought Brutalist architecture to Baltimore in 1967, pleasing to very few as it was soon voted one of the top three ugliest buildings in America. Taken as whole, the Charles Center plan offered if not perfection, a glimpse into what the city could be. Its largest benefit seemed to be not what it offered visually, but how it helped restore to the citizenry a new level of confidence in the future.

Like most American cities at the time, Baltimore's suburbs were growing. But with the language added as an amendment to the Maryland Constitution in 1948, restricting annexation, there was no practical way Baltimore City could physically grow with them. A population shift to the County was generated by multiple factors, and residential preference was one. But expansion-minded employers followed a 20th century trend of seeking spacious suburban business property, offering them room to grow, room to park, room for deliveries and shipping. When an employer relocated, the jobs they offered went with them, creating a desire for many of their employees to relocate closer to their workplaces, from city to suburb. This relocation of businesses, jobs, employees, and homes was in no small part facilitated by automobile ownership, once a luxury, by this decade quickly becoming a necessity. Shops, stores, and restaurants took note that their customers had moved, and so must they. Some moved entirely, others merely established additional suburban locations. All this movement was at the expense of the city, making Baltimore a city with a shrinking population and eroding tax base. The city had already peaked in population, 949,000 in 1950, and thereafter the change in city population would consistently be measured in negative percentages.

Like any migration, even this ultra-local movement from city to county, there were two factors: both a push and a pull. The employer and jobs exodus were luring city residents away, creating a pull, but the push of the population was far less innocuous. Baltimorean's exodus to the suburbs included a racial aspect that added a powerful urgency to the trend. The city had long been "red-lined", first formally and later by custom, with reference to the red lines around blocks and neighborhoods drawn on maps used by lenders to determine who received home loans. Black and White communities were well-defined, with separation by race along understood but unspoken dividing lines. Baltimore's Black population was burgeoning and needed access to additional housing, but was compressed into a restricted area. It was understood in the White community that if that dividing line between communities was some-how breached, a reaction would likely occur, its dimensions unknown. Sensing opportunity, real estate speculators moved into action. Once a home vacancy in the White community occurred, these opportunists would purchase the property, then breach that invisible dividing line by steering an unknowing Black family into the area. It didn't take long for members of the White community to notice, worry about a racially changing neighborhood, and then react. Panicked home selling followed, and "white flight" was underway, heading to Baltimore's suburbs. Real estate speculators purchased more houses at bargain prices as White residents fled, the speculators reselling or leasing the acquired properties at profitable rates. "White flight" was a relocation push, a phenomenon doing enormous damage to every member of the community, both Black or White.

In the earliest days of the 1950s, suburban communities continued to maintain connections to the center city. Suburban shoppers, some residing at great distance from the core of the city, soon demanded retail and home services closer to home, beginning a decline in center city shopping. The city had in many minds become inconvenient, and visiting it was becoming unnecessary. Suburban living was becoming self-sufficient as automobile ownership increased. Public transit was inconvenient and time consuming; downtown parking, less available and expensive; and the mix of local, regional, and interstate traffic on city streets slowed the pace of everything. The suburban retail demands were first met when the outdoor Edmondson Village shopping center at the western edge of the city was constructed, followed in 1958 by the region's first enclosed shopping mall, eight miles south of the city at Harundale, combining indoor climate-controlled retail with acres of free parking. More shopping malls quickly followed, as the downtown anchor department stores such as Hutzler's and Hochschild, Kohn gradually expanded to occupy those malls and were joined by retailers offering every conceivable item. Now at the suburban malls, shoppers could have it all: major downtown department stores, free parking, easy road access, and indoor weather-proof shopping. This combination of conveniences gave suburban residents even fewer reasons to come to the center city. The suburban transition included the grocery industry as well. Small retailers that occupied city street corners first yielded to modest self-service stores, and then came the "supermarket": up to 25,000 square foot emporia, soon growing to double that size, according to grocery industry historian, Jeremy Diamond. Both regional and national chains like the Great Atlantic and Pacific Tea Company (A&P), Food Fair, Acme, and later Giant and Shop Rite, offered self-service, convenience, and as always, a generous supply of free parking. The worst blow to the city may have been when the city-county borders had become the demarcation line between high and low taxes. The contiguous county real estate taxes, though not perfect indicators but certainly of note, were half the tax rate in the city. Population statistics became measures not of the city, but of the "Baltimore Region", showing the region growing some 17 percent from 1950 to 1960, while a closer look at the city population alone showed a decline of 10,000 in the same period.

POLITICS 1950S-STYLE

Baltimore's mayor, Thomas D'Alesandro, Jr., took office in 1947 and remained mayor through the 1950s decade. D'Alesandro had held appointed or elected political positions since 1926, becoming a member of Maryland's House of Delegates, the Baltimore City Council, and by 1939, the United States Congress. It was said that the power behind the mayor was in fact his wife, Nancy. She ran his home and his office, organized his campaigns while bearing their six children, including a son who would also become mayor and a daughter who became Speaker of the U.S. House of Representatives. He had inherited a city in disarray, but a place with great expectations. Ever ambitious, he considered a run for governor in 1954 but dropped out when his name was linked to a parking garage owner convicted of fraud. A bid for election to the U.S. Senate in 1958 was unsuccessful. D'Alesandro was a classic Democratic big-city mayor who recognized that constituent service was vital, and knew a storm drain was neither Republican nor Democrat, but did need to be unclogged. There were rumblings, rumors never proven, of transactions taking place during his administration that bordered on the edge of legality and propriety. The mayor spoke his mind and the people loved him for it. Years earlier, he had publicly challenged President Franklin Roosevelt to support Raoul Wallenberg's rescue of 200,000 Holocaust survivors and the birth of Israel those survivors represented. During his time as mayor, a *Baltimore Sun* reporter asked on behalf of his editor's desk why the mayor was spending money on a new desk. D'Alesandro placed his ear to the desk and replied, "My desk tells your desk to [*expletive deleted*]." He knew the game of politics well and worked to get results, finding friends where and when needed. On his watch, the city opened new highways planned by his predecessors, opened an airport, and had a hand in bringing major league baseball back to Baltimore. Perhaps his biggest achievement was how he enabled a cadre of dedicated civic leaders to re-build and re-invigorate the city. And perhaps he stayed too long, losing his bid for re-election to a fourth term to a reform candidate in 1959.

Behind the politics of the city, the mayor and the City Council, there existed an unelected government, powerful citizens whose influence, financial control, and decisions exercised an outsized influence on all things Baltimore. The influential members of this group were businessmen, bankers, even religious leaders, identified in a later essay by writer Frank de Filippo as 133 power brokers, most with names unknown to the people whose lives they impacted. Here were the heads of the Mercantile Trust Company, the Archdiocese of Baltimore, and the Alex. Brown Brokerage, among many local leaders whose powerful influence resulted from their control of the financial resources of the community. The budget of the State of Maryland had yet to reach the one-billion-dollar mark, yet the Mercantile Bank controlled twice that much. The head of the Equitable Bank doubled as State Treasurer, while his son served as City Treasurer. This was the "establishment", often meeting under the auspices of the Greater Baltimore Committee, making determinations of policy through the financial power they held. Elected political leaders sought advice, even consent, of these select Baltimoreans. Over time, the power of these leaders would fade as national firms acquired and controlled from afar the businesses they had previously run, ultimately making Baltimore a "branch office" city.

In 1951, a television-savvy junior Senator from Tennessee brought his anti-organized-crime investigation hearings to America, and Baltimore. Televised hearings with alleged crime bosses caught the attention and imagination of America, as Senator Estes Kefauver led what he called a national crusade, bringing the spotlight on citizens who would generally prefer to remain in the shadows. The hearings were riveting television, as millions watched, but the result was little more than an 11,000-word report. Even Las Vegas escaped virtually unscathed, the hearings wrapping up after one day, as the connections between crime bosses, casinos and politicians proved to be elusive. The organized crime hearings made it to Baltimore, this time in a closed door format, with an unexpected twist at their conclusion. The key witness at the local hearing was Black businessman, former gambling racket head "Little" Willie Adams. Adams, granted immunity to testify in this federal investigation, was reported to have told the committee how he had become the criminal head of the gambling trade as a teenager, conducting the business for many years, but had retired to become a wealthy entrepreneur working to finance and build Black businesses in Baltimore. With the grant of immunity, Adams spoke freely and openly about his connections to illegal gambling and the nature of the "racket" in Baltimore. In a surprise move, at the conclusion of his testimony local law enforcement arrested Adams, justifying the arrest as a local matter in which federal immunity did not apply. Found guilty of state charges the trial verdict was appealed, leading to a U.S. Supreme Court decision that the federal immunity granted to him was all-encompassing, and immunity granted by the committee applied to all jurisdictions and all activities exposed in the hearings.

Political theater in Baltimore continued as Congressional hearings of the House Unamerican Activities Committee (H.U.A.C.) arrived in 1957. Baltimore had previously been the subject of some testimony and hearings in 1952, but the 1957 investigation clearly was the high point (or low, depending upon one's point of view) of the committee's work in the region. The committee took the trend of the decade, anti-Communism, to a new intensity. Initiating a series of investigations across the country, the H.U.A.C. displayed its penchant to circumvent citizens' guaranteed rights to due process, freedom of speech, and presumption of innocence. The Baltimore hearings were no exception to these usual methods. In a week-long Baltimore hearing, the chief targets of their wrath were the presumed Communists operating at the Sparrow's Point steel mill. Undercover investigators had been placed in jobs at the mill for the purpose of uncovering anti-American thoughts, words, and deeds. Included in testimony were references to infiltration, the election of 1948, and the Progressive movement. Names were named, "comrade" often used as the honorific, with the fifth amendment repeatedly invoked by witnesses. In May 1957, the results of the investigation and hearings were delivered: a half dozen (of the 30,000 employed there) mill employees were "exposed" by the headline-grabbing H.U.A.C. pronouncements. Employment at the steel mill was terminated for those accused. The H.U.A.C. committee's politicians and staff, their task in Baltimore completed, moved on to their next city and their next investigatory hearing.

ENTERTAINMENT: MUSIC, SPORTS, MOVIES, TELEVISION

At the start of the 1950's, the music of the times reflected the musical tastes of a former era, which would soon be resigned to the past. For the past fifteen years, jazz and big bands, solo crooners, and orchestral arrangements were in vogue. Music heard on the radio was that of a passing older generation: Rosemary Clooney, Nat "King" Cole, Guy Lombardo, Teresa Brewer, and others. These entertainers were the inheritors of a musical tradition that had originated in the early 1940s, gradually replacing the swing and jazz of Benny Goodman and Glen Miller. To the youth of the 1950s the music seemed stale and like so many previous younger generations, they sought their own style. By the early 1950s, the music that appealed to younger listeners was a marriage of urban blues, country, rockabilly, and jazz that soon became rock and roll. A musical revolution was underway. It brought with it new artists, a new style of phonograph record, television images in homes that made singers and groups more visible, and importantly a willingness on the part of the youth (if not their parents) to cross racial boundaries to explore new sounds. A few groups rose early to nationwide attention: one was Fats Domino who in the mid-1950s said he'd already been playing the new sound for fifteen years in New Orleans. A disc jockey by the name of Alan Freed broadcast a radio show he called "Moondog's Rock and Roll Party", and the "rock and roll" part stuck. Chuck Berry and "Little" Richard Penniman contributed their own styles, as did bandleader and occasional vocalist Ike Turner. Turner is credited with the first rock-and-roll song, "Rocket 88", released in 1951.

Rock-and-roll became a phenomenon with local groups forming, perhaps the most popular the Orioles, known for their doo-wop harmonies, and Ronnie Dove and the Beltones. These groups began playing Baltimore clubs in the mid- to late-1950s. The Orioles styles led directly to rock-and-roll, and in the years of their activity, 1948 to 1954, the group produced multiple hit records, including "Chapel in the Moonlight". Ronnie Dove, originally from Herndon, Virginia, was a U.S. Coast Guardsman stationed in Baltimore, establishing his local connection. Dove left the Beltones at decade's end and headed to Nashville where a recording contract awaited him. The Van Dykes were a local band from Anne Arundel County, a group of family and high school friends who made their mark on the teen center and local nightclub circuit. Led by Albert Brown, the interracial group of eight played doo-wop and horn-driven soul music. The band became one-hit wonders when "Stupidity" hit the mid-Atlantic charts, but the band was known throughout the region for covering all the latest hits. National acts played in Baltimore as well. Budding rock-and-roll superstar Buddy Holly arrived for a one-week engagement at the Royal Theater, the largest suitable venue in the city at the time. Holly played multiple shows to packed houses in August and September 1957. Under contract with General Artists Corporation, he and his two bandmates, the Crickets, delivered their hit songs, like "Peggy_Sue", compensated at the very modest rate of $1,000 per week.

Baltimore's teenagers were listening as radio stations began changing their formats away from talk, variety, soap operas, and news to the constant rhythms of rock and roll. Television disc jockey and video dance party host Buddy Deane became king of the local afternoon airwaves, offering a live local teenage dance show. He played the latest hits while his program regulars "The Committee" mixed and danced with ticketed local high schoolers. Musical guest artists visited to promote record sales, lip-syncing to their latest recording. Teenage music impresario Dick Clark out of Philadelphia went unseen on Baltimore television, preempted by Deane.

Deane, with his southern roots, was broadcasting to a city with its own southern roots. Racial segregation was the practice, but integration would soon to lead to the demise of the "Buddy Deane Show". Deane's segregated program and the local broadcast station were squarely in the bullseye of people's growing interest in integration. Would Black and White kids dance together on the air? Baltimore's schools were desegregated, at least in theory, with young people sensing an integrated future. White students conducted stealthy disruptions of the show's segregation, writing-in for show tickets, receiving the two free passes, then sharing the passes with Black students. Their first effort failed, but on August 17, 1963, a second attempt got results. Pass-bearing students staged an integrated mass arrival, rushing the doors. The hosts were overwhelmed. The show had to go on and a racially diverse dance party was aired. The station tried to censor the broadcast images, offering squiggly lines in a darkened studio rather than the usual crystal-clear images of kids having fun. Ultimately, the program was in Deane's own words "…the victim of an *insoluble* integration problem." Clear accounts of the decision-making process at WJZ-TV are not available: station managers and Deane offered conflicting versions. Did Deane call it off? Or did his broadcaster? The program shut down early in the next decade, 1964.

The Ringling Brothers Circus was an annual visitor to Baltimore, having resumed its travelling shows soon after World War Two ended. Taking over the city's Fifth Regiment Armory, this was a family entertainment extravaganza: trapeze artists high in the air, clowns cavorting on the main floor, dazzling animal acts, and equestrian acrobatics circling the center circus ring. Audiences were thrilled by performances by lion tamer Clyde Beatty, the high wire work of Karl Wallenda and his family, and the antics of the most famous circus clown of them all, Emmett Kelly. The show was a true descendent of the tent circuses of a generation before, an event which both children and adults could enjoy. The circus had moved to indoor arenas by the 1950s in the aftermath of a 1944 tent fire in Connecticut that had resulted in hundreds of deaths and injuries. Arriving in the Baltimore by train, the circus unloaded near North Avenue, formed a parade of performers and animals, and headed to the nearby Armory, taking up residence for a week. In later years, the circus parade headed to the new Baltimore Civic Center, with the elephants taking a detour to enjoy their special prepared outdoor lunch at the Lexington Market. The annual visit concluded after the visit's final performance in Baltimore, with the elephants, lions, horses, clowns, acrobats, vendors, and more journeying north to the train awaiting them for travel to their next host city.

There was a Davy Crockett craze in the mid-1950s. Crockett, a Tennessean who lost his life in battle at the Alamo in Texas, became the subject of a story and legend in film and on television, produced by the major media company, the Walt Disney Company. The television series of programs aired with 6-foot 6-inch tall actor Fess Parker playing the role of 5-foot 8-inch Crockett, an oversized story about the life, morality, heroism, and death of the man who died at the Alamo. The Disney Company made Crockett a folk hero in a three-part televised mini-series, telling the story in Hollywood style, avoiding a disheartening death scene by showing him as the last man standing, swinging his rifle at the on-coming enemy whereupon the scene fades to an unfurled Texas flag. A plethora of Crockett themed items were created for purchase by fans: first on the list for every boy, and a few girls, was Davy's favorite "coonskin" cap. In Brooklyn Elementary School in South Baltimore, like many others around the city and the nation, elementary age fans sang the popular television theme song, "The Ballad of Davey Crockett" at the end of school year ceremonies.

Baltimore became a major league sports town in the 1950s. Arriving first was the city's entrant for membership in the National Football League, when in 1953 the Baltimore Colts took up permanent residence at Venable Stadium, soon to be expanded and renamed Memorial Stadium. The opening game of the fall season against the Chicago Bears saw the Colts winning by a score of 13-9. This auspicious start was not long-lived, however, as the team lost 9 of the 12 games they played that season. The team had the elements of a future championship group, but it would take time and experience for those elements to come together. Included among the names on the team's 1953 roster were such standouts and future all-stars as Art Donovan, Gino Marchetti, Bert Rechichar, and future coach Don Shula. Better days and many victories lay ahead for the team: by 1956, John Unitas had taken over the position of quarterback, replacing the injured George Shaw. With Unitas as team leader and a few player additions, the Baltimore Colts claimed two consecutive championship seasons, 1958 and 1959, with the 1958 championship game often hailed as the greatest football game ever played.

Late in 1953, the Saint Louis Browns baseball team, a losing team with a fan base that had largely moved away, became a candidate for relocation. Baltimore, as well as major league baseball management, were interested in relocating the Browns to Baltimore. Major league baseball stipulated local ownership for the move to be approved. A prominent Baltimore attorney, Clarence Miles, stepped forward and then recruited additional partners, National Brewing Company president Gerald Hoffberger and real estate developer James Keelty. By the start of the 1954 season, the former St. Louis team was playing at the refurbished Memorial Stadium as the Baltimore Orioles.

Baltimore had become a major league baseball city once again, but the city was unprepared for at least one of the consequences. Baltimore's hotels were segregated, forcing Black and White players to be accommodated at separate hotels. Both Black and White players protested. The Governor of Maryland spoke against the separation policy, but the Baltimore hotel association stood firm and the segregation policy continued. The pressure to integrate team lodgings continued until 1957 when major league baseball awarded the Orioles and Baltimore the right to host the annual all-star game, which occurred just eleven days after the segregation policy was revoked by the local hoteliers.

One million happy Baltimoreans went through the Oriole's turnstiles that first year, but the box office success of 1954 was not matched on the field. The team won their first game in Baltimore and not many more. They finished exactly as badly as in the prior year as the St. Louis Browns, winning only 54 of their 154-game schedule. Despite the best efforts of Manager Jimmy Dykes, a baseball veteran who had begun his playing career in 1918, the Orioles season's highlight may have been not finishing last, a dubious honor reserved for the Philadelphia Athletics who won just 51 games. Dykes did not return to the Orioles in 1955, as former player and manager Paul Richards took over leadership, leading to more productive years for the remainder of the decade.

The Orioles sustained a tragedy at the end of the 1956 baseball season when a highly touted player prospect, Tom Gastall, took advantage of a weather cancellation on the field to fly his newly purchased used airplane. The weather was marginal, apparently the airplane not much better, but Gastall confidently took to the air despite teammates urging him not to fly. Ninety minutes after takeoff his plane crashed into the Patapsco River, with his last words heard from his radio, "I'm going down into the water." The loss of this 24-year-old man shocked the team and the city's sports fans. As sports editor Bob Maisel wrote in *The Baltimore Evening Sun*, "The home runs and no-hit games eventually fade, but the sight of other players casting sidelong glances at a locker they knew would never be used again is something that can't be forgotten."

Baltimore welcomed television with just 700 sets when it arrived in October 1947, but the entertainment habits of Baltimoreans really began to change in the 1950s. At the New York World's Fair of 1939, President Roosevelt was the first president to speak on television, broadcasting in the area to anyone with access to a set, although only 1,600 had been sold so far. The first test pattern broadcast locally came from Baltimore's Channel Two, WMAR-TV, and was soon followed by a horse race broadcast from Pimlico Racecourse, with just four to five hours of actual entertainment daily. Two new stations were added, WAAM and WBAL, both in 1948, creating a greater demand for television sets and programming, and an increase in home viewership. By mid-1954, newspapers reported that over 500,000 sets were in use in Baltimore. National radio networks from the 1930s and 1940s had created television networks in order to affiliate local partners. WAAM joined both the American Broadcasting System and the Dumont network, broadcasting the 1948 election returns on its second day on the air. The station dropped its Dumont affiliation and was sold to Westinghouse Broadcasting in 1957, its call letters changing to WJZ. Local station WBAL signed on with the National Broadcasting Company while WMAR signed with the Columbia system, CBS. Mirroring the radio experience, network affiliation allowed local broadcasters to offer a wide selection of programming.

Television had elbowed its way into Baltimore's living rooms as citizens turned off their radios and turned on their televisions. There followed a change in the way people in Baltimore spent their leisure time and interacted with one another, modifying their sense of community. Front porches where neighbors might formerly have chatted after dinner were deserted, while residents stayed inside watching the latest shows. The advent of home air conditioners, almost simultaneous with the growth of television, meant those porches were abandoned. Local and network programming quickly followed the growth of television sets in living rooms. The networks offered comedy to the nation: Milton Berle was the king of Tuesday-night, variety arrived in the form of Ed Sullivan's hour-long program on Sundays. *Gunsmoke* offered dramatic Westerns, often using recycled and rewritten radio scripts. ABC offered Disney programming, introducing Davey Crockett to the world of television, and setting off a Crockett craze in 1955. In Baltimore, a program for preschoolers called *Romper Room* was offered by Claster Productions, ultimately to be made available through syndication to other local stations nationwide. Nancy Claster was Miss Nancy, teaching a small group of children in person and reaching many more preschoolers over the airwaves. Miss Nancy asked, "Are you a Do-Bee or a Don't-Bee?" A regular local star of the airwaves Stu Kerr appeared regularly on Baltimore television. Kerr, a New Yorker who had just completed a combat tour in Korea, went to work for station WMAR in 1952, at various times appearing as Bozo the Clown, Professor Kool, a news and weather presenter, and as host of the interactive *Dialing for Dollars* program. Stu Kerr was versatile, an early television jack-of-all-trades.

While the stations were aligning themselves with networks and creating programming of interest to new audiences, television signal reception was often still a challenge. Station signals were transmitted by the individual station over the air to be received by home television antennas, some mounted on the television set itself, or mounted on a rooftop. Clear reception was highly dependent upon the home antenna directly facing the broadcasting antenna, but with three stations each broadcasting separately from different locations, a clear signal meant adjusting the antenna with every channel change. Rooftops across Baltimore soon sprouted rotating antennae, powered by small electric motors, their controllers inside the house atop the television set. In 1959, to provide convenient, better reception, the three stations jointly built a 530-foot tower atop a local high point that became known as Television Hill.

Television had become a formidable competitor to local theaters and the motion picture industry. Television offered entertainment for the cost of just pennies for electricity and the interruption of a few advertisements. To miss a popular show might mean being excluded from the water cooler chat at the office the next day, the shows from the prior evening nearly always a topic of conversation. Theaters were plentiful, with 119 of them in 1950 Baltimore, but for the consumer there were multiple costs. Cost of tickets was merely the beginning, but with transportation, refreshments, perhaps parking, each cost factored into the decision to leave home for entertainment in a theater, or stay home in front of the small screen. The motion picture business found itself in dire straits with the five big production companies (Paramount, RKO, Warner Brothers, MGM, and Fox) cycling through leadership changes, company ownership changes, coping with limits on content, and internal dissension. Seeds of their decline were sown when to create income, production companies sold their inventory of early films to television syndicators, making thirty years of films available to the television viewer almost free of charge. Motion picture producers searched for solutions while hanging on, often buoyed by the occasional hit (Hitchcock in his prime, any film starring Elvis Presley), experiencing renewed attendance for screen epics (*The Ten Commandments, Ben Hur*) or specialty films (3-D features: *Creature from The Black Lagoon, House of Wax*).

Drive-in movie theaters leveraged the great outdoors, love of the automobile, vacant land, and low-cost entertainment to offer a unique product. Richard Hollingshead received a patent for the drive-in concept in 1933 when he experimented with a projector on the hood of his car, a sheet pinned to some trees for a screen, and a radio to offer sound. Moving from his back yard, he opened the more formal Park-In Theater in Pennsauken, New Jersey, the prices a reasonable twenty-five cents per car and twenty-five cents per person. He licensed his idea to Lowe's Theaters, who then began opening a chain of drive-in theaters. His patent was over-turned in 1950 leading to an explosion of copy-cat outdoor theaters. Baltimore had no fewer than nine drive-in theaters spread around the region, most of them along the border of the city. One of the earliest may have been the Lowe's Governor Ritchie Drive-In in Anne Arundel County, opening in May 1939. At the Bengies Drive-In, opened in 1956 on Baltimore's east side, a 150-foot-wide single screen for viewing was constructed. Most drive-in theaters accommodated automobiles with a sloped parking spot tilting the vehicle slightly uphill, allowing full screen viewing through the windshield. In this era, an in-car speaker was hung from the side window and eventually, to extend the viewing season, small electric in-car heaters became available. The refreshment stand may have been the biggest money-maker for the drive-in but for those intrepid or hungry enough, heading to the refreshment stand meant overcoming two challenges: watching one's step in the dark and finding the car on the return trip! Families were welcomed, with the kids able to enjoy an on-site playground and picnic area at nearly all the Baltimore locations. Shows were seldom first-run features, and typically a double feature, with two different motion pictures shown consecutively. In between were a few advertisements, always including one encouraging a visit to the theater's snack bar, followed by the separate late show (often more mature in content), with a combination to keep viewers on-site for many hours.

FIGHTING FOR EQUALITY

World War Two had done much to improve the treatment of African Americans. Executive Order 8802 had been signed by President Roosevelt in June 1941, mandating integrated employment in the defense industry and thus creating opportunity where there had been none before. It was an important beginning, leading to a next step in 1948, when the United States military was desegregated under Executive Order 9981 by President Harry Truman. It would take years for full implementation of the language included in the order: "This policy shall be put into effect as rapidly as possible…" There would be no turning back the clock on civil rights. The 1950s became a decade where much of the legally protected status of segregation would be dismantled.

Baltimore was typical of many cities where the laws regarding segregation may have been changed, but changing the hearts and minds of the populace was slow. Resistance was typical, even by those working in government agencies. The pace of change seemed to be for every step forward, at least a half step back. Education and government policy offer examples of the pace of this change, forward and back:

- Loyola College received the Hollander Award in 1950 when it admitted Black students. The Hollander Award was a Baltimore-based program recognizing those who made substantial contributions to racial equality.

- Integration had become the law of the land in 1954 with Baltimore City Schools taking a leading position to integrate. But over time, even the city school system's willingness to change began to falter, and it would be years before city schools were integrated in a meaningful manner.

- Baltimore City's Housing Department led the move to integration. The Housing Department fell victim to the changes within the city: a majority Black neighborhood could be created by citizen mobility, block-busting practices, or other events, but the result was often a noticeable withdrawal of public and private services, leading to community deterioration.

- The city's Park Board restricted Black access to just one of the city's public golf courses. Under pressure, the Park board in 1956 set aside one day per week at all courses for Black citizen use.

In 1952, Baltimore's Polytechnic High School offered an advanced college preparatory curriculum. The curriculum was unique in the city and as Polytechnic was a White-only school, Black students were denied access the program. When thirteen Black students applied, they were denied admission. Their parents sought legal redress. A compromise was soon proposed: a separate but equal program for the boys would be started at a Black high school. Convening a school board meeting, arguments both for and against the separate program were offered, with Polytechnic High School principal Wilmer DeHuff arguing an alternate program for Black students would satisfy the Constitutional demands of the 1899 *Plessy v. Ferguson* Supreme Court decision. Countering that argument, the families' attorney Thurgood Marshall, legal counsel for the N.A.A.C.P. , argued that a separate program was risky and created an unnecessary cost burden to the city. The school board admitted the students to Polytechnic High School, arguing that a separate course would not be equal, and therefore the students could be enrolled in the upcoming semester.

Read's Drug store operated a chain of local pharmacies, many of which offered a lunch counter and soda fountain service to shoppers. Those counters were segregated: a Whites-only policy prevailed. In the post-Christmas season of January 1955, a group of African American students were in the downtown shopping district of Howard and Lexington Streets in Baltimore. On that corner stood the flagship store of the Read's Drug Store chain, complete with its large lunch counter. The students, a small group from Morgan State College, seeking warmth and refreshment, entered the store and sat at the lunch counter in anticipation of service. The Whites-only policy was asserted and service was denied them. The Black students remained, peacefully, only leaving the store much later. This was the first civil rights sit-in in the United States, serving as a model for future such demonstrations elsewhere. Closer to the college, similar demonstrations were taking place. Soon, Read's management announced a new policy: "We will serve all customers throughout our entire stores, including the fountains..." The local *Afro-American* newspaper published a simple headline: "Now serve all".

TRANSPORTATION FOR THE FUTURE

By Air. Since 1930, Baltimore's airport had been Harbor Field, located in the southeast corner of the city. Harbor Field, ideal for an earlier time, had replaced Logan Field, but it slowly became outmoded, unable to handle bigger aircraft, and outliving its functionality. Harbor Field was initially envisioned and operated as a seaplane base: it was an airport without runways in its first years of operation. By 1950, a new Baltimore airport, conceived by Mayor Theodore McKeldin in 1943, was opened and named Friendship Airport after the Friendship Methodist Church, located in the center of the property acquired for the airport. The new airport was on a high plateau that offered less fog and fewer obstructions than other sites while its location would allow it to serve the aviation needs of both Baltimore and Washington, D.C. Its first flight arrived from Washington in the form of Air Force One, a DC-6 aircraft that was bringing President Harry Truman to the opening day dedication. Friendship Airport, owned and operated by the city but located in adjacent Anne Arundel County, opened just in time for the advent of the jet age, becoming the region's first jet port. By 1957 the facility was operating just 52 flights per day, with transcontinental service provided by Trans World or United Airlines, and more regional service provided by popular airlines of the era such Eastern, Allegheny, National, and Piedmont.

By Rail. From the beginning of railroading, Baltimore and surrounding areas had been a honeycomb of rail-lines extending in virtually every direction. Freight lines shared the tracks with long distance passenger and commuter services. Passengers could arrive from Hagerstown, Maryland, in a few hours on the Western Maryland Railroad. Hourly service connected Baltimore, Washington, D.C., and Annapolis via the electrified Washington, Baltimore, and Annapolis Railroad trains (W.B. & A.) The Maryland and Pennsylvania Railroad operated freight and passenger service over 75-miles of track, weaving its way through the farm country between York, Pennsylvania, and Baltimore, the two cities just 45 miles apart. The Ma and Pa, as it was known, operated milk runs with trains making stops at dairy farms, the morning southbound train picking up milk destined for delivery at one or more of the bottling plants in the city, the northbound afternoon trip dropping off the empty containers. These local railroads were a half century in the making by the 1950s, with their milk runs, passenger trips, and general cargo, but they were all doomed to be replaced by faster, more cost-effective highway transportation.

On the Highways. With suburbs growing, and one-car families becoming two (or more) car families, additional highways were on the drawing boards at federal, state, and local planning departments. An expanding Baltimore, reaching miles into what had been the countryside, had become increasingly automobile dependent. The Baltimore Beltway, a circumferential highway initially conceived by Baltimore County, gradually became the region's Main Street. The lure of Federal Interstate Highway funding available after passage of the Interstate Highway Act in 1956 converted the local roadway idea into an interstate highway. Throughout the decade, the Beltway was an incomplete circle around the city, limiting its value as a city by-pass. South of the city, in Anne Arundel County, the highway included a traffic intersection complete with traffic light and a W.B.& A. railroad grade crossing, albeit seldom used, both at a location where construction costs would have soared had they been eliminated. Long-distance highways began to radiate from Baltimore, becoming the new normal route for a trip west to Frederick, Maryland, a Parkway jaunt down the forty miles to Washington, D.C., or the scenic interstate highway drive north to York, Pennsylvania and beyond.

In this expanding automobile age, navigating the traffic on Baltimore's streets was complicated by the combination of local traffic sharing streets with long-distance travelers. Motorists travelling through Maryland on U.S. 1 or U.S. 40 met the bottleneck of Baltimore's traffic-filled streets, where they encountered a total of fifty-one traffic lights and seemingly endless delays as they tried to pass through the city. Regional planners developed a solution that would by-pass the city traffic, constructing a high-speed tunnel passing under the harbor on the city's east side. By 1957, the Baltimore Harbor Tunnel had opened, its underwater "tubes" having been built at the nearby Bethlehem Steel Sparrow's Point shipyard, then lowered to their underwater positions. The road offered a limited access highway for motorists, a north-south connector bypass road available for just a forty-cent toll. Mayor Thomas D'Alesandro, Jr., proclaimed the tunnel to be "one of the modern wonders of the world". Promotional materials proclaimed, "This bottle neck is broken forever" but within months, the city traffic backups had moved to backups at the tunnel. Calls for a second tunnel soon began.

To unsnarl the city's traffic problems, Mayor D'Alesandro hired traffic engineer Henry Barnes, recently the traffic engineer for the City of Denver, for a one-month traffic consultancy. He stayed for nine years. Barnes quickly became a one-man frenzy of activity, setting to work rearranging traffic flow, painting the town with yellow traffic paint, and lining street edges and lanes with orange barrels, all to streamline and redirect traffic flow. He created one-way streets, erected left-turn and no-turn signs, and installed an electronically controlled signal system that continued to function effectively long after ever-increasing traffic should have brought everything, including the system, to a halt. In the interest of clearing the way for traffic, he took on the transit company, especially its streetcars, the post office and their double-parking vans, and the sponsors of the city's Flower Mart, an annual event that closed the critical north-south thoroughfare of Charles Street. When Barnes refused to close Charles Street for the event, the influential ladies who hosted the Flower Mart protested to the mayor. Barnes lost the battle of Charles Street: the street would close for the ladies and their festival. Barnes did battle with anyone and everyone to move traffic, saying "You can't be a nice guy and solve traffic". He made a few friends, but mostly he made enemies. Mayor D'Alesandro, citing his own interest in being re-elected, refused the very unpopular Barnes a $2,000 pay raise. Barnes soon left Baltimore for the challenges offered by New York City traffic.

Baltimore had pioneered street lighting courtesy of Rembrandt Peale, an artist, entrepreneur, museum owner, and in this case, visionary, who created a first-in-America system of flammable gas manufacturing, underground pipes to transport it, and lampposts topped with gas lights to illuminate the city. Peale had seen the innovation of curb side lights lit by flammable gas during a visit to London and brought the idea back to Baltimore in 1817. His gas streetlights lit the streets and boulevards of Baltimore while he also used gas lighting in his Peale Museum on Holiday Street in center city Baltimore. It is impossible to determine which of these two applications of gas lighting were more dazzling to the public, but most certainly they both transfixed the local population. By the late 19th century, gas fixtures were being replaced first by arc lights powered by the 1881 Monument Street dynamos of the Charles Brush Electric Company, themselves soon replaced with incandescent light bulbs in modern electrical fixtures. Gas lights had survived in Baltimore in slowly diminishing numbers over the intervening years until August 1957, when Mayor D'Alesandro came to his home neighborhood of Little Italy to shut off the city's last gas streetlight. The gas lights were historic, nostalgic, perhaps scenic, their soft glow appealing, but they no longer met the lighting needs of a modern city. When Baltimore's last gas lamp was turned off, the city's march toward streetlight electrification was complete.

FINS, FADS, AND FUN

Perhaps the most enduring images of the 1950s were the work of American automotive designers. Cars of the 1940s were an uninspired, simple, enduring design continued from the late 1930s: a passenger box atop chassis box, by the late 1940s adding chrome adornment. Models from the early 1940s were never built, as war time production diversions ensured, but by the post-war period, the automobile industry had picked up the pieces and moved with great hopes into the future. Car design seemed to be stuck in neutral, however, with each vehicle offering little in the way of modern "curb appeal" and virtually nothing in the way of innovation.

The designers and engineers were playing catch-up, a problem that time would cure. The world of industrial design, led by Raymond Loewy, Harley Earl, and Virgil Exner took automotive design by storm, leading New York's Museum of Modern Art to call one model, the Studebaker Starliner, a work of art. By the middle of the 1950s, new designs, new shapes, new features on automobiles had appeared. Engines became more powerful V-8's, air conditioning became a frequent option, and two-tone paint jobs adorned car bodies. After mid-decade, the models began to sprout fins. Whether the fins were nautical or aeronautical would be in the eye of the beholder, or perhaps the designer, but they did add interest. Cars got bigger, then bigger again: the 1951 boxy sedan became the sleek 1956 model, which grew again to the outsized 1958 model. Some called them living rooms on wheels. People loved almost all of them, the exception perhaps being the oversized, strangely designed and poorly made Ford Motor Company's Edsel. Overall, industry production soared, with Baltimore's Chevrolet plant operating 24 hours a day, employing 7,000 workers. The mill at Sparrow's Point labored to keep pace, producing the sheet steel used to form car body parts.

The list of fads and fun combined the innocence of childhood, building on fashion statements of an earlier decade, created hairstyles for the ages, and college shenanigans that came and went faster than the 1950s decade. There were toys like the Hula Hoop and the Bob-a-Loop, poodle skirts, and beehive hairstyles, and for the over-18 set, phone booth stuffing and the panty raid.

By the best estimate available, children and adults began using an early version of the Hula Hoop around 500 B.C. The Wham-O company began making colorful rings of plastic in 1958, and from that point, everyone shimmed to either keep it spinning or failed to keep it spinning at the waist. Some could, some couldn't. Wham-O named its plastic hoop the Hula Hoop, somehow equating the shimmying necessary to keep the hoop waist high with the graceful hula dancing of Hawaii. Hula Hoops become a late 1950s obsession. A less successful 1958 Baltimore entrant to the toy fad marketplace was the Bob-a-Loop, a handheld toy demanding "coordination and skill", with a stick, string, and miniature barrel to flip and catch. At 99 cents and a money back guarantee, "America's newest game sensation" met with initial public interest, but the hopes and expectations of the local inventors went unfulfilled. Some 250,000 Bob-a-Loops were produced for retail sale, but interest soon waned and most remained unsold.

In response to a Christmas season wardrobe crisis, New Yorker Julie Lynn Charlot created the first poodle skirt. She crafted a swirly skirt, decorated it with doggy images, and made the poodle skirt a new, major fashion statement for young women of the 1950s. Usually a full circle of felt decorated with contrasting poodle cutouts, it was a simple design that could easily be made at home. The skirt was accessorized with multi-tone saddle shoes, white cuffed "bobby sox," and a cardigan sweater, sometimes worn backwards, occasionally adding the "letter sweater" of an athlete boyfriend.

For the men and boys, there were frequent visits to the local barber. Often living in quarters above the business, the barber operated a shop marked by a red, blue, and white helix of stripes, the barber pole symbol that had marked the trade since the Middle Ages. Every local neighborhood had one shop, often several, with patrons appearing in greater numbers just before holidays and school picture days. Young men's hairstyles were unique to the times. There were options! Haircuts were often a short, military style, sometimes a "flat top" with upright hair cut parallel to the ground. Summertime might yield to the "whiffle" with closely sheared hair, said to beat the heat. Others wore a much longer style, held in place with a pomade or "grease", and thus they became known as "greasers". With long hair slicked and curled to the back, meeting in the center, when viewed from behind the style resembled the aft end of a duck. Thus, it was called a "ducktail".

Women's hair styles were widely varied, but the most impressive of all was a beehive. This was an extravaganza of hair spray: start with longer hair, backcomb, pile it high, and twirl it atop the head, adding copious amounts of hairspray to keep it all under control. When finished the coiffeur looked for all the world as if there was a beehive atop the wearer's head. Hair pins and the occasional head scarf completed the look, which many housewives on

Baltimore's east side adopted. They were known by the way they greeted friends and strangers alike, "Hello, Hon!" These were Baltimore's "Hons".

For some newly emancipated young people, the 1950s were a time of playful hi-jinks, and college campuses were a made-to-order setting. One international competition grew in the decade around telephone booths, very much a part of the 1950s streetscape. How to determine the number of students who could squeeze into a booth, a space designed to be comfortable for one or perhaps two, uncomfortably? Groups of students competed for the record by squeezing a dozen or fifteen bodies into a booth. College shenanigans continued with the fad of boys raiding girls' housing, entering usually-locked dormitories and houses under cover of darkness, searching for trophies. Had the door been purposely left ajar? Or even unlocked? There often seemed to be an inside co-conspirator to assure the evening raid succeeded. The raids' trophies ranged from actual trophies, group sorority photos, and even women's undergarments in a "panty raid".

New times in this new decade meant some new eating habits, as fast food arrived. In 1955, Ray Kroc began franchising a chain of restaurants known as McDonalds. Marylanders could visit a McDonalds by 1960 with the first Maryland store located in the Washington, D.C., suburbs. Baltimoreans were not excluded from the fast-food trend, as Baltimore Colts player Gino Marchetti, with several other Colts player partners, had already created a local version called Gino's Hamburgers. The first store opened in 1957 in the southeast Baltimore suburb of Dundalk with a menu that would mirror McDonalds stores and new consumer tastes. Burgers were fifteen cents, French fries were sold for a dime, and milkshakes cost just twice that, twenty cents. For some customers who found eating in their car more desirable, Gino Marchetti's teammate Alan Ameche opened burger-centric restaurants with curbside service. Intercom ordering, food delivered on trays which then hung from the car window, Ameche's Drive-In restaurants became a young person's social destination. Parking lots circling with young drivers showing off their cars to see and be seen at some fast-food spots was standard at Ameche's. Cruising Ameche's or one of its competitors such as the Varsity Drive-In was a nightly event, particularly hectic on the weekends. Hamburgers and gasoline appeared to be the perfect teenage combination.

The 1950s seemed to be all about "keeping up with the Joneses". If a neighbor bought something, others wanted it, too. Products were promoted nationwide from New York's advertising mecca on Madison Avenue, but in Baltimore television advertising featured local celebrities. Local personality Royal Parker extolled the virtues of Chesapeake Clear Vinyl Slipcovers: "Hey you kids, get off that furniture…" A sofa protected by slipcovers was available "just $59 down" by calling Mohawk 4-3404. One business owner took to the airways himself: Mr. Ray advocated his hairweave as "absolutely undetectable", tugging on a model's hair to prove the point. East Baltimore's Gunther Beer was the "Happiest Taste in Beer". Sportscaster Chuck Thompson was known to exclaim after a happy on-field moment, "Ain't the beer cold!", summer or winter, Orioles or Colts, touting his presumed favorite, National Beer. The W.B. Doner advertising agency of Detroit had secured National Beer as a Baltimore client, leading National to offer Doner local office space. The local agency branch opened its doors in 1955 with Baltimore's sports teams sponsoring its premier clients.

Many 1950s trends were consumer oriented, but not all. For an anti-commercial trend, the Beat Generation's anti-materialistic, "bohemian" lifestyle movement offered an alternative. Artists, poets, and musicians joined a nation-wide movement led by Jack Kerouac, Alan Ginsberg, and Lawrence Ferlinghetti, attracting like-minded experimenters in freedom of expression. Baltimore had its own modest "Beat" movement and meeting place, a tavern and former speakeasy run by Morris Martick. His tavern catered to an eclectic, non-traditional patronage: Baltimore's artists, musicians, and poets all came to Martick's with patronage changing by the time of day: early morning drinkers were followed at midday by awakening artists. By 5 p.m. writers and editors from newspapers, stockbrokers, and street dwellers wandered in, followed in the early evening by the "gay crowd". Very late in the evening, it was often a college bar. Billie Holiday sang there. So did Hank Williams. Local Beat movement followers, along with writers and the occasional Black or homosexual patron drank there. Serving a Black individual in the early 1950s would place Martick's liquor license at risk, as would service to homosexuals, inviting a police department raid. Nevertheless, both groups were regular patrons. Martick later closed the tavern, studied cooking in France, and converted the tavern to a fine French restaurant.

A DAY IN THE PARK

Baltimoreans were blessed with a broad selection of diverse outdoor recreation available on a very accessible local scale. For a spectator or a participant, the city and its suburbs offered parks, amusements, sports, and the world class Baltimore Zoo. There were multiple amusement parks, one of them even called "Enchanted"; numerous public parks with golf, tennis, softball, picnicking, a few with swimming pools; and for the modest cost of ticket, cross-Bay ferry rides to daytime or overnight resorts on the Eastern Shore of Maryland. Waterfront beach parks lined the Patapsco, Magothy, and Severn Rivers, with 800 miles of river, creek, bay, or inlet waterfront in the city and its suburbs. Most of the beachfront parks were privately owned, all of them segregated, each with sand, salt water, and netting surrounding the swimming area to deter stinging sea nettles. Carr's Beach catered to the African American community, offering more than a beach: the resort booked name entertainment on the local bill. Publicly owned Bay-front parks at North and Sandy Points completed the list of nearby family outing adventures.

The Baltimore Zoo. The city zoo was located in Druid Hill Park, its director the very capable and entrepreneurial Dr. Arthur Watson. The zoo had the usual array of animals, with elephants in their own house, snakes contained in the eerie reptile house, and off to one side Betsy, a chimpanzee imported from Liberia. Betsy became a star, the chimp who when presented with paint and brushes for her amusement, took to finger painting. Seizing an opportunity, Watson sold Betsy's paintings to generate income in support of the zoo. Betsy and Watson journeyed to New York City to boost the zoo and Baltimore when they appeared as on-air guests for the N.B.C. network's national morning *Today Show*.

Amusement Parks. Local amusement parks dotting Baltimore's landscape were long a staple of a family outing. Most included a midway, thrill rides, a dance pavilion, and a picnic grove, all just a short trolley ride away. The notorious Hollywood Park in Essex ("No opium smoking permitted in the Mill") was long closed; Riverside Park had been sold, the land now occupied by a Western Electric plant. Amusement parks from the early years of the century, Carlin's and Gwynn Oak, both segregated, featured all the usual amusement park rides, from ferris wheels to tunnels of love. A longer trolley ride took families to New Bayshore Park on the Chesapeake Bay, opened on a new site in 1954 and offering swimming and amusements. The original Bayshore property had been sold to an expansion-minded neighbor, the Bethlehem Steel Company.

The Enchanted Forest. One month after Disneyland opened in California, Baltimore got a theme park. Though it was on an entirely different scale, with no thrill rides and no commercialized characters, it was a new park designed specifically for small children. Built west of the city near the Patapsco State Park with its river, bridges, and picnic groves, the Enchanted Forest began on 20 wooded acres, expanding later to 50. Here the childhood storybook characters, placed in their nursery rhyme settings, were installed across the landscape: Hansel and Gretel's House; the Old Woman in a Shoe, with an exit sliding board; Snow White and Little Red Riding Hood at home in their homes; Humpty Dumpty complete with his wall; and more. Amusement rides were added later and contributed to even greater success.

Public Parks. Many Baltimore parks were designed by the Olmstead firm, widely spaced across the city. Several large parks, including Carroll, Clifton, Druid Hill, and Gwynn's Falls/Leakin, offered trails, fields, and picnic areas in a green space to families away from their otherwise congested urban surroundings. Parks offered welcome summertime relief from Baltimore's sweltering heat, especially to families living in flat-roofed homes in the era before air conditioning. Patterson Park, created in 1827, once a bulwark of the defenses of Baltimore in the War of 1812, was named for wealthy Baltimore businessman Willian Patterson, banker, merchant, founder of the B&O railroad, and like many of his peers, a slave owner. The park was created on five acres of land donated by Patterson to which the city later added land purchased from the Patterson family. The park offered green space to the surrounding urban community, with walkways, trees, and recreation facilities. The Gwynn's Falls Park, created in 1901, was developed at the urging of the Olmstead Brothers design firm, expanding in the 1920s with the addition of the adjacent Crimea, former estate of Thomas Winans but by then owned by the Leakin family. The Carroll family's Colonial-era estate and Mount Clare Mansion became the city's Carroll Park which included a nine-hole golf course, desegrated in 1951 in response to local protests. Scores of playgrounds were found in pocket parks across the city, often added to the city's public squares. Public swimming pools were a welcome respite for swimmers, particularly after Jonas Salk's polio vaccine largely negated fears of contracting polio from swimming at public pools.

Cross Bay Sailings. Daily sailings departed Baltimore, usually from the Pratt Street Piers, travelling across the Chesapeake Bay and most landing at resorts on Maryland's Eastern Shore. Families appeared at the pier early on a summer day, picnic baskets in hand, bathing suits and towels packed, for a two-hour eastbound trip across the Chesapeake Bay to the Tolchester Amusement Park for a family-friendly day, or to the Town of Betterton, a location offering more recreation and dining for adult interests. Half the fun was the ride on a diesel-powered steel boat cruising eastward at perhaps 15 miles per hour, two hours "at sea" with a welcome Bay breeze. For a day at the beach, a picnic, midway and amusement rides at Tolchester, then a westbound return trip, the nominal cost offered an accessible family and friends summertime holiday. The trip home always somehow seemed shorter than the eastbound morning journey. The same boats often doubled up in the evening by offering moonlight harbor cruises, a romantic cruise along Baltimore's industrial waterfront.

Western Shore Beaches. Baltimore and Anne Arundel Counties offered mostly privately-owned beach facilities. Some such as Kurtz Beach took advantage of the appeal of legalized slot machines in Anne Arundel County, while others like nearby Mago Vista refrained from the slot machines but posted an entry sign, "Gentiles Only"; Blacks were presumed to know not to try to enter. There were no fewer than ten such segregated facilities in the region. African Americans ventured a bit further south to Carr's Beach on the Chesapeake Bay south of Annapolis. Carr's was overwhelmingly successful: when rock star Chuck Berry played there in 1956, a capacity crowd of a lucky 8,000 were allowed into the park, a fraction of the 70,000 that had converged on the site hoping to get in.

When the Chesapeake Bay Bridge opened in mid-summer 1952, many of these local attractions found themselves with new competition from the growing resort town of Ocean City, Maryland, with locals heading down to the ocean or "downee ochun" in Baltimore's unique dialect. The ocean front town of Ocean City, Maryland, had been a speck on the sand, attracting mostly deep-sea sport fisherman. The town of 1,200 residents, self-proclaimed "White Marlin Capital of the World" would see a modest summertime population increase, but the completion of the Chesapeake Bay Bridge changed everything. The ocean front resort town became more accessible, a few hours away. Baltimore was left behind, ahead were ocean breezes and resort recreation. By the summertime of 1960, the town hosted 100,000 or more weekend visitors on a regular basis creating a new holiday standard: seven days at the beach became a new family vacation norm for Baltimoreans. Amusement parks opened, miniature golf offered after-dinner family recreation, apartment rental units were built on previously vacant sandy parcels of land, and restaurants with modest beginnings grew in number and size. The famous Phillips Seafood restaurant opened as a carryout shop, a four-seat crab house in 1956. Within a few years, Phillips could seat 1,400.

This ocean-front growth happened at the expense of Baltimore's attractions, recreation, and holiday-making. Having fun in Baltimore became the second choice as much of the population took their wallets east to what they perceived as bigger and better fun on the ocean front. The Baltimore region's recreation stopped growing and began a slow decline. Tolchester Amusement Park soon closed when the cross-bay ferries full of day-trippers stopped in 1962. Local amusement parks, beset with smaller crowds and perceived civil rights pressures, hung on by a thread. One at a time, the river and bayfront beach resorts closed. When gambling was outlawed in Anne Arundel County in 1968, the loss of slot machine revenue probably drove decisions to close the county's beach resorts more than any other single factor. African Americans, largely shut out of Ocean City in the 1950s, continued to patronize Brown's, Carr's and other nearby Black resorts until the mid- to late-1960s when laws prohibiting segregation opened more possibilities for Black patrons.

LIVING WITH FEAR

While the citizens of Baltimore had likely anticipated the 1950s as a time of prosperity, peace, and good times, those expectations would be shadowed by threats unanticipated, even unimagined. The decade of the 1950s would become a decade of anxiety. New and intense post-war competition between the United States and the Soviet Union had arisen, each country armed with nuclear weapons, as these two nations competed to become a "superpower", a term originated during the reign of Queen Victoria, when Great Britain dominated one-fourth of the world both militarily and economically. But in the 1950s, "superpower" held a modern and more ominous connotation with atomic and hydrogen bombs and intercontinental missiles playing their part in the international competition. An atmosphere of fear emerged with the realization that these weapons of mass destruction could be used, with citizens never knowing which moment might be their last.

By 1950, the horror of the atomic bomb detonations in Japan that ended World War Two had been reported in detail to the citizens of Baltimore. Scenes of complete devastation in the targeted cities of Hiroshima and Nagasaki with accompanying death rates were followed by personal stories of the civilians caught by the blasts. Survivors' stories of radiation poisoning, pictures of massive scarring from burns, and accounts of children maimed by the A-bomb were published. Baltimoreans were besieged with film of yet more atomic bomb tests in the South Pacific, showing houses blown apart, test dummies buffeted by winds from the blast, and vehicles and ships tossed about like toys. The tests were conducted to study the bomb's effects and to facilitate the building of even bigger bombs. Then came the news that the United States was not the sole possessor of this enormous destructive power: our enemy, the Soviet Union, had detonated their own atomic bomb. To the average Baltimorean, this was unsettling news. When President Eisenhower delivered his "Atoms for Peace" speech before the United Nations General Assembly on December 8, 1953, it did little to assuage the public's fear of nuclear attack and its consequences. Peaceful uses of atomic energy were entirely too remote to calm an anxious public. A Doomsday Clock (1947) publicly assessed nuclear risk, everyone fearful of "midnight", as the clock reset forward or back depending upon news of our nation's and our enemy's nuclear capability, an on-going reminder of the current risk of a nuclear holocaust.

The potential for a local atomic bomb blast demanded local preparation. While political leaders secretly carved out shelters to save themselves, the recommendation for school children was to "duck-and-cover": duck under their desk and cover their head if they saw a bright flash outside the schoolhouse window. Baltimoreans took faint comfort in the reopening of Civil Defense bomb shelters from World War Two, restocked and reprovisioned with fresh canned water and food. In a move to reassure the public, the military proudly reported that they would be able to shoot down most (but probably not all) attacking Soviet bombers by launching the latest version of ground-to-air Nike missiles from nearby missile bases surrounding the region, a partial reassurance offering small comfort. Air raid sirens across the city were tested at 1 p.m. each Monday, the blast of sound serving two purposes: a demonstration that the warning system was operable and a reminder, lest one somehow forget, that an atomic bomb air raid this week or next was within the realm of possibility.

What was there for Mr. and Mrs. Baltimore to do? Personal initiative was called for. A few citizens opted to head for rural, isolated areas, taking a hint from their government leaders to live or at least prepare to flee far from what they perceived to be civilization and its dangers, perhaps near or under a mountain. Alternatively, many built bomb and fallout shelters in the basements of their homes. They read books such as *Fallout Shelter Handbook*, one of multiple publications offering advice on surviving a nuclear attack. Cans of food lined the walls of their basements, a hedge against a time when food might be unavailable. While President Eisenhower addressed the potential benefits of nuclear power harnessed for the greater good in his Atoms for Peace plan, the military in that same era had developed a hydrogen bomb, one thousand times more powerful than the atomic bombs that had killed 100,000 in Japan. Shelters and canned goods aside, citizens had to learn to live with the threat of nuclear war, nuclear fallout, and a nuclear winter.

Fear was not limited to a distant threat of atomic weapon use, for there was an unsettling condition much closer to home. Polio, a crippling and often fatal disease, was insufficiently understood, it's means of transmission still a mystery. Fear was such that many made major adjustments to their lifestyles. The poliomyelitis virus had been infecting humans since at least ancient Egyptian times, reaching epidemic proportions in Europe during the Victorian era. With major epidemics in the United States in the 19-teens, 6,000 died in New York alone. The disease came and went, varied in severity, and appeared to strike almost randomly. In the late 1940s and earliest days of the 1950s, the viral disease had become epidemic in the region once again, with the warmer months of the year producing the largest number of polio cases. People with severe illness experienced paralysis, making them unable to breathe, with the threat of permanent disability and even death. It was a fearsome disease, attacking mostly children, with those under five years old most at risk.

Prevention was the solution, but the average person really did not know the cause of the illness, how it was transmitted, and the safety practices to avoid infection. Lacking good information, parents did what they could to protect their progeny, often responding to rumors, and sometimes useful suggestions. The City of Baltimore closed swimming pools. Quarantines for those infected were initiated. Mothers taught children to avoid crowds, or better yet to just stay indoors. Advice to avoid getting worn out, overtired, or chilled meant children were sent for afternoon naps and dressed in unneeded sweaters. As the disease might be spread by insects, houseflies were to be avoided. Most of all, one must stay clean. Baltimore never quite got around to DDT spraying, though many other areas did. It was eventually learned that the polio virus is communicated person to person, entering the victim either orally or via airborne droplets.

The reprieve everyone hoped for was discovered by a researcher working in Pittsburgh. Dr. Jonas Salk developed a polio vaccine that stopped polio transmission cold. He worked with the disease, observing its replication, using human test calls originally obtained in Baltimore. A cancer patient, Henrietta Lacks, was under treatment at Johns Hopkins Hospital in Baltimore when it was discovered that her cancer held unique characteristics. Her cancer cells offered quick and perfect replication, the ideal tool for medical research. Doctors at Johns Hopkins harvested some of the dying Lacks' cells, omitting the intermediate step of asking the patient's permission. Her cells became the gold standard, the "He-La" cell lines replicated many times over for sale to research laboratories, including Salk's.

When the vaccine was released to the public in 1954 and 1955, lines of children escorted by their parents waited to receive a lifesaving dosage of the Salk polio vaccine. The earliest version of the vaccine was injected with several doses over a few weeks to achieve full protection. A campaign was launched to prevent vaccination hesitancy with singing star Elvis Presley and other popular figures photographed while being inoculated. The Salk Vaccine offered the promise for a polio-free future, and 140,000 Baltimore youngsters soon received the vaccine. An oral version appeared mid-decade, the Sabin vaccine, avoiding the trauma to children of receiving polio shots.

A SPACE RACE BEGINS

Exploration beyond the earth was a longstanding source of public fascination, and in the decade of the 1950s science fiction was becoming reality. The path to a space program riveted Americans, even as they feared the potential consequence of powerful rockets aimed not toward space, but toward the United States. *The Baltimore Sun* declared "things will never be the same again…October 4, 1957…" as local citizens scanned the skies with binoculars searching for the first earth-orbiting satellite, the Soviet Union's Sputnik. Baltimore would be front and center in what would become a race to put satellites into orbit and a man on the moon, partly through the efforts of the Martin Company.

The United States military had been developing guided missiles with the assistance of German scientists liberated from Europe after World War Two. The Army, Air Force, and Navy each created independent programs to build reliable missiles, conducting test launches in competition with one another to place a man-made satellite in orbit around the earth. The strategic advantage of a grapefruit-sized satellite was not immediately apparent, given that it wouldn't really do much except orbit. But in launching the device, the capability of rockets would be proven. Rockets called Jupiter, Thor, Titan, Atlas, and Hercules all appeared in newsreels of the launches, shown widely in theaters. But much of the interest in rocketry came from the spectacular images of launch failures. Public anxiety increased when the Soviet Union proved their rocket technology with the launch of a satellite, Sputnik One, on October 4, 1957, followed soon after by a second satellite with a canine passenger, Laika, launched to his inevitable death. The source of much of that anxiety was the Soviet Union's demonstration of rockets capable of transporting nuclear weapons. In the opinion of the U.S. Senator from Maryland, John Marshall Butler, the best response to the Soviet satellite was "…the United States should take a good aim and shoot Russian Sputniks out of the skies as fast as they appear…".

The Space Race, as it began to be called, continued when the United States countered with the launch of a Navy Vanguard rocket on December 6, developed with the assistance of the local Martin Company. With the Explorer satellite atop, the launch reached an altitude of just under four feet before it fell and exploded. The satellite atop the rocket was not destroyed, but blew free and landed safely in some shrubs where it soon began transmitting its signal. One correspondent suggested going out and just shooting the "failed thing". America's anxiety level rose again. The press called it "Kaputnik". Explorer One was salvaged from the Vanguard failure, and the Army's Juno rocket eventually placed America's first satellite into orbit almost two months later, January 31, 1958.

In the aftermath of these embarrassing scenarios, rockets, satellites, and technical education for youth became national priorities driving policy. In a letter to the editor of *The Baltimore Sun*, Baltimorean Bertha DeGraw echoed the sentiments of many in the face of what she viewed as humiliation at the hands of the Soviet Union, calling for fewer school vacation days, increased pay for teachers, and the development of the "brain power" to become competitive with other nations.

INDUSTRIAL BALTIMORE

The destructive result of World War Two was a Europe and Asia with limited industrial capacity, The major combatant countries, Germany, Italy, Japan, and Britain, had sustained major damage to their industrial infrastructure, while the countries they occupied fared as badly as the war raged over and through them. Virtually unscathed was the industrial Western Hemisphere, with the most prominent country among them, the United States, the most industrialized of them all. Times were perfect for domestic production to thrive, as foreign competition was minimal while peacetime demand and domestic consumption were increasing. Post-war households were being formed, requiring nearly everything for living, basement to attic, inside and out. Even war industries, whose prospects would have otherwise been dim, were benefitting from the adversarial relationship of East and West, as the arms buildup of what would come to be called the "Cold War" began.

These were good times for American business and for Baltimore. The broad industrial base of the city offered a multitude of jobs, from highly skilled machine operators and highly educated electronic engineers, to manufacturing experts in dozens of settings, to builders able to construct, pave, or reconfigure the fabric of the city. In the post-war period, business, industry, and employment found itself increasing, modernizing, and changing with few exceptions.

Bethlehem Steel was operating multiple facilities in Baltimore, employing tens of thousands of workers. The steel mill at Sparrow's Point which had been expanded and then expanded again to meet war time demand, by 1950 was the largest steel mill in the world. Raw steel and products such rolls of thin steel sheet, nails, pipe, wire, and more came pouring out of the mill. Steel products with a galvanized coating and produced with other variations in chemical composition, customized for its specific intended use with varying strength, weather resistance, hardness, all shipped from the plant daily by truck, train, and ship. The war time shipbuilding yard in Fairfield, South Baltimore, closed immediately after the war and was restored to its original purpose, manufacturing storage tanks. Bethlehem's city yard along Key Highway specialized in ship repair and reconfiguration. The Baltimore yard increased the cargo capacity of older World War Two era vessels by adding large mid-sections in a process known as "jumbo-izing". At Sparrow's Point, the shipyard adjacent to the steel mill continued ship construction at a steady pace, if not the frenzied war time pace of the prior decade.

General Motors returned to their pre-war automobile manufacturing business, meeting pent-up demand for vehicles. By the 1950s, the two-level assembly plant was producing at or near its capacity of 8,000 vehicles per year. The upper level of the factory created the car body, from sheet metal sides to fabric interiors, dashboard to rear bumper. Downstairs, workmen assembled the chassis: a painted frame, axles, motor, wheels and more. At a key point, the body descended through the ceiling, delivered onto the waiting chassis to be bolted in place. More workmen soon drove the car away. The factory was just 15 years old in 1950. Five of those were war time years with the facility upstairs making aircraft components, and downstairs a parts logistics hub. When the factory returned to its original automobile production purpose, it began riding on the crest of an automobile revolution. Cars were ascendent in America, and that upward trend would only continue. From boxy 1950 sedan models, the factory was by the end of the decade producing sleek, winged 1959 and 1960 models.

The Glenn L. Martin Company. As the end of the war had reduced the aircraft assembly business, a new plan was needed. Prototypes for Cold War aircraft came and went: the Canberra bomber, built for Britain, and several models of piston engine military patrol planes were built in sufficient quantities to maintain production. The company added to its capabilities the design and building of commercial airliners. The Martin 202 was built as a more modern replacement for the 1935 vintage Douglas DC-3, with company officials confident the 202 would be the aircraft of the future for Martin, the Martin employees, and the airline industry. Almost fifty were built, but confidence in them was destroyed when metal fatigue caused the loss of several 202s, the first in August 1948 when a wing detached over Minnesota with the loss of 37 lives. Martin redesigned the aircraft, creating the Martin 404, a slightly larger aircraft pressurized for higher altitude flying. When Glenn Martin passed away in 1955, the company was renamed the Martin Company and changed its direction, turning by 1957 to aerospace manufacturing. Rockets, including the Project Vanguard satellite launch vehicle, were the new output for the Martin Company and its employees. Early in the next decade, it would merge with another company, the Marietta Corporation.

The Port of Baltimore. A shipping revolution occurred in 1956 when Malcom McLean, a North Carolina trucking company owner, developed containerized shipping. Tractor-trailer-sized cargo boxes, equally able to be fastened to trucks, trains or ships, became the shipping mode of the future. No longer would ropes, baskets, nets, and cranes hover over ships where longshoremen in cargo holds waited to stack packages, boxes, and bins by hand. McLean's new company, Sea-Land, pioneered the use of straight-sided ships transporting the containers, which were lifted by cranes onto specially designed trucks and railcars for inland movement. By decade's end, the Port of Baltimore had reacted to this evolution in cargo handling by opening the Dundalk Marine Terminal. Some of Baltimore's ten thousand longshoremen found themselves now redundant, and thus began a long, slow attrition in numbers. The container revolution added efficiency and security previously unknown through a shipping process in which the shipper packs and seals the "box", which is then moved to a destination perhaps half a world away, and only then unsealed by the recipient. Transporters rebranded themselves, offering logistics services which managed cargoes from shipping or receiving, to warehousing and distribution. The Port's business measured in cargo volumes and monetary values in and out of the Port, all grew as the Port reaffirmed its role as the heart of commercial activity in Baltimore.

Formstone. Baltimore would become the world's capital of Formstone houses, "the polyester of brick" in the words of boundary-breaking Baltimore filmmaker John Waters. Baltimore's row houses were typically brick fronted, but as older brick deteriorated, preservation was needed. Homeowners painted their brick red, then drew white masonry lines onto the finished red surfaces. But Formstone was a faster, longer-lasting alternative. Salesmen conducted business door-to-door, enticing homeowners by the tens of thousands in aging rowhomes. They touted Formstone or competitors such as Permastone as more than a decorative change, promising insulation and preservation for surfaces underneath. Teams of workers descended upon house after house, with only a day's work at each to transform the aging brick: nail a wire frame to the house front, apply a colorized stucco product to the netting, and finish it with an embossed stone-like decorative pattern. Workers of the city found jobs applying Formstone during the era. Decades later, when styles changed, it may have been their offspring who found jobs removing it and restoring the brick underneath.

THE FIFTIES COME TO A CLOSE

The end of the 1950s concluded a peaceful and prosperous decade for many citizens of Baltimore. This era of optimism, tempered with a wariness of nuclear confrontation, saw an ascendent industrial and commercial community that offered opportunity almost for the asking. National leadership seemed trustworthy, if tethered to the past, America's middle class had grown, and Baltimore's residents were no exception. Baltimore at mid-century largely reflected the culture of America. Despite having made some progress toward a just and equitable society, the decade's peace and prosperity were by no means universal as minority groups continued to be marginalized in many ways. A certain homogenization of Americans from many regions of the country occurred through sharing the wonder of the age, television. To miss an episode or program left one out of touch with neighbors and co-workers the next day. Television advertising and sponsorship meant there were favorite automobile makers, each brand with its adherents; new "ethnic" foods allowing experimentation in a hungry population's diet, even if the recipes were Americanized. Motion picture and live entertainment was shared from city to city, and professional sports teams competed to represent communities, though their participants were seldom natives of the place they were paid to represent. Baltimore had its unique features, with a harbor, diverse architecture, and long-established cultural attractions. But the suburban ring around the city would offer the same homogenized vistas found in any number of American cities with streets, shops, homes, highways, and signage sharing a recognizable look. America, Baltimore included, was becoming a unity, a single place, a comfortable and recognizable place.

CHAPTER SEVEN:
UNSETTLED TIMES

The 1960s

Baltimore in the 1960s? This was still a city of streetcars rumbling through a downtown alive with shoppers at Howard and Lexington Streets. Cars on the streets were mostly domestic models, the Chevrolet automobiles likely made at a local factory with steel produced at the Sparrow's Point mill. Parades on special occasions marched through the city. Eager to stay cool, many city homeowners discarded their window fans, fitting new air conditioners into both windows and budgets. James Brown, later dubbed America's "Godfather of Soul", played the Royal in 1963. Broadway came to town at a new theater, the Morris Mechanic. Though the decade meant an unhappy ending at WJZ-TV for television disc jockey Buddy Deane, the British music invasion of the 1960s arrived with the Beatles playing several shows in 1964 at the newly opened Civic Center. In 1967 singer-songwriter Jim Morrison played rock n' roll at the Lyric Theater.

Baltimore's "big four" department stores on Howard Street, Hochschild's, Hutzler's, Stewart's, and Hecht's, offered a broad array of products in multi-story buildings on the westside of downtown. Baltimore's garment industry stocked the men's department as well as specialty men's clothing stores along nearby Baltimore Street. At one point there were eight variety stores downtown: H.L. Green, J.G. McCrory, Silver's, G.C. Murphy, S.S. Kresge, Schulte, Woolworth, and W.T. Grant. These "five and ten cent" stores lined up along Lexington Street alternating with several motion picture houses. At the corner of Liberty and Lexington Streets, a Planter's Peanut Shop sold their snacks "hot and fresh".

This was the sixties in downtown Baltimore, a hometown for almost a million, not counting the suburbs. It was a city of unique accents where the question, "Where did you go to school?" meant high school. Long before the state started a lottery, a daily numbers "racket" thrived and made a millionaire out of the man who ran it. It was a peaceful, unassuming city with something of an inferiority complex, a place from which local citizens left to seek something better elsewhere, but once gone, realized the virtues of the place they had come from.

POLITICAL LEADERS OF THE 1960S

In the first years of the 1960s, Democrat J. Harold Grady was the mayor of the city, having been elected in 1959 as a reform candidate. Baltimore's Democratic voters felt a need for a change, turning to a non-politician. Grady, a former FBI agent and State's Attorney who was drafted by the party, was joined by candidates for City Council President and Comptroller, Phillip Goodman and Walter Graham. The group ran as the "Three Gs for Good Government", though future events would cast an unfortunate light on the slogan. Grady, Goodman, and Graham were unable to cooperate with one another and the political bosses who helped put them in office were unable to bridge the divide among the three. Irv Kovens, the man most responsible for the Grady candidacy, had recently been convicted of mail fraud and racketeering. Though his conviction was later overturned, by then the "Three G's" were each heading in different political directions. Grady's candidacy and election did mark a change in the political fortunes of machine politics of the era: Kovens had replaced the perennial kingmaker and Democratic party boss, Jack Pollack. Pollack had lost much of his party influence when Kovens' candidate Grady ascended to the mayor's office.

For generations the city's politics had been tightly managed by these bosses in an era when they were able to deliver city jobs, city services, food for the needy and most importantly, an ability to deliver votes for their preferred candidates. Each district in the city had its own set of political bosses, leaders who could deliver winning votes to ensure the success of candidates. Beneficiaries of their efforts included Thomas D'Alesandro, Jr., who prevailed in twenty-three consecutive elections. D'Alesandro held office in the Maryland House of Delegates, the United States Congress, and the Baltimore City Council, before he became mayor of Baltimore in 1947 (the first of three terms), each time relying at least in part on the "get out the vote" capabilities of the city's political bosses. The names of the bosses were familiar to politically aware Baltimoreans, including Pollack and Kovens. By the 1960s, the influence of these leaders was beginning to fade as local television was making it possible for a candidate to take their message directly to the people. Minority groups were organizing politically, offering substantial competition to the status quo. Baltimore's political times were slowly changing.

The new mayor, J. Harold Grady, worked to assure the good government promised in his campaign, while assuring the financial stability of the city and guiding redevelopment construction including the new Jones Falls Expressway and the city's new Civic Center. As a non-politician, Grady was uncomfortable as mayor, as the forces of political intrigue in city hall routinely creating dilemmas in governance he was not prepared to deal with. By late 1962, in the midst of his term, Grady resigned to accept an appointment as a judge on the Supreme Bench of Baltimore. The political community lauded him as a nice man, fair and honest, and then turned their attention to his very short-term successor, City Council President Phillip Goodman. Goodman was mayor for only a few months, running for his own full term in May 1963, and losing his bid to the ultimate outsider in Baltimore politics, a Republican.

Theodore R. McKeldin was a popular candidate, a self-made, progressive Republican. He was a hometown graduate of Baltimore City schools, subsequently attaining a law degree by attending the University of Maryland at night. Twice elected as Governor of Maryland (1951-1959) after he had served an earlier term as Baltimore mayor in the 1940s, McKeldin returned to local politics in 1963, winning a four-year term as Baltimore mayor. His election as a Republican mayor with 51 percent of the vote was a solitary victory: the Democrats swept the rest of the ballot.

The energetic McKeldin was at once a practiced politician and a visionary leader. He pushed a renewal agenda for the city's infrastructure and a civil rights agenda for its people. The Inner Harbor renewal project took shape under his administration, with the plans shown publicly for the first time in 1967. McKeldin spent energy and time inter-acting with and listening to the city's residents, habits which in part insulated the city from civil unrest occurring in other cities during the years of his term. He did a good deal more than listen: under his guidance, legislation assuring equal opportunity in employment, education, housing, and social services was enacted. While violent protests were occurring in New York City; Cleveland, Ohio; South Central Los Angeles, California; Newark, New Jersey; and even nearby Cambridge, Maryland, Baltimore remained peaceful. In his *Afro-American* newspaper column, political commentator Max Johnson reported McKeldin was "walking a tight rope all the way", fighting a reluctant City Council, while his handshaking, good-natured friendliness, and genuine concern as he visited Baltimore's poverty-stricken neighborhoods was clearly paying off. McKeldin had earned the trust of the people.

In 1967, McKeldin chose private life over elective office, returning to his law practice while accepting occasional appointive government assignments. In his place stood a new Republican candidate for mayor, Arthur Sherwood, founder of the Chesapeake Bay Foundation. Sherwood was a businessman with several political connections, but his candidacy never resonated with Baltimore voters. Sherwood received just 17 percent of the vote, losing to Thomas D'Alesandro III. The Democratic stranglehold on city politics seemed to be stronger than ever: the retiring McKeldin would be the last Republican mayor of the city in the 20th century.

Thomas D'Alesandro III, the son of three-term Mayor Thomas D'Alesandro, Jr., became mayor at a crucial moment in Baltimore history. His single term as mayor was marked with a series of events and decisions that make many other Baltimore mayoral terms seem almost insignificant. Perhaps only in the early 20th century, at the time of the Great Baltimore Fire was the office of the mayor handed a greater challenge than those presented to him. D'Alesandro was an activist mayor who built schools, advanced civil rights, made the Inner Harbor Plan possible with appropriate legislation, and cancelled many of the controversial highway plans threatening Baltimore's future livability. The mayor began his term on a positive note that was quickly disrupted when just four months into his term, the city was struck by violent protests precipitated by the 1968 assassination of Martin Luther King, Jr. With martial law declared and control of the city largely taken over by Maryland Governor Spiro Agnew the mayor's plans for a successful, peaceful, progressive term dissolved. His vision for the city, "to rid our society of every vestige of discrimination" was a continuing goal, but after one term as mayor, he returned to private life, his term coming to a close in early 1971.

A CITY IN TRANSITION

In the late 1950s, an urban renewal project known as Charles Center had been approved by the voters. By the 1960s, Charles Center would become a center-city reality. Bulldozers had leveled acres of well-worn properties, making way for new apartment houses, office buildings, a hotel, and a theater, while preserving and re-purposing several existing structures. With construction of Charles Center underway, new life was breathed into the center of the city. Several super-blocks were involved, east-west through streets were reduced to just two, three pedestrian friendly plazas were created, and new and refurbished older buildings were joined by skywalks. The first modern skyscraper in Baltimore, One Charles Center, was the work of famous modernist architect Mies Van der Rohe who designed a tower 23 stories tall in the International Style of steel and dark glass. *Fortune Magazine* named One Charles Center one of the "ten buildings that point to the future." The Charles Center project would operate on a ten-year redevelopment timeline, with revisions and adjustments to the plan continuing for years into the future.

When Republican Theodore R. McKeldin came into office in 1963, another renewal project, more ambitious than Charles Center, had entered the planning stage. Baltimore's Inner Harbor waterfront at the beginning of the 1960s was an unfortunate combination of aging warehouses, buildings, and piers fronting a heavily polluted Patapsco River.

Heavy industry such as chemical processing, chromium extraction, ship repair, and more dotted the shoreline. The piers themselves were largely underutilized as the ships that might have docked at them had grown too large for the space available. A steamship network that had linked Baltimore cargo and passengers with cities and towns throughout the Chesapeake Bay region had largely fallen victim to an improved highway network. Only a few seasonal excursion vessels and a single overnight steamer to Norfolk remained. The Light Street piers they sailed from had long since been razed, leaving only a handful of Pratt Street piers to serve the needs of the remnants of a one-hundred-year-old regional waterborne transport system.

In his prior 1940s term as mayor, McKeldin had been an initiator of infrastructure and renewal projects. Now in his second term some sixteen years later, he would continue those interests. It was clearly time for another change for the city and Baltimore's Inner Harbor became the logical next location for rebuilding, changing the waterfront from an embarrassment to an asset. The timing was right: the renewal at Charles Center had a bolstered confidence in the city's future and McKeldin supported infrastructure modernization. Heavy harborside industry was rapidly departing, and remediation of environmental damage was being made possible through new governmental intervention.

In the decade of the 1960s, a clean-up of the polluted Patapsco River was deemed impossible by many. The harbor was considered a dead zone, beyond the scope of any mitigation efforts. Industrial pollutants continued to flow in, raw sewage found its way to the river, and every possible contaminant in the entire 500-square-mile river basin had settled into Baltimore Harbor. A river that at one time had supported abundant fish and game was reduced to no more than stinky waste water, covered in places with foam, oil or worse.

Near to downtown, the Fell's Point-based Allied Chemical plant, the largest chromium plant in the world, faced the Patapsco River. The waterside plant supplied virtually all the chromium needs of the United States and much of the world, its chromium used in the manufacture of stainless steel, paints, pigments and tanned leather. Chromium was extracted from the chrome-rich ore, but the refining process left a waste product of toxin-laden residual tailings. For the 100 years of the refinery's existence, the tailings were used on the twenty-acre site of the factory as fill material to expand both their own property as well as the waterfront property of others in locations around the harbor. This major polluter was leaking toxins and chromium into the Patapsco River before and during the entire decade of the 1960s.

On the harbor's south side, a Bethlehem Steel shipyard occupied the waterfront at the foot of Federal Hill's east face, on Key Highway. Founded in the 19th century as the Skinner Shipyard, the shipbuilding division of the Bethlehem Steel Company had acquired the yard in 1921, operating the Baltimore Yard as a ship repair and conversion facility. By 1960 the yard had perfected the process of enlarging ships by halving them, installing an additional midship portion, and reassembling the pieces, thus increasing the ship's capacity and economic viability. The ships were said to be "jumbo-ized". At the busy yard, ship repair and refurbishment operations would inevitably create toxins and pollutants which ended up in the harbor. Ships were stripped of paint, especially the heavy metal paints used for anti-fouling, then repainted, with other oils, wastewater, debris, and storm water from the yard's grounds entering the harbor. Perhaps most critically, the asbestos insulation that was removed, relocated, or otherwise disturbed, found in virtually every vessel appearing in the yard for repair or renovation, became waste products from the ship refurbishment. These were identifiable sources of pollution, with damage done to both the workers and the Patapsco River.

Pollution made the Patapsco River a near hopeless case. Heavy metal and other toxins had seeped into the harbor's mud bottom, covered by a layer of pesticides and industrial waste that permeated a body of water no longer able to support aquatic life. The Maryland Department of Natural Resources in 1967 termed the river "grossly polluted". Dr. Donald Pritchard of the Johns Hopkins Chesapeake Bay Institute said in a 1967 interview, in response to the question could the river be cleaned up, "...somebody's got to get the ball rolling, people say 'we don't clean up because the fellas over there don't clean up'." Resistance to environmental change was strong in the smokestack industry city of Baltimore where too much environmental action might place jobs at risk. The environmental movement was still in its infancy in 1967, its beginnings in the 1962 publication of Rachel Carson's *Silent Spring*. Pollution remediation would become the subject of governmental intervention, but it would be years before efforts to clean the Patapsco had a substantive impact. Environmentalists in the region, of which there were many, continued to petition, lobby, and act to improve the quality of the water, but their work was always a struggle.

The re-development of Baltimore's waterfront, the Inner Harbor Plan, was the next step for the city's renewal. The massive effort created parkland, a promenade, and a one-block-deep 130-acre renewal area, which would involve the purchase of 1,000 buildings and the relocation of 700 operating businesses. The plan necessitated negotiations with twenty government agencies, and the complete relocation of the city's wholesale produce marketplace to a site twenty miles away. Not surprisingly, the move made access to fresh produce for resale exceedingly difficult for the few remaining "A-rabbers", vendors of produce that had travelled the city streets in horse-drawn wagons for one hundred years. In exchange the city would have a jewel, a tourism focal point, and for everyone, access to the waterfront that had long been hidden behind those wooden offices, warehouses, and piers. Baltimoreans had become believers, converts to the principle of renewing their city. In the era just before the Charles Center Plan, according to Eugene Petty of the Greater Baltimore Committee, the average comment he heard was "I'll never see it in my time", but once the project was underway, a few new glistening buildings complete, and the Inner Harbor Plan unveiled, skeptics asked, "Why is it going to take so long?" It was a 20-year plan, to which would be added more time and more amenities as its success became apparent to late-comers with dollars to invest.

HISTORIC BALTIMORE

Modernizing a city is not without peril, as its heritage, its beauty, and many of its stories are written in brick and mortar. The preservation of the city was on the minds of groups like Preservation Maryland (organized 1931) and Baltimore Heritage (organized 1960), the latter with a stronger local Baltimore-centric interest. Baltimore Heritage was created, in the words of John Foster of the city's Junior Association of Commerce, "because nobody else seemed to be doing anything to stop this senseless waste of Baltimore's heritage." From these beginnings emerged a new city agency, the Commission for Historical and Architectural Preservation (C.H.A.P.), soon followed by the naming of the first protected historical district, Mount Vernon. Both preservation groups as well as C.H.A.P. would have their hands full. Highway planning, seemingly always on one or another engineering and construction agenda, became a priority issue in this and the following decade.

The creation of Charles Center and its modern urban cityscape had offered the city and its residents much in the way of improvement and civic pride. But these did not occur without significant risk to pieces of history, the tangible remains of the businesses and people that had been there before. Charles Center was almost unique in American urban renewal in that it preserved multiple but aging buildings amid its 33-acre footprint. These buildings within the renewal area were reinvigorated or repurposed, yielding a modern urban landscape within which there remained vestiges of Baltimore's business and architectural history. Between the saved properties, the bulldozers did their job of clearing the land, making new development possible. Despite the buildings that were saved, properties declared beyond reclamation were simply demolished, including a few of Baltimore's dwindling number of cast iron-fronted buildings, and Fayette Street's historic Miller Brothers Restaurant.

Preservationists faced a monumental task in the years ahead, but their morale remained high as progress had been achieved. Their efforts led to the creation of multiple local and federal historic districts resulting in thousands of properties gaining protected status. Urban renewal was a more controllable threat to historic preservation than the more robust threat to build new, high speed, limited access highways in, around, and through the city.

HIGHWAY PLANNERS PLANNING

Plans to build expressways to and through Baltimore were entering their 20th year in the early 1960s. Road builders had since 1942 been proposing routes that pleased some political figures and many road construction executives but very few citizens. The highway builders offered multiple successive plans for new routes. Most of the proposed highways had one overriding goal, to move people who didn't live in Baltimore into, out of, or more likely through the city, as quickly as possible. Despite mandatory public input, there seemed to be lacking a critical look at the impact of highway plans on the citizens of the city or the larger needs of the city itself. As highway opponent and future United States Senator Barbara Mikulski said during her highway battles, the highway planners always promised input on the roadway plan, but they usually meant "we could choose the color of the guardrails." That disdain for citizens' opinions was at least as motivating to the opponents as were the highway plans themselves.

Baltimore had a long history of indecisiveness and disagreement leading to an inability to create a highway plan that would meet the multiple needs of local, regional, and long-distance travelers. At issue was a path for a road free of cross traffic, intersections, and delay through the center of the city. Solutions were sought and rejected, studies were made, and still no consensus was achieved. Nine different routing proposals were advanced between 1942 and 1957, covering the entire period from when the automobile had become a city planning force to be reckoned with. The ultimate objection was somehow never properly or thoroughly considered: the division of the city into separate and distinct parts by building highways that would form walls between them. Traffic had priority over community. These early highway plans were appropriately termed East-West Expressways, with cross-town routes passing north of the Central Business District. Philip Darling became head of the Baltimore City Planning Department in 1958 and advocated various routes through the city. He likened the importance of a highway system as equal to the impact of the 1825 opening of the Erie Canal when, to compete with the New York canal, the city backed construction of the Baltimore and Ohio Railroad. Darling felt the city had to act to counteract a new threat, this time the Baltimore Beltway, lest businesses flee the city for the more accessible county environs. Darling's routes were carefully drawn and gained early and wide support by community and business groups, but when consultants were hired to conduct further planning, each report in turn began to dismantle the consensus on a northern route, and then a central route.

Each of the routes seemed to garner opposition, as one would have clipped a bit of the Walters Art Museum and then continued through the Mount Vernon district. Another would have leveled parts of Federal Hill. A third moved the west side highway route further north through Leakin Park. Analysis of these plans demonstrated that they solved little. Then the consultants began to disagree with one another over priorities beyond the route itself, with cost and preservation becoming considerations. Darling ultimately resigned his post, worn down as his Department of Planning was marginalized while the highway battles continued. His plan, a series of highway spokes entering the city from multiple directions, would have offered complete access to center city, but in so doing would have brought destruction to thousands of Baltimore homes.

By 1960 studies and alternatives (twenty of them if one counted the options within the plans) moved the highway through the city but to the south of the Central business district. Engineers were hired to study this new routing on behalf of the politicians and planners acting as decision makers. The myriad alternative routes usually included an Inner Harbor bridge crossing or a highway to skirt the southern edge of downtown following the Pratt Street corridor, or even further to the south, to level a portion of Federal Hill for a highway route. The proposed bridge across the harbor would collect traffic from multiple interstate highways, an astonishing fourteen traffic lanes wide, with the connecting highways bulldozing the historic communities of Fell's Point and Canton. One of the feeder highways, U.S. Interstate 70, would wipe out parts of several minority communities while passing through and destroying portions of the west side's Leakin Park.

One decision was finally made in 1961 as the controversy continued to roil. The Baltimore City Council, tone deaf to the last, enabled condemnation and destruction of houses in the proposed path of a piece of highway that was intended to be a section of Interstate 70 just west of downtown. Despite the absence of a firm plan for any portion of Baltimore's highway system, construction began, an African American neighborhood was leveled, and the new high-speed roadway was built. The road ultimately was not to be a part of the final highway design, leaving it connected only to adjacent city streets, and earning the 1.39-mile, multi-lane stretch the name "Highway To Nowhere."

The battle over the highways would continue into the next decade. Citizen resistance was fierce, and one opposition technique was to shield Fell's Point by creating a historic district there. Compromises were reached and by 1985, the highways were completed by crossing the city through the industrial districts well to the south. A tunnel had replaced the bridge, only a handful of the access routes entering the city were built, and most importantly, the historic districts, the vulnerable park land, and most neighborhoods were spared from destruction.

A CHANGING DEMOGRAPHIC

Racial segregation had a long history in Baltimore. Early in the 20th century, a demarcation line had been codified by the City Council, dividing the residential map of the city into separate Black and White communities. Declared unconstitutional by the courts by 1917, the law lost its legal teeth, but the practice of White residents held to its principle, which meant continuing segregation. In the 1950s, a practice known as blockbusting began to break down the informal but very real dividing lines between Black and White residential areas. White homeowners sold out quickly, brokers picked up the real estate pieces, then rented or sold the properties at profitable levels. White flight would continue into and beyond the 1960s.

Increasing the pressure on the minority community was the loss of city housing in general. Families were used as pawns in the blockbusting schemes, often forced into unwanted and undesirable relocations because their homes were condemned, with entire neighborhoods bulldozed for slum clearance, public housing projects, new schools, and proposed expressways. In the early 1960s, the destruction rate was about 800 units per year; by the end of the decade, it had reached 2,500 units per year. The vast number of those affected were the poor and African American populations.

By the 1960s, northern cities including Baltimore had received large numbers of African Americans migrating to better jobs available there. A few statistics from 1960 to 1970 help to tell the story:

- Baltimore's minority population increased from almost 35 percent to over 46 percent.

- The city's overall population declined from 939,000 to 905,000.

- The region's (city and county) population increased from 1.1 million to 1.4 million.

Blockbusting was taking its toll, as fear triumphed over reason, and entire neighborhoods such as Edmondson Village on the west side went from all White to virtually all Black in ten years. Suburbs were growing, taking away shopping districts and their customers. Factories and their workers left the older brick factories in the city, replaced by the campuses of suburban indzustrial parks. Baltimore was shrinking, the starting point of a long city population change.

Racial bias beyond the housing issues was a continuing source of friction for the African American community, leading to protests throughout the decade. The most visible was gaining full access to the downtown department stores. Efforts to gain access to lunch counters had begun in the mid-1950s, but the tea rooms and restaurants of several of the major center city department stores remained closed to Black shoppers. In a manner reminiscent of the sit-ins and integration of those early lunch counter successes, students from Morgan State visited the Hecht Company store in suburban Northwood. The response was quick: the department stores throughout the city and suburbs were thoroughly integrated by 1960. But attitudes persisted. The tragic story of Hattie Carroll is instructive, in both the events that took place and the legal system's reaction. Carroll was working as a barmaid in the Emerson Hotel. A patron felt she was responding too slowly to his request for service, and struck her with his cane. She fell, gravely injured, and died soon after. The assault led to the arrest and conviction of the patron. But his request to have his imprisonment be postponed until after his farm's harvest had been brought in was granted. Two standards of justice clearly existed, with the minority community not the beneficiary.

The march toward equal rights met a detour in Baltimore in the 1960s. Resistance to change was neither universal nor in every section of the city and the region, but it existed widely. Racial relations were evolving too slowly in the minds of some, and for others, as a revolution. When *Brown v. Board of Education* was argued before the U.S. Supreme Court it was Baltimorean Thurgood Marshall who made the case for desegregating public schools. Marshall was a pragmatic attorney, whose philosophy in taking the case before the Court was "...do what you think is right and let the law catch up." In the Brown case, that is exactly what he did, and the law caught up by banning school segregation as of May 17, 1954.

Baltimore City Schools adopted a laissez-faire approach to desegregation: students would be allowed to select and attend any school of their choice. Freedom of choice did not necessarily bear fruit. Some White parents immediately protested, picketing with signs bearing messages such as "Segregation is Our Heritage", and then withdrew their students. Yet resistance was not universal: at Southern High School the football team captain and the president of the student body joined Black students as they walked into the school, acting as a bodyguard escort. Other parents and students voted with their feet, moving to private schools or suburbs. In 1960, the student population in city schools had become majority black and by 1961, three-fourths of the city schools were 90 percent Black. The city's White population was moving away, with blockbusting and resistance to school desegregation motivating a rapid retreat from integration.

While the Black community had historically been compressed into limited portions of the city based first on legal segregation and later on informal red-lining, Baltimore's White community had virtually unlimited housing possibilities. A 1962 Executive Order created a mandate for civil rights in housing and the 1964 Civil Rights Act assured non-discrimination where federal programs and guarantees were applied. Both impacted White citizens' unlimited housing possibilities, viewed as threats to what was usually a family's greatest financial asset, their home. Into this chasm of fear came a perennial Maryland political office seeker, George P. Mahoney.

George P. Mahoney entered the contest for Maryland governor in 1966. He had previously been a candidate for governor (1950, 1954, 1962) and the United States Senate (1952, 1956, 1958) and while he did prevail in some primary campaigns, he lost in every general election. Mahoney had listened to the housing concerns of many White Marylanders and built his 1966 campaign for governor with definite racist overtones. His campaign slogan, "Your Home Is Your Castle, Protect It" was a direct rejection of the prevailing trend of equality in access to housing. His campaign would be conducted on an anti-open housing platform, but Mahoney had to first win a primary election. He ran against two more traditional Democratic candidates who split the anti-Mahoney vote, Mahoney winning with only 31 percent of the vote. Another Democrat reacted to Mahoney's segregationist candidacy by entering the general election as an independent candidate. Baltimore City Comptroller Hyman Pressman, himself a unique gadabout as an elected official, became a third gubernatorial candidate.

In the general election, the presence of the third candidate skewed the election result. Voters supported Pressman and his more traditional Democratic party positions with 10 percent of the vote, but the election was won by the Republican candidate, Spiro Agnew. Agnew had campaigned as the most electable, progressive candidate, a short-lived progressivism that would change in a matter of months. Agnew was the ultimate "New Right" suburban leader and won the governorship statewide with 49 percent of the vote, an overwhelming 70 percent of Black voters supporting his candidacy. Mahoney's candidacy, his "home as castle" campaign and his segregationist views were defeated, but still received over 40 percent of the state-wide vote, including 37 percent of the votes cast in Baltimore City.

APRIL 1968

Martin Luther King, Jr., was assassinated in Memphis, Tennessee, on April 4, 1968. The hopes and dreams of many had been dashed with a single shot. King had long espoused a non-violent approach for the civil rights movement, his leadership offering hope to the nation. His death was a lightning rod for seemingly every American: the White community was divided between those who mourned his loss and those who celebrated his death, many describing him as nothing more than a troublemaker. In the African American community, great sadness and disillusionment begat anger which became, for some, the justification for a violent reaction.

Baltimore schools, workers, and churches spent the time after King's death in discussion, reflection, and mourning. At Northwestern High School, 300 students sat in the darkened auditorium in meditation. At the Social Security Administration in Woodlawn, an afternoon memorial service drew 1,500 people. A Baptist ministers group planned a memorial service for the afternoon of April 6, but before it occurred, Baltimore exploded. Crowds had formed on east side streets, where a few broken windows led to the looting of a dry-cleaning business, followed by a nearby fire in the 700 Block of Gay Street. *Baltimore Sun* reporter James Bready observed, "We drove along North Avenue, and I remember seeing kids running along from store to store with lighted torches to touch them off." A curfew declaration proved ineffective, leading Maryland Governor Agnew to declare an emergency. Soon the first of 6,000 militia troops, which over the next week grew to 12,000, entered the city to assist the police in tamping down the violence. For the next five days, arrests increased, looting became rampant, and fires went un-extinguished due to violence directed at the fire service.

By April 11, the violence had ended, the militia left the city, but the human and property toll remained: six people were dead, six hundred were injured, and over 1,000 mostly small businesses had been damaged or lost, the financial losses exceeding $100 million in 2023 dollars. The events of 1968 did more than scar the streetscape: burned-out shells of buildings remained standing for years after the violence had ended. There was another major casualty, almost unspoken, with the introduction of fear into the lives of those who had not felt it before. They had lived through an out-of-control event, a week of unpredictability, not knowing where the next fire would start, where the next group of rioters would appear, and whether their own lives and property were at risk. The fear lingered, and the psyche of the city was damaged, some said beyond repair. White flight continued, even increased, desegregation was challenged, and progress in race relations effectively stalled.

The impact to African American residents was severe, as much of the Black community found themselves trying to survive while living in the midst of a war zone landscape. Commercial districts they had relied upon were burned out, the jobs in those businesses gone when the buildings burned. It was often a selective burning, where Black owned businesses survived while nearby White owned shops were reduced to ashes. The mayhem was perhaps fueled by a sense of retribution as payback for shopkeepers taking advantage of their customers. Thousands of protesters had been arrested, mostly for curfew violations, potentially placing their employment prospects in further jeopardy. While the uprising was seen as unjustified in the White community, Black citizens saw and understood the compounding of bias, segregation, inequality, and exploitation that had even before the King assassination created conditions ripe for an uprising, which is what occurred.

It was these conditions and circumstances that led to the ascendency of a newly formed and more militant group, the Black Panther Party. Arriving in Baltimore in late 1966, the group fed the hungry and created needed resources for the community, while their militancy raised suspicions among many of those in authority. One of the anti-poverty groups that were formed in the era was Walter Lively's U-Join, Union for Jobs Or Income Now. It grew out of an anti-poverty effort founded by the Students for a Democratic Society (S.D.S.). So racially divided was Baltimore that the S.D.S. program maintained two offices, one for White workers and impoverished White communities, the other for Black workers in similar Black communities. Lively at the time was a strong activist leader who many predicted would one day become Baltimore's mayor. The group he formed in the words of journalist James Dilts was "committed to letting people decide…a militant group because it's biased toward working, poor, Black people…radical group because it wants democratic control and basic change." Lively was advancing the cause of equality, but his promising future and leadership were extinguished when he died in the mid-1970s, age 34, of an aneurysm.

The long-term implications of the April 1968 events were to spell even harder times for the city. In the following decade, the city's population declined an alarming 120,000 residents, from over 900,000 to fewer than 780,000. Businesses fled in like numbers, taking their jobs with them, leaving transit-dependent residents long commutes over a tottering transit system. Merchants boarded up the burned-out shells, took their insurance proceeds, and left, while the downtown shopping district with its major stores and shops slowly withered and died as their customers took their money to suburban centers. The city needed a champion to help it find its way again. Fortunately it found one whose name was Schaefer, a prickly, exacting man of many dispositions. He would take over the reins of power in the 1970s.

A POTPOURRI OF THE 1960S

In the decade, random but memorable events, people, and fashions arose that no history of the decade should be without. They demand mention, so here are few of them:

The Baltimore Orioles. The local baseball team had arrived from St. Louis, at the time a losing club known as the St. Louis Browns. The team and its fans endured a slow start, losing more than winning until 1966 when the team became the envy of baseball. It was in that year the Orioles won their first baseball championship, defeating the Los Angeles Dodgers in four consecutive games to win baseball's World Series. The team was led by an amazing array of talent with two stars on the team, unrelated but with the same Robinson surname, Frank and Brooks, leading a potent lineup of players and pitching staff, winning 60 percent of the games played that season.

I Am an American Day Parade. Continuing a fifty-year tradition, Baltimore was one of many cities that hosted a September Sunday afternoon parade celebrating all things American. Begun in 1942, encouraged by newspaper publisher William Randolph Hearst, the annual celebratory day was a blend of patriotism and in Baltimore, a celebration of its immigrant population. With a modest beginning just 24,000 attended the first parade, but the very next year, perhaps heightened by World War Two enthusiasm, spectator attendance grew to 75,000 along with the size of the parade, with marching bands and marching groups. The parades took marchers from Fell's Point to Patterson Park in a three-hour long event, passing through east Baltimore neighborhoods and crowds. By the 1960s the parade had reached its apex of popularity with crowds numbering in the hundreds of thousands.

John Waters. A locally born baby-boomer became a nationally known satirist of tradition and decorum through his career as film maker, actor, and author. As a student at New York University, on-campus marijuana smoking led to his sudden departure from school in 1966 and sent him home to Baltimore seeking a vocation. He soon began filming short programs around the city, his imagination, friendships, and local support allowing him to hone his film-making craft. By 1969, his first feature length film *Mondo Trasho* appeared, a raunchy dark comedy starring cross-dressing drag queen Glenn Milstead as "Divine".

The Baltimore Beltway. A new circumferential highway knitting together Baltimore's burgeoning suburbs was conceived by Baltimore County highway planners in the late 1940s, ultimately becoming a part of the newly authorized (1956) Interstate Highway system. Short segments of the highway were completed in the late 1950s then united, effectively creating a by-pass of the city. Funding for one segment was limited in Anne Arundel County, and so the Beltway design included a traffic light and a rail crossing, complete with warning lights, crossing gates and an occasional train bound for Glen Burnie. Reconstruction in the early 1960s eliminated this design deficiency.

John Coltrane. The music of John Coltrane was heard for the last time when he appeared at Baltimore's Left Bank Jazz Society's Famous Ballroom in 1967. Coltrane, a saxophonist, orchestra leader, and composer was a notable contributor to the American jazz music scene, exploring and innovating until his death at the age of forty. In his final appearance, no one in attendance had any idea that this world-famous jazz saxophonist would be dead of liver cancer in just two months. His appearance before the eclectic group of Baltimoreans that gathered on Sunday afternoons on North Charles Street alternatively hushed the crowd, then led to standing ovations. Coltrane played through his pain to electrify the gathered jazz aficionados.

The Playboy Club. In 1964, the center of male chauvinism in Baltimore was the Playboy Club, beginning its thirteen-year run in Baltimore at 28 Light Street. Built on the premise that every man could enjoy the life of a would-be lothario, as espoused by the male adult themed *Playboy Magazine*, the club became a center of social interaction and nationally known entertainment. Membership was required, upscale apparel required for admission, and food and drink were served by uniquely, minimally attired young women known as Bunnies. The Playboy Club in Baltimore prospered through several social movements, including the loosening of sexual constraints after the introduction of oral birth control, but a concurrent move toward equal rights for women created a more challenging environment for the Playboy experience. The club closed in 1977.

Jerry Turner. Television news was in its heyday in the 1960s, where trusted voices related the latest stories to an awaiting public. In Baltimore, amongst the three primary local television news outlets, it was a highly trusted, popular news reader on station WJZ, Jerry Turner, that was most notable in the era. Turner, a Mississippi native, came to Baltimore in 1962, quickly making what had been the least popular local news outlet into the number one news outlet among Baltimore viewers for the ensuing twenty years. Turner worked with other popular local newscasters, especially Al Sanders with whom he was paired in 1977, solidifying the station's news dominance.

Harley Brinsfield. Brinsfield operated a chain of twenty-four-hour sandwich shops across the Baltimore region, forty shops featuring his famous Harley Burger: hamburger patties simmered in a tomato-based sauce developed from a recipe he created while he was in the Merchant Marine. The popular Harley Burger financed his true passion, a night-time radio program featuring music he curated, broadcast in the late evenings with a blend of smooth jazz and pops. Harley's radio show on a succession of radio stations, WITH, WBAL, WCBM, featured his deep-voiced personality and his vintage record collection, accompanied by more contemporary jazz late into the night.

Baltimore Polytechnic, Class of '61. The Baltimore Polytechnic High School, located at North Avenue and Calvert Street, had been one of the city's premier education venues for decades. In a moment that amazed many, the school awarded 17-year-old Jack Burkert a high school diploma in a ceremony held in the school auditorium. Burkert, author of this history text, was most certainly not an award-winning student, having slowly descended through the class rankings in his four-year career at the school. For the diploma, his parents were thankful.

Hon. The citizens of Baltimore often speak using a unique accent, pronunciation, and slang known locally as Bawlmerese. Letters may be added, or omitted from spoken words: "Bawlmer" for the city's name, "Patapsico" for the name of the river upon which the city is sited, the Patapsco. One commonly used honorific is a gender neutral, affectionate greeting derived from the more intimate "honey", the greeting "Hon", used by Baltimoreans for generations. It was made most popular by the hair-sprayed housewives or waitresses of East Baltimore through the 1960s in combination with "Hello…Whatcha havin'…?" and "How are ya….?"

Earl "Poppa Bear" Banks. A legendary builder of men, Earl Banks was the long-term head coach of the Morgan State Bears football team. Morgan State, a public urban educational institution in Baltimore, is a Historically Black College with a long history of creating leaders in the Black community. Under his leadership, the Morgan football program thrived through the 1960s, into the early 1970s. Banks' excellence was honored with multiple awards for coaching and community service, extending beyond his prime coaching years. He headed up or was a major contributor to a half-dozen local philanthropic and charitable organizations, from the Boy Scouts to the Salvation Army.

The Club Venus. At a time when entertainment venues were leaving intimate settings for major concert or oversize stadia, the Club Venus bucked the trend of the times. A traditional and upscale supper club, the Club Venus was a 500-seat dining and entertainment nightclub opened in 1966 in a Baltimore suburban shopping center. Other clubs like Hollywood Park in Essex offered first class entertainment in an unadorned setting, but the Club Venus went upscale in every way, hosting an array of well-known acts and luminaries of the entertainment world. Comedians Sid Caesar and Rodney Dangerfield, The Temptations, and The Platters all played the Club Venus. In late 1968 alone, the array of talent was typically diverse, offering in successive weeks, The Four Tops, Ray Charles, and Frankie Laine.

Little Tavern Shops. This chain of hamburger purveyors had been in the restaurant business since the late 1920s, featuring compact shops that were built on the concept of a quick lunch. Little Tavern Shops and their lesser competitor White Castle restaurants offered counter seating, a limited menu focused on small hamburgers cooked in advance and stored in a warming oven, and rapid ordering for in-store or carry-out, all at modest prices. These shops dotted the Baltimore landscape, but in the 1960s, ran into the competition offered by drive-in restaurants. The arrival of automobile-oriented fast-food purveyors changed consumer habits, making the Little Tavern's days numbered.

Pimlico. Horse racing was a longstanding tradition in Maryland and Baltimore, dating perhaps to the late 1600s. The Pimlico Racecourse in Baltimore was opened in 1870, marked by the construction of the course's members-only clubhouse. Remodeled in the 1950s, the iconic clubhouse caught fire and burned to the ground on the night of June 17-18, 1966. Lost in the eight-alarm clubhouse fire were the almost one-hundred-year-old building, collapsing onto itself within a few hours of the start of the fire, along with valuable horseracing records and a collection of priceless racing artwork. The age and construction of the clubhouse doomed the structure, brought to ruins by "an electrical malfunction". With the loss of the Clubhouse, one spectator opined that the fire had ended a "way of life for racing fans".

Verda Welcome. A community and civil rights leader, Verda Welcome came to Baltimore in 1929 and graduated from both Coppin State normal school and Morgan State College. She was elected to the Maryland State House of Delegates (1959) and then the Maryland State Senate in 1962, only the second Black woman to join that body. On

April 10, 1964, she was wounded in an assassination attempt when a group of men attacked her. There were opinions that a political rival in the General Assembly had apparently contracted a hit on Senator Welcome, but while the unsuccessful shooter was convicted, the indicted political rival was acquitted. Welcome went on to serve twenty years in the Maryland Senate.

Frank Zappa. Music of many styles and genres were a created by this Baltimore born (December 1940) performer. Zappa composed and performed music from doo-wop to avant-garde in his own unique style. He began his early career not unlike other musicians of the era, moving from group to group. In May 1965 he created what would become his signature group, the Mothers and later, with new membership, the Mothers of Invention, a group that honed its musical style and catalog with a six-month New York residency at the Garrick Club in Greenwich Village. Some of his work was successful, some not; some unique, others politically incorrect. But in every case, it was always pure Zappa. His New York experience began years of music creation for this Baltimorean until his death from cancer in 1993 at a youthful 52 years of age.

VIETNAM RAISES THE TEMPERATURE

When the French Army left French Indochina, Vietnam, in 1954, it was with the assurance from the United States that the "Domino Theory" of a cascade of nations becoming Communist would not result, that America would stand tall to prevent that eventuality. This was the beginning of the United States' involvement in Vietnam, a commitment of twenty years, billions of dollars and 50,000 American lives. The American guarantee was little noticed, perhaps only by policy experts and a few State Department leaders, perhaps even them not understanding the implications of these simple promises. How bad could it get? Vietnam was a small, not particularly wealthy nation at war with itself, with a cipher of a revolutionary leader named Ho Chi Minh.

Successive American presidencies continued the 1954 commitment of Dwight Eisenhower, his departing advice of not being involved in a land war in Asia ignored first by John Kennedy with his placement of military advisors on the ground, followed by Lyndon Johnson's belief that what was a Civil War in Vietnam, one side indeed Communist, was winnable if only sufficient resources and manpower could be applied to the conflict. It was 1964 when two Gulf of Tonkin incidents became the pretext to escalate the U.S. role in Vietnam. A covert American mission resulted in a brief skirmish between Vietnamese and American naval vessels, the destroyer *Maddox* virtually undamaged. But misinterpreted messages later led to reports of a second attack two days later directed at the destroyer *Turner Joy*. It was this second attack, an attack that never happened, which authorized military retaliation: the battle was on.

In the mid-1960s, every American male was required to register for the military draft, making himself available for military service at the request of his government. There were exceptions and exemptions, deferments, and medical categories leading to a non-draft-eligible status, but many young men were destined to fight, and some die, in Vietnam. A reluctance to fight and die in Vietnam was equated by some with a lack of patriotism, or perhaps worse, cowardice, especially in the opinion of many members of an older generation. These veterans and elders were accompanied by many other young men who found duty their dominant trait, all of them running head-on into a youthful generation willing to question the need, the logic, and the rationale of participating in a minor war in a meaningless (to them) country, all based on a theory that if Vietnam became Communist, the entirety of Southeast Asia would soon follow. To the youth who would be called upon to fight a distant battle, this "falling domino" theory seemed dubious at best.

In Baltimore, as in many places, college campuses were a central point around which anti-war, anti-draft protests could be organized. Sit-ins, teach-ins, any sort of mass movement proliferated.

Resistance to the war led some young men to take refuge in Canada. Others, especially those in school, parlayed educational deferments from service until their time ran out, hopefully until a time when the war was over. Where peaceful demonstrations took place, the anti-war protesters were often met with counter demonstrations, loud, boisterous, and threatening. It helped matters not at all when a few of the anti-war protesters would light an American flag afire, incendiary to the flag and offensive to the patriotism of their opposition.

In May 1968 nine anti-war protesters gathered at the Selective Service Office in Catonsville, Maryland, the place where young men registered for potential military service and the records of those registrations were maintained. The draft board office on Catonsville's main street was the target for a "hit and stay" break-in led by two Jesuit priest brothers, Philip and Daniel Berrigan. The Berrigans were accompanied by a group of seven supporters who would enter the draft board office, remove some individual files, destroy them, and then remain to await arrest. The press was on hand as the plan was carried out. One office clerk was restrained as she resisted the removal of the files, which were taken outside and burned. All nine were arrested as planned, and their point had been made: citizens would resist the smooth operation of America's war machinery. From prison, the nine sent an apology letter to the clerk they had restrained, accompanied by flowers. These were the Catonsville Nine, sentenced to prison, a cumulative eighteen years for the group members and a $22,000 fine. Daniel Berrigan refused to turn himself in to serve his term, proving to be an embarrassment to the F.B.I. when he would later make anti-war public appearances while a fugitive. He was eventually arrested and served his three-year term, one of several such imprisonments resulting from his continuing protest efforts. Subsequent draft board break-ins occurred in six more cities, each modeled on the Catonsville experience.

It was in 1965 that an anti-war activist named Norman Morrison, a Quaker from Baltimore, horrified Secretary of Defense Robert McNamara in his protest of the Vietnam War. Dousing himself with kerosene, he set himself ablaze beneath McNamara's office window. Morrison had been deeply moved by a Vietnam-based French priest's account of a U.S. bombing of his church and the deaths of women and children sheltered there. He took his opposition to the Vietnam War to an extreme, choosing the site of his symbolic suicide carefully: adjacent to the Pentagon office of one of the government's primary supporters of the war and its escalation.

The war was physically fought in Vietnam, but it appeared nightly on American television news programs, home television screens filled with close-up scenes of battle and victims. It wasn't always easy to tell who was innocent, who a civilian victim, and who a combatant in this unfamiliar style war, viewed so intimately. The war dragged into the 1970s, but the war story of the 1960s had set conflicting and irrevocable paths into the future for supporters and opponents of an entire generation.

JOBS: CHANGING AND GOING

Baltimore industry was changing, as were the available jobs. As the 1960s continued, Baltimore's role as the economic hub of the state eroded as businesses and jobs moved away. Local employers experienced significant changes during the 1960s decade, with some of the losses a consequence of forces well beyond the city's control:

- The garment industry found international sites offering lower cost production accompanied by adequate quality;

- The canning business watched with a wary eye as the prolific Central Valley of California began its year-round vegetable production;

- The steel industry, locally centered in Baltimore County was blissfully unaware of how changes were coming which would upend its dominance.

In 1959, a major economic driver for the entire city, the steel mill at Sparrow's Point, went idle. Labor actions had always been on the agenda at the mill, but this was a strike different from most: it was nationwide, and a settlement based on the formula of "give a raise – raise steel prices" was out of reach. The strike became a four-month shutdown of the entire steel production of the United States. Steel consumers were unprepared for a strike of that duration. In the absence of this vital raw material, steel users faced production shutdowns themselves as week-by-week, their reserve steel inventory slowly depleted.

Steel produced overseas had been making marginal inroads into the domestic market in the United States, but when a nationwide steel strike shut down virtually all the country's steel mills for nearly three months, and domestic sources were unable to meet demand, steel users searched for alternatives. The absence of domestic steel production opened the door to a new source for this much-needed material. World War Two had disrupted, and even destroyed foreign steel-making capability. But by 1959, former combatants had rebuilt their steel capability, producing high quality steel in newly constructed mills. Domestic steel users began to buy steel from overseas. The steel strike ended and the Sparrow's Point mill re-opened, making and shipping steel again. But it went unrecognized by employer and employee at the time, that the future of Sparrow's Point steelmaking was no longer assured. The domestic steel strike had given German and Japanese suppliers an entry into the American market. A monopoly on steel by domestic producers had been broken, a monopoly that would never reappear.

Steel next began to face further competition from alternative materials. Plastic began replacing steel in automobile body and interior parts. Aluminum beverage cans became the new normal once the aluminum industry pointed out the advantages of their lightweight metal. Construction engineers found concrete beams fabricated with a few steel rods inside could often replace steel girders. The Sparrow's Point steel mill employed 30,000 workers in the 1960s. It was hard to imagine it would disappear, but imagination was needed and sadly, lacking.

At the Port of Baltimore, times and methods were changing. In 1956 shipping containers first appeared, offering higher efficiency and greater security, while lowering the cost of shipping. In the earliest days, the containers were complete highway truck trailers. New, specialized equipment led to only the container boxes being left for the shipper to load. Shipping became a matter of a shipper loading cargo containers, many 40 feet long, that could be secured for transport by highway, rail, or water. The shipper would pack and seal a container, then forward it by truck or rail to the port where at shipside, in a mechanized choreography, cranes would lift containers, one by one, to be stacked on-board a vessel, then securely locked together with universal safety connectors. At their destination, this delivery process was reversed. Trucks gained importance as thousands of containers arriving on ships were off-loaded and sent on their way, travelling inland along new interstate highways. If the container was not trucked, railroads serving the port regularly pulled away trainloads of container boxes.

Employment at the containerized Port of Baltimore inevitably changed: an industry that had employed 10,000 longshoremen operating slings and nets to handle bags or to stack boxes was reduced dramatically. The efficiency brought about by the use of containers led to a reduction of the waterfront workforce, ultimately reaching 75 percent in losses. To move the cargo beyond the port, demand for trucks and drivers soared, as did the need for workers to maintain them. Each container transported by highway demanded for the duration of its handling, a dedicated truck, trailer, and driver. The number of transactions at the gate, vehicles coming and going, soared into the thousands monthly, with the original facility at the Dundalk Marine Terminal being supplemented by the opening (in 1990) of the Seagirt terminal, an additional dedicated container facility. Railroads developed and deployed special equipment to handle this new mode of shipping: boxcars were largely displaced by container carriers, equipment upon which containers could be securely stacked. These new types of equipment and the methods used to deploy them made it possible to transport hundreds of containers in one departing rail movement. The new logistical demands, workers' roles, and equipment utilized allowed containerization to bring about the safe and secure movement of goods in many multiples of the cargo volumes previously moved by hand.

Baltimore's spice producer McCormick and Company was thriving, but their headquarters, offices, and manufacturing building were centered in the Inner Harbor redevelopment area. The location pleased many Baltimoreans as the aroma of spices being processed, ground, and packaged would pleasantly perfume the downtown air. Every day a different spice, a different downtown scent, a far superior choice to the smells to those of many other center city downtowns across the country. For that, Baltimoreans counted themselves lucky. By the early 1960s, manufacturing on a changing waterfront was difficult, as access to the plant via truck or train was limited, and often only possible overnight. When the waterfront was an industrial center, McCormick seemed to be at home there, but the company saw the future and a McCormick factory on Light Street was not a part of it. In 1962, the company created the 435-acre Greater Baltimore Industrial Park, later Hunt Valley Business Community in Baltimore County, eighteen miles north of downtown Baltimore. The industrial-park streets were named by McCormick: Pepper Road, Schilling Square (after a spice company acquisition), Gilroy Road (after the garlic capital of the U.S.), and of course, McCormick Road. The company's offices and headquarters moved to Hunt Valley in 1967, soon a second manufacturing operation was opened there. Hundreds of jobs had moved with the company to the Baltimore County location where the parking was free, though for the non-driver, transit service was abysmal. The Light Street location continuing production despite logistical problems, finally closing in the late 1980s.

By 1969, Baltimore's iconic Bromo Seltzer Tower was all that was left of the once thriving Emerson Drug Company. The company was sold, and reasonable estimates are that a few hundred factory and office jobs in Baltimore City disappeared with the company's move. Isaac Emerson, usually Captain Emerson (after he used his yacht in the defense of the Chesapeake Bay during the Spanish American War, declaring himself captain of his yacht as a Naval Auxiliary vessel) created Bromo Seltzer, a fizzy headache-hangover medication in 1888. The medication struggled at least twice when some of the compounds in its formulation were found to be harmful, one substance even toxic. Reformulations followed and Bromo-Seltzer continued in its cobalt blue bottles, made at the Emerson-owned Maryland Glass Company. He had built the fifteen story Emerson Tower in 1911, his six-story manufacturing plant abutting it on two sides. By 1967, the Emerson Drug Company was sold to a Pennsylvania firm, with the headquarters tower protected by deed stipulation when it was acquired by the City of Baltimore. The factory building was razed in 1969, a fire house erected in its place, with the new structure surrounding but not directly abutting the Emerson Tower. The Maryland Glass Company separately changed ownership and survived for another decade.

CULTURAL CHANGES

By the late 1960s, a new generation was coming of age, with expectations and behaviors changing in response to a war in Vietnam, much as the changes wrought in the 1920s in the aftermath of the brutal First World War. Nationwide, young people pushed the limits where and when they found them restrictive, exhibiting a frankness and openness in all things political, sexual, musical, and chemical. Women experienced a new sexual freedom when the effective and safe oral contraceptive became available in 1960. Legal, medical, and religious objections dissolved as millions of women took charge of their reproductive lives with the birth control pill. Women began to make demands for equal rights, equal pay, and equality with men in access to credit and jobs. Controlled substances, always available just beneath the surface of polite society but not openly acknowledged, became mainstream in the social construct of the younger generation. Not everyone used the substances, but everyone knew someone who did. By 1969, the homosexual community took action to live openly, beginning in New York City with the Stonewall Riots, a spontaneous community reaction to regular harassment by city officials. The secret lives lived by many in the 1950s were no longer acceptable to many: it was time for them to "come out".

Responding to the increasing demands for freedom, legislation provided support in three areas: the Civil Rights Act of 1964 banned discrimination based upon race, color, religion, sex, and national origin (although it would be 60 years before court cases affirmed that "sex" included sexual orientation); this was preceded in 1963 by the Equal Pay Act, guaranteeing same pay for same work regardless of sex; these were followed by the Privacy Rights Act, 1965, which would become the foundation for laws guaranteeing a woman's right to abortion.

Baltimoreans shared these 1960s experiences with Americans everywhere, picketing, parading, demanding, teaching, reacting, and more. In 1969, four women in Baltimore created a journal of and for the women's movement, *Women, A Journal of Liberation*, each issue offering articles, opinions, and insights on a single topic. Managed by a collective, topics were selected to meet women's interests and needs: women's rights, peace and war, children, living alone, and more topics were examined in detail, creating in many ways a "how to" manual for living in new times.

This was a decade for the "counterculture" to make it presence felt. The Beatniks of the 1950s self-described as outcasts rejecting the mainstream in favor of their style of literature, illegal drug use, and a bohemian lifestyle. By the 1960s, a younger generation led the way to a new style of thinking, dressing, acting, and interacting, labelled "hippies". Born of disillusionment with materialism and a disdain for the value systems of their elders, this generation chose long hair, rock music, used or vintage clothing, beads and headbands, and while they and their elders both smoked, this group rejected cigarettes in favor of "weed", marijuana. Communal living (group homes with shared responsibilities and finances) became fashionable among those who rejected mainstream culture. Young men and women eked out a lifestyle, where an unemployed hippie could practice guitar most of the day while his partner supported them both with work in the local adult entertainment industry.

San Francisco became the gathering point of these young people arriving from across America; Baltimore had its hippies, those who rejected mainstream American life, but in more modest numbers. This youthful generation gathered in central Baltimore in older neighborhoods along Park Avenue, Tyson Street, Mount Vernon, and north of Mount Royal Avenue to Charles Village, often living in group homes, some in one of the dozen or so local communes. In conservative Baltimore, a counterculture crowd wasn't easy to assemble. In the spring of 1968, a Sunday afternoon "be-in" was planned (to the extent that any planning was accomplished by those likely to attend.) This was to be a gathering of anyone and everyone in the counterculture at Druid Hill Park. Hippies shared space with yippies, i.e. hippies with politics. The event featured a guerilla theater group protesting the Vietnam War, with music provided by a few local bands. One of the bands placed extra space between themselves and what they perceived as a left-wing radical element. So much for universal like-mindedness. The crowd never exceeded 1,000, and for most of the day there were about 500 in attendance. An even smaller group had gathered a year earlier in Patterson Park for a "Love-In", but just nineteen people showed up, leading a hippie named Pete to claim Baltimore was loveless. To prove him wrong and defy convention, a group soon held a double wedding ceremony in Patterson Park, all of them teenagers, the officiant a pizza delivery man. The ceremony was more a snub at conventionality than a wedding, as no one really claimed they were married. Which was fine, they said. Of the long-term result of the matrimonial links created that day, one can only guess.

Social awareness programs were a part of the hippie culture. Health care in their eyes was a right, not something granted or a part of some agency's largesse. A group of eight volunteers established the Peoples Free Clinic on Greenmount Avenue, a place where anyone could receive medical advice and treatment free of charge. The clinic was led by a Baltimorean, Barbara Ray Sweeley, Antioch College graduate, Baltimore City Schools guidance counselor, American Friends Service Committee member, and community activist. The clinic was staffed by volunteer medical personnel, doctors and nurses from local medical facilities offering services for the elderly and children, women's care, and general medical services, even dentistry.

Baltimore hippies, as well as the like-minded from Washington, D.C., had their very own Woodstock-like festival two years before the upstate New York event. The Laurel, Maryland, racecourse hosted the Laurel Pop Festival, promising a Saturday and Sunday of rock and roll. Mother Nature added an overnight and all-day-Sunday rainstorm, making day two a music and mud festival. On stage were name acts of the era: Jethro Tull, Johnny Winters, The Guess Who, Led Zeppelin and more. It was said this was no concert, this was a non-stop music "scene". The syndicated music columnist Ritchie York called the festival "…truly utopia for the young music nut. He or she gets all the music he could possibly want, at ear-shattering sound levels, and all the time." Admission was $4.50, box seats were $10.00, but with the chill from the rainstorms of Sunday, the chairs became fuel for bonfires. Woodstock's three days of peace and love (and mud) on a dairy farm in upstate New York made more news, but the Laurel event had offered much the same, just a half hour from home.

DOMESTIC ADVERSARIES

The 1960s were a time of many controversies and many changes, as citizens found a new way forward for themselves and those around them. Baltimore experienced one of the strangest episodes in the adversarial conditions that inevitably arose in the decade. It involved the Baltimore Police Department and The Black Panther Party.

The Baltimore Police Department was headed by Commissioner Donald Pomerleau, hired in the 1960s after his consulting examination of the force found the department antiquated, corrupt, and lacking any sort of relationship with the Black community. He began his leadership with a reform agenda, building relationships, hiring more Black officers, and rebuilding the department's leadership team. Things were improving in the department and the community but for reasons of his own, Pomerleau instituted a reactionary program to the cultural changes, disputes, and violence found in the city. He created the Inspectional Services Division (I.S.D.), a support function of the department, essentially an investigatory group that infiltrated presumed "enemies" of the city and state, as determined by Pomerleau.

The Black Panther Party was formed in Oakland, California, in a response to perceived police brutality. Espousing second amendment rights for the Black community, the group was viewed as a threat and labeled a Communist front, so there began nationwide efforts to dismantle it, led by J. Edgar Hoover's F.B.I. A Baltimore chapter formed in 1968, their activities including feeding programs, political education, and working to help citizens find resources to better their lives through challenging times. Regardless of their local activities, the Black Panther Party with their militant reputation were a target for the Baltimore Police Department's attention.

The Inspectional Services Division (I.S.D.) set about examining the lives and the activities of those persons and groups they perceived responsible for the upheavals of the times. There was no consideration on their part as to whether the targets of their examination had broken, were contemplating breaking, or would even consider breaking the law. The I.S.D. infiltrated the offices of civil rights leader and future Congressman Parren J. Mitchell, with paid office informants, wiretaps, and photographic surveillance. They spied on the American Civil Liberties Union, even the American Friends Service Committee, all with no provocation. If one can characterize this work as having a noteworthy accomplishment, it would be their infiltration of the local Black Panther Party by law enforcement. Between autumn 1968 and summer 1969, the president and founding member of the Baltimore Black Panther chapter, Warren Hart, was also an active law enforcement informant. In the opinion of many at the time (and in retrospect, the theory is undisputed), the activities of the local Black Panther Party were guided in whole or in part by the Federal Bureau of Investigation. Sadly, there is no mention of a corresponding infiltration of the contemporaneous National States Rights Party, a group of anti-integration citizens that rallied in Patterson Park, despite integration being the law of the land.

CHAPTER EIGHT:
RENAISSANCE CITY

The 1970s

IT WAS THE DECADE THAT would make or break Baltimore. A city since 1729, settled even earlier, the city on the Patapsco has seen good times and bad, prosperity and depression. All that history had come down to a moment in time which would determine what sort of city Baltimore would be twenty, thirty years hence. A racial divide, the consequence of a hundred years of neglect or worse, had ignited a fire in American cities, Baltimore included. That fire had burned buildings and more importantly, people's spirits. Unrest in Baltimore following the King assassination had been bad enough to give pause to even the most optimistic. Was the city to survive, or would it become an urban shell? Was Baltimore an island, or was it the center of a region? Citizens in the city, those that remained, recognized an urgent need to rescue the city by rebuilding the structures while building new bridges to one another. The city was at a turning point, and the next few years would write a new story in the history of Baltimore.

A POLITICAL CHANGE

Thomas D'Alesandro III seemed to have taken the challenges personally. Elected in 1967, his interests in governance were civil rights, advocacy for the poor, actively meeting with his constituents, and helping to repair the damage from years of racial discrimination. His civil rights advocacy had led to threats on his life, such that when riots in Baltimore began in April 1968, he felt personally lost. In his book, *William Donald Schaefer*, Fraser Smith character- ized D'Alesandro as a mayor who built community relationships and had "…been so open and flexible, this was the thanks he got. He fell into despair." Yet, in the years of his term of office that followed, he did his utmost to calm the situation. As Walter Orlinsky, former City Council president said, "Tommy pulled the thorn of racial anger out of the city's paw." The lure of private life was strong, enough that by the fall of 1970, fully a year before the next mayoral election, he called City Council President William Donald Schaefer to his side, telling him in confidence, "I'm not going to run again." It had become Schaefer's turn.

Schaefer ran for mayor in 1971. He won the primary election handily, then the general election by a landslide, receiving 87 percent of the vote. It seemed just about all of Baltimore wanted Schaefer to take over. Schaefer as mayor had a role model for his new job, Chicago Mayor Richard J. Daley. Daley had reminded every citizen of Chicago of his role in their lives and how he had directed improvements to their city with appropriate signage placed at every opportunity. Schaefer did the same, taking charge of the city, and assuring that every citizen knew it. He would transform the city, reinvent the city by leaving behind a declining and disappearing industrial economy, remaking the city as a tourism center. He was a demanding leader, "do it now" his mantra, with *Baltimore Magazine* describing him as "Irascible. Opinionated. Unpolished. Obsessive. And most of all: impatient", every one of those descriptions confirmed by those who worked with him. Schaefer served as the city's mayor for a transformative 16 years, through the 1970s and beyond, re-elected by majorities of 85 percent or more in each election. While he did much to build the city physically, perhaps his most important contribution was the way the citizens believed in him and followed his lead to believe in the city. He was named "America's Best Mayor" as he brought the redevelopment plans created in prior administrations to fruition, adding improvements of his own, while taking citizen service to a new level. He rebuilt the city while his special public works team worked tirelessly at his behest to respond to problems he encountered as he drove through the city: fix the streets, fill the potholes, tow abandoned cars, clean the trash from an alley, and more. A classic Schaefer moment: he notified public works he had found and they needed to remove an abandoned vehicle. When asked where he had seen it, his response was: if I found it, so can you. Public works towed about a dozen abandoned cars over the next few days before they found the one the mayor had called about.

A CITY FAIR

The challenge of luring crowds back into the city in the aftermath of the 1968 riots and another lesser-known disturbance at the city's Flower Mart in 1970 led to a remarkable solution. There was the usual upbeat publicity program, on-going news about renewal of the city, casting in the best possible light continuing urban renewal and the changing city-scape. There were activities like Sunny Sundays, using the recently cleared waterfront park-like land to attract kite flyers, ball players, and family friendly picnics. There were the reminders of the long-standing institutions among town attractions, from the venerable Walters Art Museum to the *Constellation* at its newly refurbished dock. There was, however, a group of individuals who were thinking bigger and better, led by a very dynamic Hope Quackenbush. Quackenbush was part of the Citizens Planning and Housing Association (C.P.H.A.), a non-profit dedicated to assisting Baltimore's neighborhoods. She put forth an idea for a festival of the city's neighborhoods, describing the city not as a melting pot, but a vegetable soup, a delicious combination of many ingredients. Supporting her were Housing Commissioner (and father of the city's "dollar house" program) Robert Embry; Christopher Hartman, an editor at *The Baltimore News-American* and future Executive Director of C.P.H.A.; and Sandy Hillman, head of Baltimore's tourism agency, responsible for generating positive messages about the city. The idea grew and became the Baltimore City Fair, an event that did the most to convince Baltimoreans, from both the city and its suburbs, that it was not only safe but also fun to come back into the heart of town.

The City Fair became a reality: an urban version of a country fair, emphasizing the best of the community with attractions, displays, and entertainment. By September 1970, the very first Fair was held in the renewal area known as Charles Center. Skeptics predicted disaster, but 350,000 Baltimoreans came over three days, taking in the highlights of the city, from neighborhood exhibits, booths from city and non-profit service organizations, a few carnival rides, and lots of ethnic foods. Mayor D'Alesandro, fearful of another disturbance and under pressure from more conservative voices, considered cancelling the event, relented, and the weekend's events went forward. The only disaster was from the weather: a storm blew through overnight leaving exhibit wreckage in its wake. The result became proof that the city could and would work, as neighboring exhibitors who had never before met pitched in to help one another, repairs were quickly made, tents re-erected, and the Fair went on. Chairman of the Fair, Chris Hartman commented on the cooperation, "It was really a mess…Union Square helped restore Gay Street and Mount Holly helped restore Charles Village." Fireworks ended the Fair on Sunday evening, as 65,000 gathered to watch and the Fair as an annual event was underway.

Every September through the 1970s and beyond, a City Fair took over the interest of all of Baltimore. The Fair would usually be held on a weekend that would include at least one good rainstorm, keeping volunteers busy through the night, obeying the lesson first learned in Charles Center in 1970: get the accumulated water off the tent tops. The Fair moved from the confined quarters of Charles Center, landing at the newly cleared Inner Harbor, a vast combination of asphalt parking, busy streets, a grassy expanse, and an embryonic waterfront promenade. With more space, the Fair grew, with sixty or more neighborhoods sharing their happy stories, institutions displaying the ways in which they aided the city and its residents, an arts district offering locally crafted goods, multiple stages for the performing arts showcasing a constant flow of local and in the evenings, national acts, a vast carnival area for those who needed that country fair feel even in an urban setting, and food, seemingly every type of ethic food from every corner of Baltimore. The entire assemblage was fenced, with admission just a dollar to make the Fair self-supporting, at least in theory. At noon on a Friday, crowds would gather for the grand opening of the Fair with ribbon cutting, a few speeches, and then the "Opening Act": Karl Wallenda tight-roping his way across the harbor, the Great Zucchini human cannonball shot from a cannon, or Doug Jones diving from a tower 170 feet above into a 25-foot-deep pool. Even King Kong made an appearance one year, an inflatable high atop the World Trade Center, illuminated at night by a National Guard operated spotlight.

By the mid-1970s the event was drawing 1.5 million visitors over its three-day run, and largely created by volunteers. A steering committee of 50 or more, each with their own special skills, would coordinate with the chairman, a volunteer drawn from the steering committee, and an executive director, an executive on a one-year assignment whose services were donated by a local company to the Fair. Plans for the Fair site were drawn and an electrical contractor chosen to wire this temporary city. Entertainment agents were contacted: would the Four Tops be available? How about Roberta Flack? Others lined up dozens of local acts, bands and other entertainers. The financials were arranged, including a request for Crown Petroleum to sell admission tickets via their network of filling stations. Security from the City Police Department was aided by private agents and a team of steering committee trouble shooters, each radio-dispatched to investigate problems from broken fences to arguments over booth spacing and aisle width. Logistics were always on the minds of organizers, from ticket-taking to resupplying the food vendors once the crowds had departed. The city pitched in making an enormous contribution though its Department of Public Works teams, from emptying trash cans to spreading wood chips over inevitable muddy spots and much more. Many of the volunteers moved to the site for the week prior to the event, staying overnight in caravans on site or in nearby donated hotel rooms. The City Fair was an event in which everyone could have a role, directly through a leadership effort or as a participant in the exposition itself. Every Baltimorean could be a part of the Fair by spending that admission dollar, enjoying events, and helping to prove that the city collectively was more than its individual parts. This pioneering effort gave rise to several other city-wide festivals and events, each thriving by following the path the Baltimore City Fair pioneers set, a unique way of making the city whole again, one event and one year at a time.

DOLLAR HOUSES

They were abandoned and neglected. There were entire neighborhoods filled with them, often row homes that had been purchased by the city along the rights-of-way for highways that would never be built. They were usually structurally sound, but some would need complete rehabilitation. Of sturdy brick construction, eighty or more years old, they could be made into a home for some family, if only there was the incentive and the financial terms to make it happen. Buyers had to make promises, to rehabilitate the houses promptly and then to occupy them after completion. In return for their dollar, these urban homesteaders did indeed earn the deed to their property, receiving financial assistance in the form of loans that might not otherwise be available in what lenders deemed to be distressed communities. The Baltimore program experience was positive with the new homeowners able to rehabilitate their homes, gain the benefits of home ownership, and have their cost versus home value ratio remain positive. There were no loan defaults through the course of the program.

Baltimore's Dollar House program met with success in several neighborhoods where planning and city services were assured, and a concentration of similar available homes was to be found. Otterbein, Ridgely, and Barre Circle were most successful, as these homesteader participants could transform their own home while others did the same, transforming the entire community. The Dollar House program was a creative solution to the vexing problem of ridding the city of real estate it had no interest in owning. The success of such a venture was dependent not only on finding those willing to homestead the property. There was no shortage of houses, but if there was no critical mass of visible shared activity or if the neighborhood was one residents had fled because of poor conditions rather than forced out by highway plans, the results were more lackluster. About 150 houses went through the rigorous process of evaluation and commitment, going from abandoned house to desirable property.

THE INNER HARBOR COMES ALIVE

Where derelict piers and ancient warehouses once stood, a new city was rising. The 1960s plan for a renewal of almost 200 acres of land adjacent to Pratt and Light Streets along the harbor, thence eastward along the Key Highway, was becoming reality. This was the crown jewel of Mayor Schaefer's dream for a bigger, better Baltimore, an area where ocean going ships had once docked, banana cargos unloaded, Belt Line freight trains travelled, and piers from which the Old Bay Line overnight steamers departed for Norfolk. It was being rebuilt, replaced, and rejuvenated with a new friendly, human-scale center. A brick waterfront promenade, in its earliest days just a mile long, was projected to join the entire city waterfront, linking buildings, shops, tourist activities, residences, and parklands. In the immediate renewal area, the waterside district was surrounded by hotels, shopping, apartments, and by the end of the decade, a harborside retail facility in two buildings to be known as Harborplace. This change wasn't without a cost: the retail district along North Howard Street was already breathing its last, but the Inner Harbor shops sealed its fate. The Inner Harbor was growing, the heart of the city was moving south and east toward it, and in this decade of the 1970s as well as decades beyond, it was the place to be in Baltimore.

It was a big undertaking to acquire property, redirect rights-of-way, raze the old, and build the new. It included a World Trade Center (1977), a 400-foot-tall pentagon shaped skyscraper erected on the Pratt Street harborside, with an observation deck on top. At the south end, the multi-level Maryland Science Center was given a prominent corner site, opening in 1976. Tourists and residents alike flocked to the Inner Harbor, dodging the Harborplace construction until late 1980. Harborplace would be a two-building retail center that was to open at decade's end, featuring locally produced products and waterfront restaurants, attracting in its first year more visitors than Disneyland. A modest outdoor amphitheater between the two Harborplace buildings was created for acrobats, magicians, and others to entertain visitors. Nearby to the east, a new National Aquarium was under construction, by 1981 a premier visitor attraction for the Inner Harbor area. Further east, the original United Railways streetcar power plant on Pier Four was mystifying developers as to how to repurpose it, so it sat vacant. An amusement park was installed, and soon closed. Later the Power Plant became home to restaurants, commercial development, and cultural spaces. Harbor shuttle boats transported riders to the south shore of the harbor and the Fort McHenry National Monument and eastward to the historic Fell's Point district. Surrounding the waterfront were a series of new buildings to the north and west, including hotels, a multi-level shopping center, restaurants and at the southern tip of the redevelopment area, the Christ Lutheran Church constructed a senior living residential facility.

The business of conventions was a great driver of tourism as delegates from across the region or the country arrived in need of lodging and meals, with diverse interests, disposable dollars, time on their hands, and an interest in the city. Convention delegates, often numbering in the thousands, were the perfect means to fill the tourist attractions with visitors, but most such events tended to by-pass Baltimore as it lacked a first-class convention facility. Mayor Schaefer led the effort and the city proposed, designed, constructed, and opened a new convention center of 425,000 square feet of exhibit and meeting space in 1979. It was just the right size for mid-sized conventions, competing with like-minded and – sized cities for the many events that business, civic, and mutual interest groups conduct yearly. (For comparison, the Javits Center in New York offers 3,000,000 square feet of space.) Hotels at the nearby Inner Harbor served the needs of the delegates, with steak houses and restaurants from Harborplace to Little Italy enjoying the trade the delegates brought to them. If there was a downside, a modest one, it was the loss of the original properties razed for the center's construction. The building of the G. Fava Company, a fruit and vegetable wholesaler, was lost but its magnificent cast iron front was saved when Robert Embry came to the rescue, having it disassembled and placed in storage to be later installed at the Front Street buildings of the (now defunct) City Life Museum.

ENVIRONMENTAL ACTION

The best-selling book *Silent Spring* had been published in 1962. Rachel Carson's environmental wake-up call documented human damage to the planet and its people. In citing names, products and places, Carson was specific in identifying the enemies of the environment, which consequently earned her enemies of her own. Her writing and subsequent Congressional testimony had an effect as her message filtered through to the general population and environmental policy changes were demanded. Congress responded with the Clean Air Act (1967), the creation of the Environmental Protection Agency (1970), the 1972 Clean Water Act and finally, the banning of Carson's primary target, the effective, inexpensive, but persistent and damaging insecticide D.D.T. Baltimore had much to gain from any and all of these changes: whether one looked to the sky, the ground or the river, the heavy industrial history of the city meant there was much environmental clean-up work to be done.

On April 22, 1970, Baltimoreans participated in the nation's first Earth Day, a focal point in the blossoming environmental movement. Earth Day nationally drew twenty-million Americans, one in ten, to the streets protesting the destruction wrought by environmental neglect. Many Baltimoreans took a dim view of the proceedings, given how many livelihoods were dependent on smoke-belching heavy industries around the city. There was a gray haze over the city, the water regularly absorbed oil and chemical spills, and litter spoiled the streets. Local power plants burned coal, emitting smoke, soot, and toxic chemicals. Phosphates from soap powder bubbled in the water and mercury made the fish inedible. At the Sparrow's Point steel plant, the Tin Mill Canal became a toxic waste site, as chemicals of every description mixed into polluted water, then seeped into the ground and the adjacent river. Evidence of environmental damage had been accumulating at Sparrow's Point for years. Hazardous substances and dangerous chemicals were a part of the landscape. Lead was pervasive. Arsenic was in the ground. PCBs, man-made carcinogenic chemicals primarily used as electrical equipment coolants were found throughout the property. And asbestos, a substance with clear connections to lung diseases and cancer, was in the air, in the buildings, and on the ground. The company made promises, did some mitigation, and made a few voluntary production changes. Enforcement of environmental regulations at the steel mill seemed to be a double-edged sword: jobs and paychecks versus the long-term health of the air, ground, and water. It became business as usual at Sparrow's Point and in Baltimore where terms like ecology, recycling, and environmental clean-up were unheard of – so far.

On that very first Earth Day in Baltimore, it was mostly the younger generation that voiced the need to improve the environment. Facing an uphill battle in this first year of awareness raising, the largely student community led the way with local teach-ins to introduce terminology and to help identify problems and likely obstacles to creating a clean, healthy environment. Ralph Nader, nationally prominent political and environmental activist, came to Johns Hopkins University to speak. From the campus of Johns Hopkins, a Charles Village clean up project was created. Maryland Institute-College of Art students planted trees. The American Friends Service Committee marched to the utility company headquarters to award the company a "Top Polluter of the Year" award. State Senator Julian Lapides offered a presentation at the Pratt Central Library, "The Never-Ending Fight Against Pollution", after which the library offered four films on pollution. The marches, teach-ins, and presentations each were held to raise awareness of the harmful effects of industrial development. Not all were convinced. It would be a long march to a cleaner environment, achieved mostly through state and federal government action.

ENTERTAINMENT

By the 1970s, Baltimoreans could select from a wide array of local, live entertainment venues, featuring everything from major league sports to classical concerts.

The Lyric Opera House. On Mount Royal Avenue, the Lyric was a traditional setting for a variety of entertainment. The oldest such venue in the city was built in 1894 with seating for 2,500. The Lyric was home to the Baltimore Symphony and Baltimore Opera productions during the decade. It would later become a more general venue when the nearby Joseph Meyerhoff Symphony Hall opened in 1982 as the home of the Baltimore Symphony Orchestra.

The Civic Center. New in 1962, this city-owned venue was a multi-purpose facility able to host concerts by Elvis Presley, The Grateful Dead, and Led Zeppelin for up to 14,000 patrons, while also offering a quick turnaround to host Baltimore Clippers ice hockey, Baltimore Bullets basketball, and once a year, the Ringling Brothers Circus. The circus would arrive via their circus train, conducting as elephant parade along Cathedral Street, gathering publicity and press coverage along the way.

The Morris Mechanic Theater. The Mechanic largely offered Broadway theater programming. Opened in the late 1960s, it struggled almost from its beginning, and as early as 1972 news headlines called for a necessary "revival". An insufficient number of theater shows, shuttered restaurant, a city liquor license withheld, a stage too small, blocked sight lines, and more led to its closure and subsequent razing. Only a few Baltimoreans mourned the loss of the Brutalist architecture the Mechanic embodied. It was voted by one group as the ugliest building in America.

The Memorial Stadium. The direct descendent of stadia built on the same site, often directly overlaid, including Municipal, Baltimore, and Venable, this was the home of baseball's Baltimore Orioles and football's Baltimore Colts. The Orioles baseball team won another World Series in 1970. The stadium's second deck was hit by a small aircraft in December 1976, just after a football game had concluded. By the 1970s, talk of needed renovations to this very basic stadium had stalled, leading to early discussions of a new downtown stadium.

The Arena Players. Founded in 1953, this African American theater group found its permanent home in 1969 on McCulloh Street. It is the senior citizen of Black theater in Baltimore and is (as of this writing) the oldest continuously operating Black theater in America. Mounting a half dozen or more productions per year, the Arena provides a voice for Black theater and performers.

The Royal Theater. The Royal had been a major venue for hosting name entertainment in Baltimore since 1922. Located in the city's Pennsylvania Avenue entertainment district, the Royal fell in 1971 to the wrecking ball. Founded as the Douglas Theater, the Royal became one of the top five entertainment sites for Black entertainment in the country. As its neighborhood had begun to decline, there was an urban renewal plan for the community, and amid that renewal, the Royal was lost.

The Hippodrome. . An entertainment palace on Baltimore's west side, the "Hipp" opened in 1914 to vaudeville and the latest in modern marvels, motion pictures. A grand palace, its ornamentation included a 45-foot mural, textured facades, statuettes from Greek mythology, massive curtains across the stage, and seating for 3,000. Early audiences enjoyed a combination of seven acts and a two-reel movie, then name acts such as Cab Calloway, Red Skelton, Frank Sinatra's debut in 1939, and many more at the Hipp, until it was only films through the 1970s.

Modest venues. Smaller theater venues with professional and amateur companies are the heart and soul of many cities, and Baltimore was no exception. Baltimoreans could attend performances of theatre productions across the city in varying venues, including those of the Vagabond Players (1916), Center Stage (1963), and the 100 seat Corner Theater (1968).

There was a wonderful diversity of entertainment in the city, something for everyone. Noontime weekday concerts in Charles Center invited office workers to slip away while enjoying their midday meal. ODell Brock opened his club in 1976 on North Avenue to become the unofficial center of Baltimore's disco dancing enthusiasts.

Another kind of entertainment was available at a series of nightclubs along Baltimore's "Block", the adult entertainment zone on East Baltimore Street. The Block was described by investigators as a vicious and lawless district where vice of all sorts was tolerated, even protected. Despite constant surveillance, with the Police Department's Central Jurisdiction located nearby on Fayette Street, the Block managed to thrive. When Oasis Nite Club owner Julius Salsbury, known as "The Lord", was arrested and then convicted of running a gambling operation from a back room at the club, the Block was stunned and law enforcement exultant. Facing 15 years in prison, Salsbury posted $80,000 in bail and was released pending the results of his appeal. Those who had brought him to justice were ready to see Salsbury finally go to prison. In 1970, Salsbury had the last word when his appeal was rejected, and he failed to appear to begin his sentence. Salsbury had many friends, and the timing of his appeal's denial and his immediate disappearance seem to suggest information had been leaked to him. His mid-town apartment was cleaned out and Salsbury was gone, soon to become a local legend. He fled first to Canada where he had stashed funds, then to Israel in the early 1970s, where he quietly lived out his remaining twenty-four years as a shopkeeper, safe from extradition. The Oasis Nite Club continued in business, efficiently run by Salsbury's ex-girlfriend, Flora "Pam Gail" Spina, a former burlesque dancer.

In contrast to business on the Block, the motion picture production business was a clean industry appealing to Mayor Schaefer and others in city government as an opportunity to build the city's national image. Following the trend of other cities, Baltimore had recently chosen for its slogan "Charm City": charm bracelets were given to visitors, the charms themselves available at tourist destinations around town. The unfortunate timing of a strike by sanitation workers, within days of the announcement of the Charm City campaign, certainly made Baltimore a bit less charming and much more odorific. The strike lasted only a few weeks, with no long-term damage, and soon the next step in image-making was underway. Baltimore would soon be "Hollywood East". With the triple lure of abundant money to be made in the film industry, jobs for local workers, and image-building, a City Office of Film Production was established, its role defined by the mayor to eliminate red-tape and costly delays for the private film industry. Enthusiasm seemed to have run amok, as the goal of that agency was effectively to help private businesses bypass or ignore the city's own regulations. Extolling the virtues of the city's (White) neighborhoods, historic sites, and architecture, advertisements appeared in various publications including *The New York Times*. The ads included eye-catching benefits such as streamlined permitting, free use of some facilities, easy parking permitting, and tax exemptions. Films were produced. Two major studio productions were listed as candidates for a new city film festival. Independent film-maker John Waters was also producing, but it came as no surprise that his work was ignored. What was also ignored, much to the future embarrassment of city leaders, were the several "blaxploitation" films that were being produced in the city. Ignoring this genre, despite its having a significant impact on the city's film-making industry, was cultural tone deafness at its peak. The film festival never took place, scheduling conflicts to blame, and so the city's version of an Oscar, the "Don" (an ego boost for the mayor) was never presented. It would be another twenty years before the promotion of film-making in the city became a prominent political effort.

Two youthful Baltimore natives were success stories in the world of motion pictures in the decade, John Waters and Barry Levinson. Waters, 24 years old in 1970, had previously been producing short subjects filmed around Baltimore, but in 1972 he released his most famous cult classic *Pink Flamingos*, a film that was "a deliberate exercise in ultra-bad taste" according to the Internet Movie Data Base. In the 1970s Levinson was writing in Hollywood with director-producer-writer-comic Mel Brooks on the well-received film *High Anxiety* (1978), after previously serving as an executive and writer on the screenplay of another Brooks film, *Silent Movie* (1976). His most prominent work would occur in the 1980s and beyond, including the Baltimore-centric *Diner* and *Liberty Heights*.

And television personality Oprah Winfrey began her climb up the ladder of national fame, appearing as co-anchor on local television station WJZ.

A BI-CENTENNIAL CELEBRATION

In July 1976, as a part of the National Bi-Centennial celebrations, Baltimore had big plans for Independence Day, July 4. Celebrations were scheduled at Fort McHenry, entertainment for the citizens to enjoy, and to pay for it all, City Council President Walter Orlinsky had a 35-ton cake baked and barged to the Fort with a plan to sell 153,000 slices of cake to the attendees. The entire episode became known as "Wally's Folly" as plans soon went awry. As Frank De Filippo, aide to Governor Marvin Mandel said, "…everything went wrong in the 70s". As for the cake: Baltimore's rats got to the cake first, 18 tons were quickly discarded, then it rained and soon 3,000 pounds of icing were floating in the harbor. There was never a chance to sell those 153,000 slices, the anticipated crowds at the Fort never materialized, as only 30,000 attended. But there was entertainment: on a temporary stage, a succession of second-tier entertainers appeared at Fort McHenry, led by the local big band orchestra of Zim Zemeral. The entire event was subject to twelve hours of continuous television coverage.

Baltimore's bicentennial fiasco was salvaged when days later the city hosted Op-Sail, Operation Sail, with tall ships visiting the port, open to the public for tours on board. These sailing ships, visitors from another time, were sailing vessels from across the world: from Europe, the Italian *Amerigo Vespucci*, the *Mircea* from Romania, from Poland the *Dar Pomorze*, the Danish vessel *Danmark*, the *Gorch Fock* from Germany; from South America, the *Esmeralda* from Chile; and from the United States, a Coast Guard barque (itself, a World War Two German war prize) the *Eagle*. The Inner Harbor promenade was filled with visitors. As event Chairman Robert Hillman said, "the main thing about the tall ships, I think, was that it felt organic to the city". This was entertainment that could only be held at a port city such as Baltimore. As for DeFilippo's "everything went wrong" comment, he was right: it wasn't long before his boss, Governor Mandel, and even Wally Orlinsky went to jail for illegal activities while in office.

TROUBLE BREWING

The 1970s were not as kind to the Baltimore region as had been hoped: both man-made and natural phenomena combined to wreak local havoc on an all-too-regular basis.

In June 1972, a summer storm was brewing off the Yucatan Peninsula in Mexico, a storm that was destined to become the most destructive hurricane (to that date) in United States history. This was Hurricane Agnes, the first storm of the 1972 hurricane season. The storm drifted eastward, then turned north, at no time more than a minor hurricane. When the storm reached North Carolina it merged with another weather feature, intensified, and Agnes became a flood maker, quickly dumping up to 14 inches of rain through the Northeast, including 8 quick inches in

Baltimore. Nationally, the resulting flooding took 130 lives and produced over three billion dollars in damage ($90 billion in 2023 dollars).

As Baltimore was downstream, the flooding began with rivers and streams overflowing their banks. The rainfall north of the city headed down the waterways to the city. The Gwynn's Falls was 10 feet above flood stage, destroying houses and lives, while the Jones Falls Valley was evacuated for fear the Lake Roland Dam might burst and send a wall of water through the city. Amtrak delayed or cancelled trains, the B&O railroad lost 10 miles of riverside track, and Ellicott City with the nearby Patapsco River State Park were both destroyed by flood waters. The Chesapeake Bay was impacted with this inflow of rainstorm producing fresh water, largely killing off the soft-shell clam and the once plentiful shad fish, while also eradicating bottom grasses so vital for the habitat of many species.

In 1973, in the aftermath of an Arab Israeli War, oil exports became an issue for Americans. The United States had assisted Israel and in response several oil-exporting Arab States were set to reduce oil exports to America. By early 1974, the international price of a barrel of oil had quadrupled and shortages of gasoline had arrived. The effectiveness of the embargo has repeatedly been called into question, as shortages may have arisen more from a public perception than a true lack of oil, but the lines of cars were there, miles long, with no gas for sale on Sundays, alternate day access to gasoline, limits on quantity, and all these limitations making driving a bit of a luxury. Conservation efforts began, a nationwide 55 mile per hour speed limit was imposed, and daylight savings time was extended to save energy. Cars averaged 12.9 miles per gallon in 1973: it would be a long, slow climb to fuel efficiency. (Average vehicle fuel economy half a century later exceeded 35 MPG.)

Traffic jams of 1973 were mostly in the vicinity of gasoline stations, while vehicle counts on Interstate 95 through the city and Maryland were reduced by 40 percent. Area police received multiple calls per day complaining of an almost previously unheard-of problem, gasoline theft. The only retail sales that seemed to increase was the purchase of locking gas caps. Gas lines and the irate motorists in them were too much for some retailers: fifty-five fuel stations closed in Baltimore alone. Soon, an economic recession filtered through the economy, driven by the shock of fuel price increases. The rising oil prices directly impacted where and how people worked and shopped. The Mass Transit Administration reported a 50 percent increase in bus ridership a year after the crisis ended, while it had been a 100 percent increase when gasoline was largely unavailable. Carpooling via computer matching became popular. Gasoline prices and advice about supplies became regular newspaper copy. Vacation advice appeared in *The Baltimore Sun*. In the Letters to the Editor section correspondence from James Hudgins urged Baltimoreans to enjoy the many local attractions available to them, accessible with little to no gasoline expenditure. Gas guzzling automobiles quickly fell from favor as Baltimoreans began a search for vehicles with a new priority in mind: fuel economy.

It was 1974, July 1, when city employees, starting with the sanitation workers, walked off the job, demanding more than double the contract pay raise the city had agreed to and a new policy on worker absences. Poor equipment, exhaust fumes, and excessive heat were complaints added to their request for a pay increase to counteract the impacts of price inflation. Their walkout began a cascade of other job actions. Within hours, they were joined by a few hundred highway and sewer workers, two days later all the highway workers went out, soon followed by the guards from the city jail, and days later, the city's police officers. Picket lines and demonstrations sparked to violence, leading to arrests by non-striking police officers. An uprising in the city jail was put down, with police refusing assistance from the striking guards. What had started as a "wildcat" strike by a few employees had become a formally supported labor union work action, one that in many ways paralyzed the city.

Mayor William Donald Schaefer was livid, and reacted accordingly. Mobilizing the city's white-collar workers, he reassigned them into teams of refuse collectors. To avoid union picket lines and possible confrontation, these newly-minted sanitation workers followed neither regular routes nor pickup points: the refuse pick-up times and locations and dumping sites were routinely changed to prevent striking workers from establishing picket lines that might prevent access. The courts declared these strike actions illegal. Fines were levied, and a July 15 end-of-strike deadline was established. Negotiations between city and labor union leaders followed. One by one, the striking unions agreed to a compromise and the strikers returned to work. A $90,000 fine against the unions was levied by the courts, the penalty to be paid by paycheck deductions from the workers. The two weeks of a city services standstill had ended.

In 1975, the *Pride of Baltimore* became a symbol of progress and hope for the city. It would end sadly. The city, re-inventing itself in 1975, created an emissary of good will, linking its past and its future. The suggestion came from Robert Embry to Mayor Schaefer to build a new Baltimore Clipper Ship, to be named the *Pride of Baltimore*. It would be built in an open-air shipyard at the Inner Harbor. The ship was to be a replica, fully operable, built using the methods of the colonial era. It would sail the world, the sole exception to the demands of authenticity the installation of a diesel engine. On May 1, 1977, the *Pride of Baltimore* was commissioned, ready to take Baltimore's message to the world.

The *Pride* sailed from Baltimore down the east coast, then ventured as far as British Columbia as the promotional material stated, "extending the hand of friendship to countless visitors." In 1986, the ship embarked on a trans-Atlantic trip to Ireland, England, the North Sea, and the Mediterranean. On the return voyage, tragedy struck. On May 14, 1986, north of Puerto Rico, the ship was struck by a sudden micro-burst of 80 mile per hour winds, sinking before even an SOS could be sent by radio. Four on board, the captain and three young hands, went down with the ship, while eight others climbed into a small life raft. They were rescued from the sea four days later. The optimistic message-bearing mission ended abruptly, the ship gone. Later a memorial service and monument were all that remained. A second *Pride* was commissioned in 1988, the *Pride of Baltimore II*, a larger ship and unlike the original, a safer design with watertight compartments below decks.

By 1976, Baltimore had endured a decade of violence. The number of homicides regularly exceeded 200 per year, with the city being named the most violent city in the United States by federal law enforcement officials. The city was shocked when Charles Hopkins entered a temporary City Hall, in use while the traditional city hall was under renovation, determined to air a grievance. His carry-out shop had been shut down by city inspectors and Hopkins wanted it reopened. He walked through the building until he found the office of Mayor Schaefer, who at that moment was behind his locked office door eating lunch. Hopkins asked the mayor's secretary if he could see the mayor. Sensing something amiss, she told him the mayor was in Annapolis on city business. When he then asked to see a city councilman, the mayor's secretary led him to the office of Dominic Leone. There, Hopkins entered Leone's office, drew a pistol and shot Leone, killing him. Before Hopkins was restrained, he wounded another office worker, and the events caused another councilman who had witnessed the shooting to suffer a heart attack. That councilman died soon after. Then the City Hall shooting was followed three days later by a sniper attack, when an individual barricaded himself in his home, from which he shot seven police officers, killing one. Homicide had become part of life and death in Baltimore.

In the 1970s, Baltimore was losing its identity as a heavy industry town. The city was shrinking, the population decreased by 120,000 residents in the decade. Manufacturing jobs were being lost at an alarming rate, led by the Bethlehem Steel Sparrow's Point mill cutting 10,000 jobs from a workforce of about 40,000. Baltimore City unemployment was impacted by both the oil embargo-led recession and long-term de-industrialization, the rate jumping from 4.6 percent to 10.3 percent in the decade. Ship building, long a leading part of Baltimore's industrial base, was struggling to survive given foreign competition and weaker demand. The intervention of the Maritime Administrator and Port of Baltimore booster Helen Delich Bentley brought some ship building activity, reportedly including orders by Greek shipping magnate Aristotle Onassis, allowing some Sparrow's Point shipyard workers to enjoy continuing employment. The Sparrow's Point shipyard built just 26 vessels in the entire decade, virtually all of them petroleum tankers, ending with the construction of the 130,000-ton *American Independence,* the last of five massive super-tankers built there. (By way of comparison, Liberty ships, a mainstay of ship construction in the 1940s, weighed in at just 14,000 tons.) Inflation accelerated to almost 9 percent by 1973, would soon rise to 12 percent later in the decade, and combined with the loss of industrial jobs, hard times had arrived for many Baltimoreans.

ASBESTOS

For thousands of years the mineral asbestos offered industrial and domestic users a means to provide heat insulation, protecting workers and others against excessive heat exposure. The material came into wide use during the Industrial Revolution as a protective covering. It was used to wrap or shield machinery, pipes, wires, or any material that could be damaged by exposure to heat, corrosion, or electrical contact and thus required a protective or insulating layer. The product asbestos comes with a dangerous downside: when loosened into the air, its fibers can be toxic if inhaled. Asbestosis is the disease from that inhalation. Discovered in 1930, asbestos was linked to cancer in 1934, and by the 1950s, the linkage between asbestos and job-related illnesses was widely accepted. This was a useful mineral that also produced serious illness, illnesses that would typically manifest many years after exposure, leading to a diagnosis of a fatal lung disease. Asbestos was widely used by the thousands of tons, having been employed in both industrial settings and in ship construction. By the mid-20th century, generations of workers had been exposed, especially those in shipyards. As a heat insulator, the mineral had been used in steam ship construction, a long-time Baltimore specialty. By the 1970s, the frenetic World War Two Liberty and other ship construction work was producing the delayed but debilitating disease, mesothelioma, in shipyard and other workers.

Like so many other industrial settings, the Sparrow's Point steel mill wrapped its pipes and wires with asbestos, with some workers in hot environments wearing heat protecting suits made of asbestos. Workers routinely went into the coke ovens (forges that reduced the impurities in coal) to clean out residue. With temperatures typically 115 to 120 degrees Fahrenheit, workers wore protective asbestos suits. To clean them, the workers took the suits home to be washed in the household laundry. As Larry Bannerman, son of a steelworker, said, "Our family got to share exposure to the asbestos fibers…" by the simple act of doing the laundry.

In the 1960s, asbestos remediation at the Sparrow's Point mill began. Workers wearing protective masks and clothing chipped at the layers of protective asbestos wherever it was found. The asbestos debris was scattered about the work area in a loose form, allowing particles of the debris to become airborne and thus breathable. The material was placed into special handling bags, again by workers properly protected, to be transported to a nearby on-site landfill where the bags were unloaded. Landfill bulldozers then took over, pushing and then crushing the asbestos laden bags, in the process breaking them open. The asbestos fiber contents spilled onto the ground to be caught in the wind, exposing other workers or nearby downwind residents to the dangers of asbestos. Proper, complete handling and remediation practices seemed to be well in the future.

By the 1970s, exposure to the insulating mineral asbestos was running head-on into the long-term health issues created by the product. Asbestos had found its way into an alarming number of products, in housing alone from floor tiles to roof shingles to the wall board dividing interior rooms. The National Gypsum Company on Newkirk Street in Baltimore had incorporated asbestos into thirty different construction products. The company, facing enormous liability though its inclusion of asbestos in its products, was eventually forced to declare bankruptcy.

An accounting by the end of the decade of deaths in Maryland directly connected to asbestos exposure ran to more than 1,000. Wherever hot or steam-transporting pipe had been installed prior to the 1970s, it was almost certainly wrapped in asbestos. By the 1970s, in recognition of the health risks and consequent business liability, jobs were created in a new industry: asbestos abatement, the proper removal (or alternatively, permanently sealing) and handling of the product that would protect future generations from exposure.

MINORITY BUSINESS AND BANKING

Baltimore's African American community was making strides in operating minority owned businesses throughout the city. A long-standing problem for Black business owners was difficulty in accessing the necessary capital to initiate a new business. Business owners or potential business owners seeking financial assistance to open or expand an operation had largely been denied loans by traditional banks, the banks maintaining that the loans were too risky.

A lack of access to commercial loans and funding led local Black entrepreneur Henry Parks, founder of the Parks Sausage Company, to seek private funding from the Black community's informal banker, "Little Willie" Adams. Parks was an experienced manager in the sausage manufacturing business, yet could not qualify (in the eyes of local traditional bankers) for a business startup loan when he moved to create his own company. Finally, in the mid-1960s, after Parks had been running his successful business for 13 years, he was able to receive a loan for a company expansion from a commercial bank.

For others seeking to start a new business in the 1970s, access to capital by Black business owners was still not easy, but there was an incremental improvement in the process. The progress was initially not through more cooperative banks, although that cooperation would ultimately arrive, but through government loan guarantee programs, many through the Small Business Administration (S.B.A.) Black-owned businesses such as the Super Pride Grocery chain, with over $40 million in annual sales and employing 400 workers in seven city locations, struggled financially in the absence of banking support. One small Black-owned business, the March Funeral Home, opened with an

S.B.A. loan of $15,000. A decade of successful operations later, in the late 1970s commercial bank financing became available for a major expansion of the March business.

Congressman Parren Mitchell was elected to Congress in 1970, the first African American member of the House of Representatives from Maryland. Mitchell fought civil rights battles beginning in his younger years, bringing a lawsuit to demand entry to the University of Maryland graduate school, where he was the first African American to graduate. Mitchell was a major backer of Black business enterprise, viewing business as an excellent path forward for the Black community. To a public works bill making its way through Congress in the 1970s, Mitchell attached an amendment that mandated a guaranteed minority 10 percent set-aside to assure government contracts included opportunities for Black, Hispanic, and native Americans. Later, he initiated a Congressional investigation of no-bid military contracts and associated bribery. That investigation and subsequent judicial findings resulted in two of his cousins, Clarence Mitchell III and Michael Mitchell, serving prison time for their involvement.

BETHLEHEM STEEL CONSENTS

Bethlehem Steel at Sparrow's Point was no stranger to lawsuits and courtrooms. In 1974, the plant avoided expensive, time-consuming courtroom trials by negotiating a Consent Decree. A consent decree provides a remedy for a dispute, often with the participants neither admitting guilt nor paying monetary damages, with those in the dispute mutually agreeing to a specific, legally binding plan of action. The 1974 consent decree had major implications for access to equal employment opportunity, first for women, then for African Americans. This negotiation affected not just Sparrow's Point: because of the involvement and participation of the United Steelworkers Union, the entire steel industry was included in the final agreement.

The employees at Sparrow's Point held jobs that had historically been segregated by race and gender, with limits placed upon promotions and wage increase opportunities for minority workers. While hiring practices were addressed by the Civil Rights Act of 1964 and other legislation, discrimination was harder to eliminate once the hiring process was complete. Promotions at Sparrow's Point were granted based on employee seniority, but only the seniority an individual had gained within his or her department or work group. The work groups at Sparrow's Point were segregated, thus this process effectively locked in minority candidates to the trade to which they had been assigned. The practice effectively allowed racial segregation to continue, mandated by seniority rules. A lawsuit in opposition to this practice was filed by African American workers and by 1974, a consent decree, an agreement by all parties to abide by a set of standards or rules, was completed. Bethlehem Steel, the Steelworkers Union, and the minority workers who brought the lawsuit to overturn the discrimination would in the future abide by an agreement that plant wide seniority was to be considered when considering any individual for transfer or promotional opportunities.

A DECADE'S END

As the decade of the 1970s ended, the city was well positioned in many ways to prosper for the ensuing years. The shaky industrial economy of Baltimore saw its future as a service-based economy, complete with a tourist-based core. Local imaginations did not stop there. As actions followed, a new economy for the city became a reality. Tourists and conventioneers flocked to the city and there was much in which to take pride, both financially and culturally. Service industries put down roots and began meeting the needs of the local population. Setbacks were many, but problems were largely resolved as only an activist mayor like William Donald Schaefer could: forcefully, directly, immediately. The city was on a roll.

Lurking just beneath the surface gloss of a rebuilt Inner Harbor and portions of downtown were problems that would have to await a new decade to be addressed. Some saw trouble ahead, but a shiny new image and glass-fronted hotels and office buildings distracted many, if not most. The distraction was certainly not universal. Rising unemployment numbers meant many formerly employed citizens lost their jobs and income, and many found day-to-day life challenging. The problems were largely focused within the city limits, where frustration was followed by a consequent sense of hopelessness. Help was not at hand from one of the city's most visible government entities, the Baltimore City Police Department. The city's law enforcement agency was in many ways unchanged from the days of Chief of Police Donald Pomerleau and his enemies-list style of investigations. The reforms of the early years of Pomerleau leadership seemed to disappear, replaced with a harsher, more confrontational brand of law enforcement. Some called it abusive. Compounding these scenarios was the reality that there were swaths of the city where urban renewal and redevelopment never seemed to arrive, where parts of the city were still marked and scarred with derelict or burned-out buildings, left over from the violence of 1968. Such was life in much of Baltimore for much of the Black community inhabiting those places, with many citizens fighting just to survive.

Mayor Schaefer did much for the city, beginning with building the citizens' sense of community and confidence. He would remain mayor for most of the following decade, but it would remain for others to address some of the missing pieces necessary to move toward creating a thoroughly healthy Baltimore.

CHAPTER NINE:
A CENTURY ENDS

The 1980s and 1990s

de·in·dus·tri·al·i·za·tion, *noun*

1. decline in industrial activity in a region or economy.

"DEINDUSTRIALIZATION" WAS THE WORD ADOPTED to describe what was occurring in many American cities at the end of the 20th century. Baltimore is a case study for the process and its effects. Textbooks tell the story of deindustrialization as a natural process: when a city such as Baltimore, founded with a focus on agrarian activity, progresses to become an industrial center, there is a subsequent progression as a mature industrial economy moves next to a service-based economy. As demand rises for more services for a more affluent citizenry, the service sector responds with growth in activities such as tourism, restaurants, financial services, or communications. The industrial sector simultaneously becomes less labor dependent, with more robotics and automation, resulting in fewer industrial jobs. Entire industries in the sector may opt to relocate to a lower-cost environment, where they build modern facilities, resulting in the loss of all the jobs.

Baltimore's experience closely matched deindustrialization theory. There was, however, a persistent failure for the affluence factor to reach all citizens: the deindustrialization process affected the city's diverse citizenry in different ways. For some, there was an overall net positive, with available services enhanced while the costs of manufactured goods were stabilized or reduced. For industrial sector workers, the consequence was very different, with fewer industry jobs, lower wages in available service sector work, and for many, in the absence of re-training, no work at all.

THE POTEMKIN CITY

In 1787 Catherine the Great of Russia toured the Crimea, a region which her troops had taken from the Ottoman Turks in battle, part of her plan to annex the entire region to Russia. She had previously appointed Grigory Potemkin as viceroy of Russia's southern regions, to which the Crimea was to be added. Potemkin needed to impress and please the visiting Catherine, both to demonstrate his prowess as viceroy and his intimate affection. The tour she was to take on the Dnieper River would allow her to view, from a distance, the new villages being added to her domain. Potemkin knew the villages were sad affairs, so it is said that he constructed fake facades for the portion of each village facing the river, then moved people and even cattle herds to visible locations, all to please and impress the touring Empress. Whether truth or legend, these became known as Potemkin Villages, with a beautiful but false front, behind it a very different reality.

Baltimore's story in the 1980s and 90s was in some ways not unlike that of the Potemkin tale, a renaissance city with a pleasant public face but some sad realities just behind. Baltimore was known as a city of neighborhoods, with multiple faces, most pleasant and habitable. But there were also residents who made their homes in those neighborhoods comprising what Morgan State University Professor Lawrence Brown called the "black butterfly": two segregated Black communities fanning across the western and eastern sides of the city, separated by a narrow white corridor, on a map resembling the two opposing wings of a butterfly. Though surrounded by Black and White middle-class Baltimore, poverty was concentrated in the two wings of the butterfly and services appeared to bypass these streets. Residents facing problems of the human condition were often on their own to find solutions.

In the 1980s and 1990s, Baltimore's story is one of both affluence and poverty. It was a city with a highly visible, rebuilt, attractive core, but with harder times just beyond. The city's leadership set different priorities, adopted for very different reasons. A dynamic Mayor William Donald Schaefer (elected to four terms, 1971-87) set the renaissance goals, and a future mayor, Kurt Schmoke (three terms, 1987-99), established progressive new priorities for a new era. It has often been postulated that Schmoke was a leader well ahead of his time, as he addressed problems that helped to guide the city into the 21st century.

The city had endured years of population shrinkage. Alongside the population decline was a more critical element, the decline in the number of jobs. In 1970 there were just under 98,000 manufacturing jobs in the city; by 1985 there were but 52,000. Corporate leaders made decisions affecting plants, work, products, and jobs in Baltimore, but those making the decisions were almost exclusively headquartered outside the city. Baltimore had become a branch office city, its industrial, employment, and investment future in the hands of those who lacked the in-depth commitment that locally headquartered businesses had previously maintained. A productive economy of 1,700 manufacturing firms in years past had been reduced by more than half by century's end. If the city was to survive, it would need to attract new providers of jobs. Otherwise, the city's economy and population would continue to shrink. Already citizens had opted to escape the city limits, Black and white alike, leaving behind a community poorer and Blacker. The numbers from 1980 to the year 2000 tell a story of a city losing 18 percent of its population, reducing it to a population of fewer than 650,000 citizens.

Reversing these trends had become a primary task at Baltimore City Hall. Through most of the 1980s the mayor was William Donald Schaefer, a driven man with a "do it now" attitude who knew that to attract the clean industry jobs of real estate, finance, insurance and the like, the city needed more than physical repairs and further expansion of the rebuilding already underway. Baltimore's image needed an overhaul as well. William Donald Schaefer had been the beneficiary, the inheritor and the promoter of an image-making process begun years before. In 1978, he and his team created Hollywood East, attracting the movie industry to the city, raising awareness of the advantages of Baltimore as a film location, and proposing a film festival complete with an award, appropriately named the "Don". Film making had the multiple advantages of bringing revenue to the city and boosting the image of an otherwise largely unheralded community. Baltimore began appearing in motion pictures.

In the early 1980s, renovating and improving the city's physical appearance focused on the Inner Harbor Re-Development Plan, a plan that had originated under the leadership of prior mayors. They envisioned a glittering array of shops, hotels, waterfront attractions and historic sites, taking advantage of something most cities did not have, nor could they manufacture, available land alongside a historic scenic vista. It was a good plan and was successfully executed. The redevelopment plan focused along the waterfront, extending just one block deep in a city that extended inland for miles. Many complained the plan had left behind the city's working poor, the disadvantaged, the neglected and the underserved in a community under the assault of a growing substance abuse problem. These were serious problems with no simple cosmetic "renewal" solution.

The Inner Harbor was new, vibrant, and alive. The restoration of the city's waterfront was well underway, with a brick promenade along the harbor's western and northern sides; a new pair of buildings called Harborplace, filled with shops offering locally themed products; and multiple restaurants. Harborplace was a major success, attracting 18 million visitors in its first year. The shopping center had a bit of an identity crisis from its very beginnings. Some of the restaurants were national chains with just a few local dining spots mixed in, and popular food court of mostly fast and later chain food offerings. The upstairs tourist-oriented shops such as "Hometown Girl" featuring Baltimore-made products competed with a first-floor vegetable market and a Hess Shoes store, catering to a local consumer far different from those who visited the center. In fact, some merchants offering shops at the July 2, 1980, Harborplace opening did not survive through the first summer. Still, the attraction drew customers, and a short promenade walk away were soon two more prime attractions, the Maryland Science Center to the south and the National Aquarium to the east, both opening in 1981. The dazzle was apparent, the tourists arrived, locals joined in, and at least one part of Baltimore was creating the image the city and its leaders craved.

A few steps from the Inner Harbor and the more sedate redeveloped Charles Center, the city was not as optimistic or glittery. There was neither glitz nor glamour in the high-rise public housing, none at the open-air drug markets that seemed to ignore police patrols, nothing shiny and new where guns and violence were the norm among the burned-out buildings lingering from the 1968 riots after the assassination of Rev. Dr. Martin Luther King, Jr. This was the side of the city that confounded the city fathers, the image makers, and city residents alike. There was much of Baltimore that was doing just fine, but these places were not. That other cities were going through similar travails in these times, and some were even worse off, was of little comfort. There was so much more to the city, but this was also an image that stuck.

Baltimore by the year 1999 was in fact three cities nestled together, with dividing boundaries overlapping at times. The first of these was the renaissance city, the city of renewal, the city of gentrification, tourist attractions, museums and theaters, a place where the row homes of South Baltimore were suddenly called "town houses" in Federal Hill, with the addition of many dollars in improvements. Nearby on each side of renaissance Baltimore was a grittier, less affluent, less well served city. This part of Baltimore was not universally segregated, and though times may have been bleak, just as often there was celebration by those who had deep generational roots in these neighborhoods and found community with one another. These two cities were surrounded by a third, the Baltimore suburbs: the place where a disappearing city population had relocated. In this period, the city lost 17 percent of its population. The suburbs gained 14 percent, becoming a home to over two million residents, each identifying themselves as Baltimoreans. The suburbs were green with grass, leaves, services, and money, the place where the jobs had gone, where the shopping offered free parking.

A GRADUAL DECLINE

In the mid-1800s, the foundations were in place for Baltimore to become an industrial giant. Henry Sonneborn had come to Baltimore where he would open a men's clothing factory, joined by a half dozen other garment industry pioneers. The 1830 umbrella factory of Francis Beeler on West Lexington Street helped make Baltimore the umbrella capital of the world. Thomas Kensett began canning oysters in the winter, switching to fruits and vegetables in the summer, and opened the way for Baltimore to become America's canning capital for one hundred years. Shipbuilding had been underway since before the early 1700s, the days when William Fell opened his Fell's Point shipyard, an industry that would produce the Baltimore Clipper and more World War Two Liberty ships than any other yard in America. By the year 1950, one hundred years after Sonneborn, the world's largest steel mill was on the shores of the Patapsco River at the Bethlehem Steel Company Sparrow's Point plant. With the advent of the airplane, aviation pioneer Glenn L. Martin began building airplanes, from the China Clipper to the post-war Martin 404 commercial airliner. Baltimore maintained more than a hundred thousand manufacturing jobs for much of the 20th century plus a hundred thousand more workers supporting the needs of those workers and their families. The city was a prosperous, joyful place. But times change, and what happened next was nothing short of disastrous, as the economic fabric of the city unraveled one factory, one industry, one worker's pink slip at a time.

Deindustrialization wasn't a commonly used word in the 1950s, but there are hints of its presence much earlier. A first tangible sign of decline may have been in Baltimore's garment industry where the decline began early, the 210 manufacturing concerns of the 1920s declining to just 75 by the late 1940s. The remaining needle trade jobs had left for foreign shores through the 1950s, with the local industry mostly at an end by 1980. The final survivor in garment making seems to have been Londontowne Manufacturing, maker of London Fog coats where, as the lights were turned out, the owners were heard to say that American workers were going to have to learn to earn a lot less money. The local oyster canning industry had declined years earlier, but canning continued in the city with vegetable production continuing well into the 1960s. Canning disappeared from the local scene more slowly as improvements in transportation and automation decentralized the industry allowing canning closer to the farms. One major industry participant, Crown Cork and Seal Company, founded in Baltimore, moved away in 1958, but smaller parts of can making and canning hung on until later. The last of this major industry closed its doors in the 1990s when Manning's Hominy Company was sold, and production moved to Virginia.

The Port of Baltimore should have been immune to the impending dislocation, as it was a hands-on, labor-intensive operation requiring manpower to function. It changed when in 1956, Malcolm McLean invented multi-modal shipping by container. Suddenly, ship loading that had been using cargo nets, cranes and hand labor was replaced with a new process of handling big highway trailer sized boxes with heavy machines. This was containerization, using large boxes to stow and seal freight, the boxes fitting and locking onto trucks, rail cars, or specially designed cargo vessels. Highly efficient, containerization reduced the number of longshoremen needed to work at the Port of Baltimore over time, declining by 8,000 jobs, from 10,000 to 2,000 over the next two decades.

The biggest job loss blows were yet to come. Deindustrialization arrived as if in a choreographed movement, with the steel mill at Sparrow's Point leading the way. What had been 30,000 steel industry jobs became 8,000 by the late 1980s, with many residents and workers unwilling to face the reality that steel making did not have a long-term future in Baltimore. Steel enjoyed a small resurgence in the late 1970s with sufficient orders to be a profitable business, especially after accounting for the cost-cutting due to employee layoffs in the prior decade. Profits were being plowed back into the Sparrow's Point mill where a much-needed rehabilitation, modernization, and expansion of capability (e.g., continuous casting, a more efficient way to produce steel) was underway. These modernization efforts wouldn't succeed for long, as a nationwide economic recession dealt a major blow to the Sparrow's Point mill. By 1982, consumer demand for steel had collapsed, sales and revenue fell, and with it mill production. Modernization at Sparrow's Point relied on company profitability; without those profits, plant modernization came to a sudden halt. Two changes in steel consumer preference added to the decline: increasing purchases of foreign steel and aluminum usurping steel as the product of choice for beverage containers. Fully 22 percent of the Sparrow's Point production was in steel specifically for container products alone. These forces combined to sound the death knell for the mill at Sparrow's Point.

Mike Stillwell spent fifty years working at Sparrow's Point. He started in a local version of Bethlehem Steel's famous "loop" training program, in which as a new hire he had visited and worked in every department, seeing all aspects of steel making at Sparrow's Point. Mike became the plant's hydraulic engineer, a vital role as many things could not move without the powerful hydraulic machines he helped maintain. Years later, he was very disappointed in Bethlehem management which led the company to bankruptcy. Like so many others he was focused on his role at the mill. He was an engineer, managing machines, while others were furnace workers, making steel, and still others were workers producing the many steel goods that flowed out of the vast plant. They were all doing their jobs. Mike asked, perhaps on behalf of many: how come top management couldn't seem to do theirs? It was never that simple, of course. Steel worker Eddie Bartee put it in different terms. He is quoted in *The Baltimore Sun* saying, "I thought Beth Steel would be here forever." By the early 2000s, the end was in sight, and all the high paying, life changing jobs at the mill would soon be gone.

For the thousands of workers impacted, loss of gainful employment was painful. There was an even more tragic side of the closing and bankruptcy of Bethlehem Steel sadly waiting to be learned by former employees and retirees. The steel mill was a heavily unionized operation, with negotiations between labor and management often contentious. But agreements were made, and the steel workers achieved significant wage levels, with guarantees for their future retirement benefits and assurances of company paid health care into the worker's old age. These two benefits were never to be delivered, as the retirement program was significantly underfunded, and the health care program not funded at all. The retirement program reverted to the United States Government's Pension Benefit Guarantee Corporation, an agency that paid mere pennies on the dollar of anticipated benefits. Bethlehem Steel anticipated delivering the promised health care benefits through payments from its ongoing operations but with the company's bankruptcy, there were no ongoing operations and therefore no funds whatsoever to deliver on that agreement. Workers lost both their jobs and their futures.

The Bethlehem Steel mill was served by a diverse array of local suppliers. Among them were two southside refractory brick producers, providing an almost invisible but critical part of steel making. Refractory bricks of many shapes and sizes were used to line the steel ovens at the mill. These two competing companies, Harbison-Walker and General Refractories were located blocks apart, each employing hundreds of factory and management personnel to supply these specialized products to Sparrow's Point. When the mill closed, the manufacturers lost their prime client and their inevitable closure soon followed. Hundreds of "brick yard" employees lost their jobs, their earnings, and for many of the senior personnel, their way of life.

The shipbuilding industry joined steel production as a lost industry in Baltimore. Commercial vessel shipbuilding met its domestic demise nationwide when the U.S. government ended subsidies to the shipbuilding industry in 1981. (Military applications were exceptions.) In the mid-1970s, despite an apparent abundance of available ships, domestic yards built 75 ships for private enterprise. After the loss of subsidies, by 1990 the entire domestic commercial ship building industry launched just three ships. Competing with subsidized foreign builders became impossible, and Bethlehem Steel operated the two biggest yards in Baltimore, at Sparrow's Point and the Baltimore Works along Key Highway. Congresswoman Helen Delich Bentley helped maintain the local industry's viability through her work with major shipping company operators. Super tankers were built, keeping the yards alive and the ship builders on the job. But it would never be enough, the problem was too big, and from a massive work force in the thousands, the Sparrow's Point yard ended its days with a few hundred workers building barges, the last one sliding into the water in 1995. The Baltimore yard, long unable to accommodate the larger ships of the late 20th century, had previously closed in 1983, idling the few thousand repair and conversion workers remaining on the site. Other local yards met a similar fate.

The General Motors (G.M.) Automobile Assembly plant had opened for business in the days of the Great Depression, 1935. But the modern factory of 1935 no longer met the manufacturing needs of 1980. Vehicle assembly work continued, albeit with a workforce well below the 7,000 employees of years past. A two-shift per day operation had become just one shift, idling thousands. Hope does spring eternal, even in the face of declining quality reviews and dwindling sales, with one worker quoted as saying, "Until they bring in the wrecking ball, there's always hope." The plant closed in 2005, with yet another loss of thousands of jobs. The wrecking ball appeared a few years later. The decline of these factories and the loss of these jobs is only a part of the story.

At the eastside General Motors plant, each assembly line production position was said to create or impact nine external jobs, from the suppliers of steel parts, materials transport personnel, even clerks in the groceries where the workers spent their paychecks. Staff reductions over a number of years became the new norm, but when General Motors finally closed the assembly plant, the community felt an outsized impact. Throughout the local economy, a cascade of secondary job loss and consequent economic loss created greater hardship. Dedicated suppliers reacted by reducing employment, with some even closing completely: a Michigan-based frame supplier immediately announced the closure of its local factory, idling a hundred more employees.

Some 1980s data can provide insight into how hard the city and its residents were hit by the constant downsizing and ultimately by de-industrialization. The decade of the 1980s created 200,000 new jobs in the region (Baltimore and surrounding counties) even with the 40 percent decline in city manufacturing employment. The economy was growing regionally, yet the city's unemployment rate soared. The city's official unemployment rate was over 8 percent, a third higher than the state and nation. The Regional Council of Governments reported that in the decade, the number of jobs had increased by 20 percent. Deindustrialization was claiming jobs, but the service sector and suburban employers seemed to be replacing the jobs lost, often adding more.

EXPLORING A LOST INDUSTRY

Of the many industries that were lost during this period of change, a close look at one of them offers insight into how even a company with extensive local roots and a history of adapting to changes in demand can decline and fail. The Hayward Bartlett and Company was a prosperous Baltimore metal foundry that by the mid 19th century had added cast iron building fronts to a product line that had previously offered stoves, fireplace inserts, even railroad locomotive components. This was a relatively new construction method that largely replaced masonry, utilizing iron sections that could be quickly bolted together, providing faster, less expensive construction, and offering extensive daylight through large windows, with unique and often elaborate design features. Hayward Bartlett helped make Baltimore the cast iron front capital of America.

One early Baltimore commission for a building front was for the fruit and vegetable business of William Thomas at 218-226 South Charles Street, while another major application of cast iron construction was the headquarters of *The Baltimore Sun*, the Sun Iron Building, a five-story edifice. The Sun Building with its cast iron beams and exterior walls of architectural cast iron sections was erected in 1851 but lasted only 53 years. It was lost in 1904 when the two-thousand-degree conflagration of the Baltimore Fire passed directly through the news offices and press room.

In this cast iron era, Hayward Bartlett employed hundreds of workers in their foundry area as well as in their extensive belt driven machine shop. Casting architectural iron fronts and building exterior walls in their foundry, production continued with the machining of the building fronts to precise dimensions and smoothness. Skilled hands worked with a robust supply of powered and manual tools allowing the company's group of highly experienced craftsmen to change the dreams of engineers or architects into physical products meeting or exceeding the desires of the designer. The whimsical, the elaborate, the classic, the essentials of iron fronts and more were the products of foundries, and in Baltimore, the number one foundry was Hayward Bartlett and Company.

Over time, the company shifted its operations to other products to meet client demands. World War Two saw the company become a leader in the casting of bronze Liberty ship propellers. Foundry operations continued but the company, later renamed Bartlett Hayward, was travelling a predictable if unsettling path. The foundry business was like much of the heavy industrial base of the city, a major employer, and an innovator. This dominant company also found that changing consumer product demands, competition from lower labor cost providers, and local, modern materials, then later nationwide environmental concerns, became a combination of forces impossible to overcome. The company was caught amid the macro shift to a service economy and like much of the city's heavy industrial base, Bartlett Hayward by the 1980s had become a part of Baltimore's past.

A WOUNDED CITY

By 1980, the people of Baltimore were enduring a sad new reality: drugs, guns, and gangs were making the streets where children once safely played, milkmen delivered, and neighbors chatted on front porches no longer quite so friendly. The drugs, guns, and gangs were linked by the money that flowed among them. Buyers came from both city and suburbs, venturing to the inner city to purchase illegal drugs appealing to those escaping or enhancing reality, relieving a mental or physical pain, fitting in with a group, being more creative or competitive, or perhaps just satisfying curiosity. The money the buyers brought with them afforded the mostly youthful dealers an unexpectedly improved lifestyle for these often-disenfranchised youth. Street corner dealers found a new economic windfall in a system they were determined to protect. But it was a competitive business: there were many customers but fewer corners to occupy, limiting opportunities and often setting up conflicts over turf. The unwritten but understood rules of drug dealing geography were enforced by the dealers, often at the point of a gun. The city was awash with easily available weapons, and bullets became the ultimate dispute settler. Every city in America dealt with these problems, but Baltimore seemed to have become the cultural poster child for them all.

Drug abuse became a true epidemic in the mid-1980s when a new, cheaper substance arrived in the form of crack cocaine, a processed form of powdered cocaine which when smoked delivers a powerful stimulant with an immediate effect, powerful enough to become extremely addictive. Marijuana, powdered cocaine, and heroin were each available, but crack created customers aplenty, and the dealers flourished. Open air drug markets, perhaps the most notorious at West Fayette and Monroe Streets on the city's West Side, were detailed by writer David Simon in his book, *The Corner: A Year in the Life of an Inner-City Neighborhood.* Simon details a stark reality of a community abandoned, a police presence overwhelmed, a social welfare system missing the mark, and a loving family scratching out an existence despite the odds against them. Simon embedded with the Baltimore Police Department to gather the stories for *The Corner* and other earlier works, *Homicide: A Year on the Killing Streets* and the television series, *The Wire.* Simon researched and wrote authentic stories of parts and people of the city that had been forgotten or ignored by the planners and builders of the renaissance Baltimore, with its tourist and convention focus of downtown and harbor front.

In 1980, Baltimore's resident homicide rate stood at 216 deaths for the entire year. The rate rose even as the population of the city declined with the mean streets of the city producing 353 homicide deaths by 1993, a rate of forty-eight murders for each 100,000 citizens. (In the same period, nationwide statistics showed a stable rate, then gradual decline of the homicide rate by the late 1990s of about 20 percent.) The Baltimore Police Department estimated at the time that 40 to 60 percent of these murders were drug related. Drugs and drug abuse created criminal activity in Baltimore well beyond the retail corner drug markets of the city. The city was a delivery point and crossroads for drug smuggling and marketing, with a port, an airport, and a highway system serving as conduits for drug movement. Distribution networks existed locally through a network of gangs, numbered at over 200 in the era by local law enforcement officials. Such an all-encompassing crime culture made the vast majority of the city's citizens innocent victims, often at risk, reluctant to participate in the normal everyday transactions of city life.

POLLUTION ADDRESSED

When Rachel Carson's book *Silent Spring* was published in 1962, it created in the public a new awareness of human pollution of the environment. The book and public pressure in the decade that followed resulted in legislation to mitigate or eliminate environmental problems. By 1970, Earth Day activities offered a means for citizens to be personally involved. People demanded action, and the demands were vocal enough that government responded. New laws such as the Clean Water Act appeared and a Clean Air Act soon followed. Regionally, the creation of the Maryland Department of the Environment made overall enforcement practical as the problems were regional in nature and environmental issues often extended across city and county boundaries. Resources were deployed to prevent future damage and cleanse the environment, air, water, and ground, of the sins of the present and the past. This activity led to the creation of a new industry, environmental remediation: spills, upsets, toxic soil, each were to be professionally addressed in clean up efforts. From major problems in the waters of the Patapsco River harbor to the grounds of the steel mill at Sparrow's Point, to the smaller but more numerous issues such as leaking fuel tanks at the corner gasoline station, there was a new resolve, and a legal mandate, to fix the pollution issue before it was able to do more damage.

In 1910, the Baltimore Harbor had been described as a "hellbroth" of dreadful odors wafting off the waters into the surrounding city. For almost the first two hundred years of Baltimore's history, no sanitary sewer system existed, horse dung covered the streets, and resident trash was openly burned. When industry began appearing in the region, the harbor became a resource and means for waste disposal, "out of sight, out of mind." In the summer, the canning of tomatoes created waste which turned the harbor red. When the steel mill opened at Sparrow's Point, slag and waste material was dumped on the ground, in the water, or in the heavily polluted "tin mill canal", a stream bed that had formerly flowed through the mill property. Chemical plants situated on the Patapsco would dump their waste, adding toxicity to the harbor. Algae blooms in the Chesapeake Bay do naturally occur, and in modest amounts they form part of the food chain, but industrial wastes, then excessive fertilizer use by distant farmers plus home lawn fertilization cumulatively added enough nitrogen to the waterways for algae blooms to become harmful, as the algae grew out of control and became toxic. As the city grew, natural waterways like the Jones Falls or the Gwynn's Falls added city storm runoff pollutants to the harbor. Once installed, the city's sewage system was subject to failures, more frequently as the system aged: broken pipes, inadequate capacity, defective treatment, and overflows. Even visiting ships would use the harbor waters to clean their holding tanks, discharging the waste directly back into the Patapsco. Sharing this environment, the fish in the Patapsco River universally had traces of heavy, toxic metals such as lead, chromium, or cadmium. These fish added urgency to the clean-up task, as the health of the fishermen (and those who consume their harvest) could easily be at risk. In a 1996 interview, Carl "Slim" Kelly, unaware of an advisory indicating the health risk of consuming the catch from the Patapsco, said he recently hooked 22 catfish in two days' time, even giving some of them away. Kelly, 62, whose residence was near the river in the Cherry Hill section of Baltimore, said he crabbed and fished frequently from the pier, catching everything from spot and yellow perch to rockfish. All the same, he observed, "The water could be a little cleaner." The clean-up challenges were enormous, and so the work began.

Enforcement of environmental regulations is the most significant deterrent to actions which pollute the air, water, or ground. In the late 20th century, many such actions were initiated, some against those who inadvertently damaged the environment, others whose actions were calculated and deliberate. Among the many enforcement actions brought by Maryland Department of the Environment, these represent the nature of the encounters and actions that precipitated the enforcement, and they demonstrate this important step in changing behavior:

- Baltimore Rustproof, Inc. The company was cited for discharging untreated chromium, cadmium, and other hazardous wastes into the harbor, after first disabling the city installed water pollution monitoring system. The owner was placed on probation and incurred a serious fine.

- American Recovery, Inc. An oil recycling company illegally discharged chemical waste into the harbor. The General Manager allegedly lied to an investigating grand jury, resulting in his receiving a six-month work release jail sentence.

- Four Maryland Colleges. A total of $700,000 in fines was proposed for schools on whose campuses there were maintained power transformers containing toxic PCBs, with failures to keep records and to notify local fire companies of their locations on campus.

The U.S. Environmental Protective Agency was also at work in the region identifying heavily polluted sites, initiating mandatory business procedural changes (if applicable) and property clean-up. Polluted properties could be identified as "Superfund" sites, enabling federal funding assistance to eliminate the most hazardous conditions. Of many, here are three examples:

- Chemical Metals Industries, Inc. Identified as a Superfund site in 1984, the company contaminated soil and ground water with heavy metals and toxic chemicals in a mixed residential, commercial, and industrial site in the Westport/Annapolis Road area of Baltimore.

- The Mid-Atlantic Wood Preservers, Inc. A company that pressure treated lumber using arsenic and chromium to the point that ground water near the plant had 200 times the maximum allowable amount of those chemicals. Clean up and on-going monitoring was initiated.

- The Allied Chemical Plant. Located in the Fell's Point area, this refinery processed ore for chromium until its closing in 1985. The heavily toxic waste post-refining tailings were used as fill for the factory grounds and surrounding areas. Toxins leached into the harbor until the property was "capped", with the installation of an impervious soil layer, to prevent further seepage.

The Sparrow's Point Steel Mill, always a focal point in pollution investigations, was subject to inspections, fines, and mandated changes at the 3100-acre plant. Demanding change at the mill became a balancing act for state officials, recognizing the need for change while acknowledging the rather precarious financial condition of Maryland's largest (at the time) employer. Sparrow's Point had a 100-year long experience as a polluter, so any clean-up effort was inevitably going to demand massive change. On the property was a "Tin Mill Canal" which followed the path of a natural feature, Humphrey's Creek. The canal became a dumping point for seemingly every other polluted, toxic liquid used at the plant, and the tons of industrial wastewater used as an essential element in any cooling process. Over decades, the canal's liquid contents began a downward infiltration, eventually reaching the ground water supply. Polluting the ground water would impact not only the plant but also nearby communities dependent on that same ground water for their water supply. So advanced were the "Tin Mill" problems that the immediate response was to simply prevent the pollution from getting worse. A proper, thorough, best possible clean-up would not occur until the mill was finally and forever shut down in the early 2000s.

In 1980, Baltimore had some of the worst air pollution in the United States. The Baltimore Gas and Electric Company and the Bethlehem Steel Mill at Sparrow's Point both consumed large amounts of coal, the power company for fueling the fires that make the steam to make electricity, the steel mill using coal as a constituent part of making steel in a blast furnace. The two polluters would each release 100,000 tons of soot particles into the air each year. That soot, a known carcinogen, would ride on the wind to settle where it would and be inhaled by anyone in its path. Pollution abatement steps were begun in the 1980s, with some "scrubbing" technology applied to the smoke and soot entering the atmosphere from the power company smokestacks. Later, these changes were accompanied by a switch to cleaner fuels. In the case of the steel mill, efforts were made to reduce its polluting processes to meet multiple air quality environmental mandates, especially with the construction of its new "L" furnace. (Production equipment at the mill was designated alphabetically and sequentially, thus the "L" furnace went into service as the last of the series in 1978). The "L" was a sophisticated, computer-controlled steel blast furnace which was said to be as pollution free as a blast furnace could possibly be. Sparrow's Point pollution was slowly reduced as the steel mill produced smaller and smaller quantities of steel, declining until early in the 21st century, when emissions problems came to an end with the closure of the plant.

LEADERS COPING WITH CHANGE

In 1980, William Donald Schaefer was beginning his third term as mayor of Baltimore. Schaefer, a "do it now" leader, accepted no excuses for delay or dawdling. The mayor would travel the city, spotting problems and issuing orders for correction, orders that would need to be obeyed with haste. But that attitude became a liability when Schaefer confronted the latest proposal in a long process of highway planning. With approvals and funding in place for only a small portion of the proposed highways, he ordered the building of a four-lane segment through the city that would become known as "The Highway to Nowhere".

Baltimore had endured forty years of highway planning, some of it during Schaefer's term of office. One of many plans called for Interstate 70 to pass through the center of the city, a plan he had favored at one point. Protests and litigation slowed much of the plan down, but one section through a west Baltimore community had already been funded. That section lacked a firm (or any) plan to become part of a unified highway system; it was a mile long segment that was completely reliant upon other unapproved, ever-changing highway proposals. When told that building the road was pre-mature, Schaefer's stubborn nature led him to "do it now", ordering the segment to be built. The connecting portions of the highway were later cancelled, the segment he had ordered built became known as "The Highway to Nowhere", and the African American community it plowed through was reduced to a memory. Its final disposition, highway, parkland, rail line right of way, remains a question into the 21st century.

He had inherited the plans for the Inner Harbor development, then made them his own. Schaefer was a builder: the Inner Harbor, the National Aquarium, and more. He was later named the Best Mayor in America in 1984 by *Esquire Magazine*. *Baltimore Sun* opinion columnist Dan Rodericks correctly assessed the years of the Schaefer administration as free of corruption. This was remarkable in an era when both Baltimore and Anne Arundel County executives, the governor of Maryland, and the vice president of the United States (a former Baltimore County executive) were convicted or forced to resign. Rodericks did note, however, Schaefer's use of a "shadow government". A group of the mayor's trusted friends and business associates were influential enough to exchange favors to help the mayor by-pass the perceived "red tape" of governmental procedures likely to delay the Schaefer "do it now" protocol. This "shadow government" of various leaders and William Donald Schaefer was unorthodox in creating a large ($100 million) fund that could be used to sponsor projects of the mayor's choice. City government had in many cases previously made loans to promising projects across the city. When repayments of those loans arrived, a mechanism to return those funds to city coffers was apparently absent. The funds received went into a mayor's project account, allowing the repayment money to be used for funding projects without the Baltimore City Council's oversight. From those repayments came the dollars to purchase land for a land fill, to make a low interest loan for the City Employees Credit Union, to bail out of a project close to default at the Lexington Market, or to guarantee loans for private developers engaged in "renaissance" projects. These were projects made possible without the awareness of the City Council, accomplished by a shadow government that transacted city business. The fund proved to be neither nefarious in intent nor criminal in appropriation, but merely a means that allowed the "do it now" directives of an impatient mayor to act on his vision, undeterred by formalities. Though the process was found not to be illegal, to *Sunpapers* journalist Fraser Smith, who wrote a series of news articles exposing the arrangement, it was "very inappropriate."

Schaefer left the city in 1986 to become the 58th Governor of Maryland. Succeeding him in the mayor's office was Clarence H. "Du" Burns, President of the City Council, who in a caretaker role continued Schaefer's programs if not his leadership style. Burns had been in elective office since 1971, first as a City Councilman, then as City Council president. A self-made man, he earned his nickname of "Du" on the basis he was always helping, <u>doing</u> something, for someone. With the rise of Schaefer to the governor's office in Annapolis, Burns had become the city's first African American mayor. Reflecting later on his replacement, Governor Schaefer described Burns while simultaneously making a dig at Du Burns' eventual successor: "He's the old-time, caring politician. He used to go out of his way to help people. That's what made him so great...Du was a man who got his degree on the street. He wasn't a scholar. He wasn't an Oxford man."

KURT SCHMOKE

Kurt L. Schmoke was an Oxford man. Born in Baltimore, his Baltimore public school education was followed by a degree from Yale University (1971), a year at Oxford as a Rhodes scholar, then a completion of his education in 1976 at Harvard Law School. He had always been a leader, first in high school at Baltimore City College, then continuing throughout his higher education years. That he fitted into a governmental leadership role came as no surprise, as he successfully ran for elective office in 1982, becoming the city's chief criminal prosecutor as Baltimore State's Attorney. His was no small victory, as the 32-year-old Schmoke received over 100,000 votes, with a high African American turnout, while his opponent, incumbent and longtime state's attorney William Swisher garnered only 59,000 votes. Swisher, a law-and-order, favorite son of Baltimore's political clubs, lost to an opponent who had seemingly risen from obscurity. The "upstart" Schmoke said after his surprising landslide victory, "It's a tremendous tribute to the Black community, and it does change politics in this city." The city's electorate had spoken, and the voice was loud and clear: a new political force had been awakened in Baltimore's Black community.

In 1987 Kurt L. Schmoke ran for mayor. In the Democratic primary, he opposed and defeated the incumbent mayor, Clarence "Du" Burns. Winning a close contest, Schmoke earned just over 79,000 votes, while his opponent Burns received 74,000. Schmoke had at one time early in the contest held a 30-point lead in local polls, ultimately winning the primary by just a 3 percent margin. He went on to handily win the mayor's office on November 3, 1987, with 78 percent of the votes cast in the general election, promoting his victory as a change to a younger generation. At the time of this election, Schmoke was just 38 years old, while Du Burns was 69. The Republican candidate was 63-year-old Sam Culotta, in his fifth losing attempt to become mayor of Baltimore.

Schmoke became a City Hall fixture for most of the 1990s, going on to two more victories, serving three terms as mayor. But April 1988 marked the beginning of a new political life, dimensions of which may have been a surprise for the new mayor of Baltimore. The youthful mayor had become a nationally recognized public figure, appearing on countless broadcast programs, granting dozens of interviews, and appearing at numerous speaking engagements. Contemporary major television hosts, including Phil Donohue, Morley Safer, Ted Koppel of Nightline, all wanted to hear from Kurt Schmoke, to question him about a speech he had made to the U.S. Conference of Mayors. In his presentation to a room filled with mayors and chiefs of police, Schmoke had declared that the nation's "War on Drugs" was a failure and that impacting the nation's drug abuse problem might be better accomplished with an alternative approach, decriminalization of drug use. The response of those gathered was perhaps predictable: first complete silence, then criticism of virtually every aspect of the speech. Mayor Ed Koch of New York City said Schmoke was "…a brilliant spokesman for a bad idea".

A former State's Attorney, Schmoke had enforced and prosecuted drug use laws, but saw no end to the problem. As he later said, "We can't arrest our way out of the problem". By 1989, two thirds of Americans viewed drug abuse as the nation's number one problem, leading to ever more draconian laws enforced by the courts. The identification of the HIV virus and its transmission through shared hypodermic needles had made drug abuse a three-part problem: the abuse itself, the criminal activity it fostered, and now an AIDS epidemic expanding when needles were shared by infected persons. Schmoke persevered, not proposing legalization but offering hope through decriminalization, pursuing treatment as an alternative to felony convictions and jail time. He won a victory when the Maryland legislature approved his plan for a needle exchange program, designed to reduce to spread of AIDS by halting needle sharing amongst drug users. Schmoke knew he might only ever be remembered for his speech in Washington, D.C., on that April morning, and he was satisfied with that legacy.

Mayor Schmoke was not without awareness of Baltimore's image. Once branded as "Charm City", it later boasted "Baltimore is Best", then Baltimore was "*balti*More than you know". The new branding for the city was a slogan that Kurt Schmoke introduced in his inaugural address. With more than simply tourist appeal, Baltimore was to be "The City That Reads". Baltimore had a strong literary past: Frederick Douglas had learned to read in Baltimore, Scott Fitzgerald wrote while a Baltimore resident, Dashiell Hammett wrote of the fictional Continental Op from the Continental Trust Building, Henry L. Mencken wrote and opined from his home on Hollins Street, and Charles Osgood, resident poet and commentator at the Columbia Broadcasting System, grew up in the Liberty Heights area of the city. It was Schmoke's plan to harness that literate past to his city of the 1990s. His strongly held belief, garnered from his years of growing up in the city, was that to improve literacy was to improve the lives of the city's residents and the future of Baltimore itself. For Schmoke, the slogan was more than mere words, it demanded action. By creating a public-private partnership to coordinate efforts designed to enhance adult literacy and working with state government to gain funding for innovative approaches to improve student achievement, the program Schmoke created behind the slogan set a direction for the city and its new mayor.

SHIFTING PRIORITIES

Under Schmoke's leadership, a change in direction began. Much of the work of the remaking of the city into a modern, tourist friendly place had been accomplished over the past twenty years. Schmoke and his administration turned to address the issues of the city's residents, directing attention to the city's human resource: its citizens, their problems, and their future. Nowhere was this more apparent than in housing. The city was plagued with abandoned houses, some owned by the city itself. The statistics are alarming: in 1990, though the city had some 300,000 total housing units, among them just under 40,000 housing units were listed as abandoned, meeting the City Code definition of uninhabitable: "an unoccupied structure that is unsafe or unfit for human habitation or other authorized use." When it chose to do so, the city could demolish its own properties, but often the abandoned home was amid a row of occupied houses. If an abandoned property was privately owned, as was more often the case, there was an extended process for the city to gain ownership and control of the property's future. By 2000, intense efforts halved the number of vacant houses to well under 20,000. The paradox was that in a city with a declining population and abandoned homes, there was still a shortage of appropriate, safe, clean, and healthy housing. Mayor Schmoke resolved to fix that problem.

Schmoke's efforts were twofold. The city-owned high rise public housing communities were well past their prime, having been built in the 1950s. By the 1990s, they met no one's definition of desirable housing. These "projects" were in some cases dilapidated, all of them subject to overcrowding, and while recreational facilities might have been included in the community design, a lack of maintenance limited their functionality. The Schmoke administration began the process of demolishing these properties, replacing them with a series of low-rise communities, designed to be cleaner, safer, and more livable. The demolitions did little to alleviate the racial segregation found in these communities, and many had seen them as a deliberate attempt at isolating the Black community. Nonetheless, the replacement housing was an improvement.

The high-rise buildings of the 816-unit Lafayette Court Housing Community were the first target for replacement. Looking little like the artist's rendering of the early 1950s, Lafayette's multiple buildings and open spaces were worn down at the end of their fifty-year life span, which ended with their controlled demolition by implosion in August of 1995. Beyond these large high rise community plans, a second approach to alleviating the housing issues was to leverage federal programs and apply them to some of the at-risk city neighborhoods. This approach was termed "neighborhood revitalization" and the results on the west side at Sandtown and on the east side adjacent to Johns Hopkins Hospital proved successful enough to attract the attention and support of President Bill Clinton, who provided the program with the designation of an Empowerment Zone. An Empowerment Zone brought with it federal financial support for community-based programs in job development, housing, and social services, with tax credits for businesses when they located their operations within the boundaries of the designated community.

While these progressive initiatives had a positive impact on the city, forces well beyond the control of a local administration hampered the overall results. The population declines of the 1970s had continued into Schmoke's years in office: by 2000 the city had lost another 3.5 percent of its citizens, declining to a population under 650,000. This population decline, accompanied by both residential and business abandoned properties, created enormous pressure on the city government to fund the city's essential services. Homeowner real estate taxes within the city, a major portion of the city's revenue, were more than double those of surrounding jurisdictions. The Schmoke administration managed to maintain control of these costs, a major plus for the citizens. Yet the fact remained that comparable houses in city and county were listed with very different prices: city housing prices were "adjusted" downward to compensate for the significantly higher city tax burden and to increase their appeal to potential buyers. Facing impossible tasks, Schmoke did what could be done using the resources available, but many of the problems he sought to address during his three terms of office, especially the high homicide rate, continued to be Baltimore issues as he left office in 1999.

BETTER TIMES

Among the excitement, convenience, or changes to life in Baltimore in the 1980s and 1990s:

Baltimore gets a subway. No big, modern American city could possibly exist without a rapid transit system, or so the conversation went in government corridors, heard loudly from Baltimore Mayor Schaefer and Maryland Governor Marvin Mandel. The original plan, from the 1960s, called for multiple spokes emanating from downtown Baltimore, with 71 miles of route trackage. Funding limitations cut the system to one line of 28 miles. An even more modest subway was built in phases, beginning with an 8-mile section, built on time (1983) and on budget, at a cost of $797 million. Later there would be two extensions, in 1987 and 1995. The completed system trackage was just over 15 miles, with the route going from the northwest suburbs to the near east side at the Johns Hopkins Hospital complex. The subway system, representing an investment of $1.3 billion, was at best a partial solution for Baltimore's largely inadequate mass transit system.

The Left Bank Jazz Society. Formed in 1964, the Society was created through the efforts of two local jazz enthusiasts, Vernon Welsh, and Benny Kearse. The society invited and hosted legendary jazz greats through the 1970s and into early 1980s. John Coltrane, Cannonball Adderley, and others entertained on Sunday afternoons at 4:00 pm at the Famous Ballroom on North Charles Street. Welsh recorded the afternoon performances, with the tapes rediscovered years later and gradually released to an anxious and awaiting public. The Famous Ballroom was a second-floor space above a former auto dealership which had become a 100-lane bowling alley, but upstairs the music took over. Local artists often played, soul food (fried chicken a specialty) was sold from the kitchen, and the music was the common language for the multi-racial audience that attended. On one Sunday afternoon, a solo Duke Ellington appeared, his band's Baltimore bound bus missing enroute to the 4:00 pm start. Ellington played for an intimate 90 minutes, introducing each song with "And then I wrote this." What could have been better? The Society lost its permanent home in 1984, then moved through temporary quarters until it was disbanded in the 1990s.

The Baltimore Orioles. The O's had been a Baltimore fixture since 1954, a reincarnation of the championship teams of the late 19th century. It was in the 1980s that the local "boys of summer" made their second baseball World Series appearance in 1983. The team featured long-time Orioles player favorites like the 22-year-old (the season's Most Valuable Player) Cal Ripken, Jr., and the top hitter Eddie Murray (runner up to Ripken in the Most Valuable Player voting), and led by their top pitcher, Scott McGregor. This World Series was billed as the "I-95 Series", with two competing teams representing cities just 100 miles apart and connected by U.S. Interstate 95. The series games began in Baltimore, where they split victories, then moved on to Philadelphia where the Orioles took all three games. Future Baseball Hall of Famer and veteran pitcher Jim Palmer, at the end of his career, appeared for the Orioles, becoming the winning pitcher in Game 3. Baltimore's faithful fans filled the 33rd Street Memorial Stadium in two sellout crowds with a total attendance of 104,000. Memorial Stadium would be left behind by the Orioles in 1992, moving to a downtown stadium, Oriole Park at Camden Yards.

Pope John Paul II visit. Baltimore's Camden Yards stadium was the site of a visit by the leader of the one-billion-member Roman Catholic Church on October 8, 1995. John Paul travelled from his visit in New York City to Baltimore, where in public pronouncements he urged a renewed spiritual vitality, and maintenance of the moral truths, passing them forward to the next generation. After celebrating morning mass at the local Basilica, the Pope travelled in a procession along streets lined with an estimated 300,000 Baltimoreans. While church attendance was in decline nationally (49 percent reported regular attendance in 1958, 34 percent by the year 2000), this was not apparent as worshipers filled the stadium in Baltimore, site of the first American Diocese (1789). Tears of joy were shed by those in attendance: "overwhelmed" was the word used by Eileen Walsh, while seven-year-old Melissa Brent recalled a feeling of warmth, comfort, and calm. His Holiness was also greeted by local political leaders, lunched at a local kitchen that feeds the poor (Our Daily Bread), and offered remarks in multiple languages during several stops during his visit.

The Meyerhoff. This new center city concert hall was built specifically for the Baltimore Symphony with a capacity of 2400, opening in September 1982. The initial concept of a new concert hall in Baltimore a decade earlier, in the late 1960s, was to replace the aging Lyric Theater. The hall found an appropriate site, the Deutsches Haus on Cathedral Street, a short walk from the Lyric, with planning then construction starting in 1978. Initially planned as the Maryland Concert Center, the facility was renamed the Joseph Meyerhoff Symphony Hall just prior to its grand opening, honoring its long-time inspirational leader, major financial contributor, and Chairman of the Symphony Board. At the grand opening, Orchestral Leader Sergiu Comissiona conducted *Housewarming*, a piece commissioned for the occasion. The nearby 1894 Lyric Theater, seen as surplus by many patrons, was spared the wrecker's ball, remodeled, and became a second, similar sized entertainment venue for the city.

The Baltimore Museum of Industry. The erosion of the industrial base of the city had attracted the attention of Baltimore's mayor and his advisors. De-industrialization was becoming a common occurrence in many cities, Baltimore included, and city fathers were determined that at least a portion of Baltimore's history, the industrial history, should remain visible to future generations. The Museum of Industry began as a travelling exhibit of industrial relics and equipment collected and curated by Dennis Zambala. In 1981, the museum and its growing collection of artifacts moved into the waterfront buildings of a long-closed oyster packing house. In this work, Zambala and his wife Anne Steele were pioneers in their avocation of industrial archeology, a systematic study of the industrial heritage of a region. The museum quickly became a destination for school children on field trips, for visiting tourists, and for nostalgia driven local citizens alike. With youth activities, exhibits that memorialized jobs of the past, and maintaining an archive of books and related memorabilia, the museum preserved significant part of Baltimore's history.

The Good Humor Truck. Good Humor featured a variety of frozen treats, including a chocolate covered ice cream bar on a stick, dispensing summer delights from trucks in seemingly every neighborhood. By the 1950s, the company was summoning customers with their tuneful bells from a fleet of 2,000 uniquely designed trucks nationwide.

But in the midst of changing times, operations declined until 1978 when the Good Humor Company closed its street ice cream vending operations. Baltimore was one of three cities exempted from the closures, where routes continued for an additional six years, until the jingling ice cream bells of summer were finally silenced in 1984. Good Humor Ice Cream trucks were idled, all 140 of them, and the ice cream plant that made the products that filled them was closed.

The Highways. The highway wars in Baltimore had created a steady diet of news articles, maps with dotted lines, and public hearing after public hearing for forty years. The wars often pitted the road builders and politicians against community and preservation advocates. Every aspect of road building was up for debate: was a proposed road a city by-pass and if so, was it really needed? If a road was indeed needed, where would it go? What form would it take, a freeway, a boulevard or something else? One question was whether the road would go through, under, over, or around the city? By the 1980s, the arguments drew to a late 20th century conclusion, ending years of discussion, rancor, accusation, demolition, and heartache. The opening of the Interstate 95 Fort McHenry tunnel brought travelers through the city by going under the harbor, out of sight if not out of mind. The route opened in 1985, but not until one last controversy, between the Federal Highway Administration and the state highway planners over the tunnel's construction design arose. Those with the money won, and the federal standards were followed.

The Block. In 1992 Baltimore's adult entertainment district came under siege. "The Block" had a long history of skirting the law, its offerings a potpourri of vices that politicians (and an occasional police officer) publicly decried while quietly accepting largesse from business owners operating there. On January 14, 1994, five-hundred Maryland State Police officers, one third of the entire force, led by Governor William Donald Schaefer (described by one pundit as taking up the mantle of General George Patton leading his troops into battle) descended on the nightclubs, the employees, the customers, and the hangers-on on the Block that evening in an effort to root out perceived evil. The planning, undercover work, and the infiltration came at a cost of $360,000 tax dollars ($780,000 in 2023 dollars), funds that produced just sixty arrests, almost half of which were soon dropped by prosecutors for improprieties in evidence, process, or enforcement misconduct. The Block was open again the next evening.

The Colts. A football drought of sorts began in Baltimore in 1984 when the uneasy negotiations between Mayor William Donald Schaefer and the National Football League's Baltimore Colts owner Robert Irsay came to a sudden halt. Conditions at Memorial Stadium, deemed outdated by 1980s professional stadium standards, were central to the controversy, with a resolution proving elusive. In the 1983 season, the team had a mediocre record, losing 9 of the 16 games they played. Their previous season, interrupted by a players' strike, saw them lose all but one game, that one ending in a tie. In March 1984, the Mayflower Moving Company arrived at the Colts training facility at Goucher College and their offices at Memorial Stadium, unannounced and unknown except to Colts officials, packed up the team and left town during an overnight snowstorm, headed for Indianapolis. The sudden team move had occurred after the Maryland legislature passed a bill that made the team subject to a local eminent domain seizure. Owner Irsay took no chances, before the governor could sign the bill, the team was spirited off to its new home city in Indiana.

A Trash Skimmer. Remediating the pollution in the Baltimore Harbor had been the subject of studies and reports, by one consultant's count 300 times over the past 30 years. Studies were often a political means of shelving an idea, "kicking the problem downstream" to some unknown point in the future, with the citizens forced to await another study, another result, another conclusion. Finally, a visible sign someone was doing something when in 1988 the city deployed its first watercraft designed to skim the floating trash from the harbor's surface. On a rainy day, the city's storm drain system delivered discarded trash and debris through its system of conduits and pipes directly to the harbor. The skimmers, known to those in the trade as "retrievers" snared everything from appliances and tree stumps to corpses. The skimmer made the water if not purer, at least more presentable for both tourists and residents as it made its daily rounds.

The Eubie Blake Cultural Center. With the mementos of a lifetime, a center to honor the contributions of ragtime and jazz giant Baltimorean Eubie Blake was proposed in the 1980s. Born of the community work of a few local moms seeking music and dance lessons for their children and a simultaneous desire by music aficionados to preserve the legacy of Blake (and later, others), a plan was drawn to unite the two efforts and create a permanent educational and memorialization center. Early plans were interrupted by a fire at a proposed site, followed by a move to an interim temporary site, and then in 2000, with the cooperation of the city administration, a permanent home on North Howard Street was located. The center had expanded its mission in 1993, becoming the Eubie Blake National Jazz Institute and Cultural Center, Inc. adding tributes to other local Baltimore talents such as Billy Holliday and Cab Calloway.

Bayview. The Baltimore City Hospital, founded in 1773 as an almshouse offering housing and health care to the poor, was granted a new lease on life when it was sold to the Johns Hopkins Medical System in 1984. The City Hospital had been underfunded and understaffed, the hospital struggling to meet the medical needs of the city's large east side population. Upon acquiring the hospital from the city, the Hopkins Medical System began a major investment program, re-naming it the Francis Scott Key Medical Center, a name change that would have an action plan behind it. Hopkins soon began a major change, expanding services, using the existing hospital while expanding significant medical services away from its more center-city but land-locked main property. A 130-acre campus of medical offices and services buildings was established along Eastern Avenue, the location commanding hilltop views of the city and the lower reaches of the Patapsco River as it intersected the Chesapeake Bay. Hopkins renamed the facility a second time in 1994 as the Johns Hopkins Bayview Medical Center.

Hammerjacks. In 1977, a rock and roll, dance party, concert venue opened its doors, soon to become something of a local legend. Other clubs co-existed, including Odell's on North Avenue and Paradox on Russell Street, but the king of all such venues in Baltimore was Hammerjacks. Located first on the southern reaches of South Charles Street, the owners soon found a more commodious space on South Howard Street. The venue was vast, and it attracted massive numbers of patrons, with major acts of the time. Singer Eddie Money was the first concert presented there in the 1,000-seat auditorium. Artist Joan Jett shot a music video on site, Peter Frampton, Kiss, and Waylon Jennings, and dozens more demonstrating diversity in music styles. Hammerjacks was the venue for the big hair, spandex wearing, leather and lace, heavy make-up youth of the 1980s and 1990s.

THE NEW YEAR ARRIVES

December 31, 1999, was a special day and night for Baltimore. It was New Year's Eve, but more significantly, it was the last day of a century and tomorrow would mark the start of a new millennium, with the year 2000. The weather was pleasant for the end of December. Though it wasn't one of those Baltimore mid-winter thaws with temperatures reaching into the 70s, it was a sunny day with an afternoon temperature of 55 degrees Fahrenheit. It had snowed lightly a few days before, but with the mild temperatures, the roads and sidewalks were clear and dry.

Baltimoreans were planning to welcome in the New Year, a new century and millennium, in various ways. Unlike the turn of the century in 1899, a good deal fewer would attend midnight church services, as religious disaffiliation had been on the rise for a half century. Unlike 1899, steamboat whistles would not sound the new year's arrival, as the port facilities had mostly moved well downstream, and the city's streetcars would not be running late to take revelers home, their rolling and coasting metal wheels along metal rails had disappeared from the streets in 1963.

Marking the occasion, some Baltimoreans chose to attend house parties, gathered with friends and family in front of television to catch New Year's Eve from around the world. Others would elect for the full celebration, attending events on the town, a drive to a hotel ballroom or club, cocktails, dinner, music, party hats, and a night's lodging, the cost of perhaps $1,000 per couple secondary to the pursuit of a unique experience on this unique evening. Some chose the memorable date to be married. There were others for whom the evening was nothing special, an artifice of modernity to be ignored. Regardless of the celebration or not, a bigger issue looked over this night. There was even some question as to whether the new millennium actually began January 1, 2000, or not until the end of the "aughts" year, in 2001.

For many in Baltimore and around the world, this would not be an evening for fun and friends, but a night to spend at the workplace attending computers and the machines they controlled, dealing with the phenomenon known as Y2K (shorthand for "Year 2000"). Digital equipment is designed to run with both internal and visible clocks. Original designers of software and equipment had generally established an internal date protocol that provided for a year abbreviated in two digits. Thus December 31, 1999, would be known internally to the computer as 991231, with the "19" of 1999 assumed. When the new year turned over at midnight, embedded date-time routines would add to this number, which yielded a new date of 000101. Since the "19" was assumed, the new date in the computer with this protocol was a century earlier: 19000101, or January 1, 1900. No one really knew what, if anything, would occur at this particular midnight, when the new year would be abbreviated "00". System analysts and programmers had worked for several years to search out and update these potential "glitches", sometimes requiring massive upgrading of both hardware and software, but no one knew where all the dates were embedded. Would digital equipment controlling elevators, heating systems, power plants, and credit card companies continue to function? Would it revert and begin to recognize the date as 1900? If so, would bank borrowers happily receive a minus one-hundred-year interest credit? Would prisoners due to be released at some date after December 31, 1999, suddenly be serving time up to 100 years after their release date? No one was sure what consequences might occur, so those clocks and the equipment they controlled could not be on auto-pilot that night. Offices, power plants, data centers, all would have to be staffed in the event of some failure. Plans were made, contingencies considered, and hundreds of Baltimoreans went to work to await the midnight hour. In the end, all went smoothly, the computer systems mostly behaved, there were vanishingly few failures, glitches, or power failures. (For a short time on January 1, 2000, some point-of-sale credit card software generated duplicate transactions, but this was quickly corrected. Most of the truly challenging issues that arose were quietly corrected and never known to the public.)

Y2k was a lesson in being prepared, expecting the worst, and hoping for the best. The new millennium was underway. It was January of the new year 2000, so a normal quick dip in the temperatures for the first day of the year was followed by a real January thaw that arrived for the remainder of the first week of the year 2000.

AN AFTERWORD

BALTIMORE BY THE YEAR 2000 was a city of mixed virtues, with all the attributes of a complete city, yet somehow on a slightly smaller scale. This medium-sized city had a long history of doing more than might otherwise be expected. A legendary history of ships of wood and ships of steel. Medical research and advances. Dollar houses setting a nationwide model. A renaissance at the harbor front. Aircraft built by the thousands. Cultural experiences and contributors in art and theater. Notable literary expertise. And yet, the residents, at least the long-term ones, also maintained the traditional Baltimore inferiority complex throughout the 20th and well into the 21st century (Are we worthy? I think so, wait, maybe not.). The city's residents, especially those long-term ones, found that other cities, Baltimore's neighbors, always seemed to offer "more". Some Washingtonians sneered, but when many discovered Baltimore and its reasonable rents and easy rail commute, they swallowed their sneers and packed their belongings. Philadelphians found the little city on the Patapsco, by the year 2000 one-third their size, merely amusing. That is, until they compared historic attractions, found themselves "toe to toe", and eventually granted a bit of respect for the smaller metropolis. New Yorkers? Visitors from the Big Apple found Baltimore charming and welcoming, almost but not quite southern in its hospitality. They did miss the delis, though, Attman's on Lombard Street not-with-standing.

Cities have a way of reinventing themselves: it is almost axiomatic that good times are followed by not-so-great times. The story you have just read (I hope you read it like the novel it was supposed to be, until facts got in the way) is most certainly one of the ups and downs of the city through the 20th century. The story began with a devastating fire, destroying everything but hope. A World War and a decade of good times was followed by one of those spirit-crushing eras known as the Great Depression. Baltimore persevered, endured, and became a major part of the World War Two arsenal of democracy, growing jobs like low hanging fruit as business and industry flourished. But the city had neglected some of the basics, too many citizens were marginalized, the city was physically a wreck, and every Baltimorean needed a hero. He arrived in the form of a stubborn, demanding leader named Schaefer. The city was reinvented, became an attraction, a destination, and times were looking up, at least until a few forces merged to send it into yet another decline. Drugs, guns, and poverty will crush anyone in anyplace, Baltimore was no exception, and yet the spirit of the city endured, loyalists stayed and continued to work side by side to build, or rebuild, well into the 21st century. As the Broadway version of Little Orphan Annie once said in song, "The sun will come up tomorrow". Optimism is infectious here in this city on the Patapsco, my hometown of Baltimore.

BIBLIOGRAPHY

Adams, Steven B. and Orville R. Butler. *Manufacturing the Future: A History of Western Electric.* Cambridge University Press, 1999. ISBN 0-521-65118-2

Ahmann, Chloe. *Future After Progress: Hope and Doubt in Late Industrial Baltimore.* The University of Chicago Press, 2024. ISBN 978-0-226-83361-3

Argersinger, Jo Ann E. *Making the Amalgamated.* Johns Hopkins University Press, 1999. ISBN 0-8018-5989-1

Argersinger, Jo Ann E. *Toward A New Deal in Baltimore.* University of North Carolina Press, 1988. ISBN 0-8078-1769-4

Baldin, Dyane. "Sailor and Canton: History of the Breed." *American Chesapeake Club*, 2023. Retrieved at: https://amchessieclub.org/sailor-and-canton-history-of-the-breed/

Baltimore and Ohio Railroad. "America's Largest Immigrant Pier." *The Book of the Royal Blue.* Vol. VII, No. 10, July 1904.

Baltimore and Ohio Railroad. "The Great Fire of Baltimore." *The Book of the Royal Blue.* Vol. VII, No. 6, March 1904.

Barry, Bill. *The 1877 Railroad Strike in Baltimore.* Amazon Publishing, 2019. ISBN 13-978-1500918637

Blum, Isidor. *The Jews of Baltimore: An Historical Summary of Their Progress and Status as Citizens of Baltimore from Early Days to the Year Nineteen Hundred and Ten.* Historical Review Publishing Company, 1910. Reprint, Forgotten Books, Ltd., 2018. ISBN 978-1-333-60103-4

Brown, Alexander Crosby. *The Old Bay Line 1840-1940.* Bonanza Books, 1940. LOC Card 77-712-12

Burt, Christopher C. "North America's Most Intense Heatwave." *Weather Underground,* August 2018. Retrieved at: https://www.wunderground.com/cat6/North-Americas-Most-Intense-Heat-Wave-July-and-August-1936

Cassie, Ron. "The Great Migration." *Baltimore Magazine,* December 2020. Retrieved at: https://www.baltimoremagazine.com/section/historypolitics/the-great-migration/

Cotter, Arundel. *The Story of Bethlehem Steel.* The Moody Magazine and Book Company, 1916. Retrieved from the Library of Congress at https://www.loc.gov/item/17007829/

De Filippo, Frank. "Baltimore's X-Rated Block Is on The Chopping Block Again." *Maryland Matters,* February 2022. Retrieved at: https://www.marylandmatters.org/2022/02/14/frank-defilippo-baltimores-x-rated-block-is-on-the-chopping-block-again/

Dilts, James D. and Catharine F. Black, eds. *Baltimore's Cast Iron Buildings & Architectural Ironwork.* Tidewater Publishers, 1991. ISBN 0-87033-427-1

Dorsey, John & James Dilts. *A Guide to Baltimore Architecture.* Tidewater Publishers, 1973. ISBN 0-87033-187-6

Fee, Elizabeth, Linda Shopes and Linda Zeidman, eds. *The Baltimore Book: New Views of Local History.* Temple University Press, 1991. ISBN 0-87722-817-5

Good Roads Magazine. League of American Wheelmen. Multiple editions, 1892-1899. Retrieved at: https://onlinebooks.library.upenn.edu/webbin/serial?id=goodroads

Gordon, Virginia and Herb Meade. "Exxon's Boston Street Terminal Cleanup." *eMDE,* September 2009. Retrieved at: https://mde.maryland.gov/programs/ResearchCenter/eMDE/Pages/vol3no12/exxoncleanup.aspx

Grant, James. *The Forgotten Depression.* Simon & Schuster, 2014. ISBN 978-1-4516-8645-6

Holian, Timothy J. "The Long Road Home: Baltimore's Brewing Heritage." The Society for the History of Germans in Maryland, Loyola-Notre Dame Library, June 2017. Retrieved at: https://loyolanotredamelib.org/php/report05/articles/pdfs/Report47-02-Baltimore-Breweries-Holian.pdf

Hough, Emerson. *The Web: A Revelation of Patriotism: The Story of the American Protective League.* Reilly & Lee, 1919. Reprint, Forgotten Books, 2017.

Johns Hopkins University. "Celebrating the Philanthropy of Mary Elizabeth Garrett." Retrieved at: https://exhibits.library.jhu.edu/exhibits/show/celebrating-the-philanthropy-o/introduction

Kahn, Philip Jr. *A Stitch in Time.* Maryland Historical Society, 1989. ISBN 0-938420-33-X

Kasper, Rob. *Baltimore Beer: A Satisfying History of Charm City Brewing.* The History Press, 2012. ISBN 978-1-60949-457-5

Keith, Robert C. *Baltimore Harbor*. Ocean World Publishing, 1982. ISBN-0-8018-7980-9

Kelly, Jacques. "Old Oriole Ballpark." Fairfield-Wagner's Point-Brooklyn Historical Society. April 2019.

Lisicky, Michael J. *Hutzler's, Where Baltimore Shops*. The History Press, 2009.
ISBN 978-1-59629-828-6

Messimer, Dwight R. *The Baltimore Sabotage Cell: German Agents, American Traitors, and the U-boat Deutschland During World War I*. Naval Institute Press, 2015. ISBN 978-1-99114-184-6

Monet, Dolores. "Baltimore's Great Fire of 1904 and Its Legacy. " *Owlcation,* January 2018.
Retrieved at: https://owlcation.com/humanities/Baltimores-Great-Fire-of-1904-and-Its-Legacy

Morris, Richard. *A History of the American Worker*. Princeton University Press, 1983.
ISBN 0-691-04697-2

Moving Picture World. July 1910.

Nast, Lenora Heilig, Laurence N. Krause and R.C. Monk. *Baltimore: A Living Renaissance*. Historic Baltimore Society, Inc., 1982. ISBN 0-942460-6

Nichols, Nancy A. "Whatever Happened to Rosie the Riveter." *Harvard Business Review,*
July-August 1993.
Retrieved at: https://hbr.org/1993/07/whatever-happened-to-rosie-the-riveter

O'Prey, Maureen. *Brewing in Baltimore*. Arcadia Publishing Library, 2011.
ISBN 978-0-7385-8813-1

Okrent, Daniel. *Last Call: The Rise and Fall of Prohibition*. Scribner Book Company, 2010. ISBN 978-0-7432-7702-0

Olson, Karen. *Wives of Steel: Voices of Women from the Sparrows Point Steelmaking Communities*. Pennsylvania State University Press, 2005. ISBN 0-271-02685-5

Petersen, Peter B. *The Great Baltimore Fire*. Maryland Historical Society, 2004.
ISBN 0-938420-90-9

Pietila, Antero. *Not In My Neighborhood: How Bigotry Shaped a Great American City*. Ivan R. Dee, 2010. ISBN 978-1-56663-843-2

Power, Garrett. "Deconstructing the Slums of Baltimore." In *From Mobtown to Charm City: New Perspectives on Baltimore's Past* edited by Jessica I. Elfenbein et al. Maryland Historical Society, 2002. ISBN 0-938420-85-2

Reutter, Mark. *Sparrows Point: Making Steel: the Rise and Ruin of American Industrial Might.* Summit Books, 1988. ISBN 0-671-68752-2

Robenault, James David. *The Harding Affair: Love and Espionage During the Great War.* St. Martin's Press, 2009. ISBN 978-0-230-60964-8

Rogers, Michael H. *Answering their Country's Call: Marylanders in World War II.* Johns Hopkins University Press, 2002. ISBN 0-8018-7126-3

Rudacille, Deborah. *Roots of Steel: Boom and Bust in an American Mill Town.* Pantheon Books, 2010. ISBN 978-0-375-42386-0

Rukert, Norman G. *The Fells Point Story.* Bodine & Associates, Inc., 1976. ISBN 910254-11-7

Rukert, Norman G. *Fort McHenry: Home of the Brave.* Bodine & Associates, Inc., 1983. ISBN 910254-24-9

Rukert, Norman G. *The Port: Pride of Baltimore.* Bodine & Associates, Inc., 1982. ISBN 910254-17-6

Sandler, Gilbert. *Home Front Baltimore.* Johns Hopkins University Press, 2011. ISBN 978-0-8018-9983-6

Sandler, Gilbert. *Small Town Baltimore.* Johns Hopkins University Press, 2002. ISBN 0-8018-7069-0

Simon, David. *Homicide: A Year on the Killing Streets.* Picador, 2006. ISBN 10-0805-08075-9

Smith, C. Fraser. *William Donald Schaefer.* Johns Hopkins University Press, 1999. ISBN 0-8018-6252-3

Springirth, Kenneth C. *Baltimore Streetcar Memories.* Arcadia Publishing, 2017. ISBN 978-1-64399-034-9

Stockett, Letitia. *Baltimore: A Not Too Serious History.* Johns Hopkins University Press, 1997. ISBN 0-8018-5670-1

The Weems Steamboat Line. *Bugeye Times.* Vol. 7, No. 4, Winter 1983.

Travers, Paul Joseph. *The Patapsco: Baltimore's River of History.* Tidewater Publishers, 1990. ISBN 0-87033-400-X

Warren, Kenneth. *Bethlehem Steel.* University of Pittsburgh Press, 2008.
ISBN 10-0-8229-6067-2

Warren, Marion E. & Mame Warren. *Baltimore: When She Was What She Used to Be.* Johns Hopkins University Press, 1983. ISBN 0-8018-2994-1

Weiner, Deborah. "German Jews Find a Safe Haven." *JMore – Baltimore Jewish Living.*
January 2017.
Retrieved at: https://jmoreliving.com/2017/01/31/german-jews-found-safe-haven-baltimore/

Westwood, Lara. "Carlin's Park: Baltimore's-Million-Dollar-Playground." *Maryland Historical Magazine, Vol. 113, No.1, Spring/Summer 2018.*
retrieved at https://www.mdhistory.org/carlins-park-baltimores-million-dollar-playground/

Williams, Harold. *Baltimore Afire.* Schneidereith & Sons, 1954. ISBN 0-9602304-1-6

Zambala, Dennis. *Baltimore: Industrial Gateway on the Chesapeake.* Baltimore Museum of Industry, 1995.

ADDITIONAL RESEARCH SOURCES

Pro-Quest Historical Newspapers

Press accounts provide primary sources for research. This work relied upon literally hundreds of newspaper articles. *The Baltimore Sun, The Baltimore Afro-American, The Washington Post*, and *The New York Times* were the main source documents in the research.

Here is a partial list of historical sources with the subject matter and publication date briefly noted. Realistically, there can only be a sampling of them, as they were gathered over a period of ten or more years, beginning long before this book was even an idea.

The Baltimore Sun

May 12, 1913 – Teacher endorsement

July 18, 1914 – Kentucky delegation

August 2, 1914 – Centennial Program (War of 1812)

September 1, 1914 – Centennial at hand (War of 1812)

September 20, 1918 – Spanish Influenza

December 21, 1919 – American Labor

June 26, 1921 – Carlin Park

January 1, 1930 – Western Electric Co.

February 20, 1933 – Bank holidays

September 5, 1935 – Works Progress Administration (W.P.A.)

May 25, 1940 – Old Bay Line

October 28, 1941 – America First meeting

January 21, 1951 – Transit strike

November 23, 1954 – J. W. Crook store armed bandits

March 6, 1960 – Alum Chine

December 14, 1963 – Buddy Deane

September 13, 1964 – Star Spangled Celebration

February 6, 1966 – Ronnie Dove

August 6, 1967 – H.L. Mencken

August 20, 1967 – Pollution on the Patapsco

August 31, 1967 – Hippies

January 31, 1968 – A Progressive City Emerges

June 11, 1968 – Bendix Radio Production

June 24, 1968 – Druid Hill "be in"

September 16, 1968 – Wedding

August 16, 1970 – Dance Marathons

July 14, 1974 – Scott and Zelda Fitzgerald

September 3, 1978 – Carlin Park Mountain Speedway

April 21, 1985 – Baltimore Hippies

October 15, 1989 – Civilian Conservation Corps (C.C.C.) reunion

June 4, 1992 – City Fair

September 27, 2018 – Tin Mill Canal

The Washington Post

October 1, 1937 – Carlin Park fire

February 1, 1999 – Blaustein Corporate History

July 7, 2017 – Five Myths

July 9, 2019 – Laurel Pop Festival

The Baltimore Afro-American

October 18, 1918 – Spanish Influenzas

November 23, 1929 – Wonderland Park to be Sold

July 26, 1930 – Bessie Smith at the Royal

July 14, 1951 – Willie Adams

January 22, 1955 – Lunch Counters

January 1, 1972 – Dr. Lillie May Carroll Jackson

The New York Times

September 9, 1906 – Baltimore Post-Fire Celebration

January 24, 1921—Isaac Emerson passes

July 8, 2010 – Charles Schwab home

The Wall Street Journal

January 22, 1937 – Bendix Forms Radio Corp

Websites

Web searches for every topic resulted in hundreds of web references. Every topic and subject area in this text was explored via website research. Wikipedia references were often used to access the bibliographies listed in the various articles, at other times Wiki research was used only to confirm basic data of the topic (date, size, location). Many,

but not all, of these listings are primary sources. Below is a sampling of the websites that were used to help develop this work:

www.dyingtotelltheirstories/home/2020/9/8/chick-webb

www.baltimoresun.com/maryland/baltimore-city/bs-md-ci-kelly-bank-20180222-story-html

www.ourdocuments.gov/doc.php?flash=true&doc=66

en.wikipedia.org/wiki/United_States_Post_Office_and_Courthouse_(Baltimore,_Maryland)

www.tulkoff.com/about-us/history/

www.historians.org/publications-and-directories/perspectives-on-history/march-2016/the

www.jstor.org/stable/3789081

www.baltimoresun.com/citypaper/bcpnews-our-town-what-the-rise-of-nazism-looked-like-in-

https://uselessinformation.org/oldsite/baltimore/index/html

https://baltimorebrew.com/2014/02/12/another-piece-of-industrial-baltimore-succumbs

www.ncdc.noaa.gov/cag/statewide/time-series

www.explorebaltimore.org/city-history/jewishheritage

https://en.wikipedia.org/wiki/Baltimore_Assembly

www.tudorheights.com/the-history-of-jewish-baltimore

www.baltimoresun.com/news/bs-xpm-2008-09-07-0809000895

www.baltimoresun.com/features/retro-baltimore/bs-md-ci-retro-armstrong-20181206-story.html

https://en.wikipedia.org/wiki/Walters_Art_Museum

http://articles.baltimoresun.com/1994-06-07/news/1994158148_1_ship-telegraph-war

https://www.baltimoresun.com/maryland/bs-xpm-2013-01-10-bs-md-backstory-redwood-street

www.fredopie.com/food/odasalens.com/2013/04/canned-foods-and-baltimores-first.html

www.hoehnsbakery.com/about-us

www.mdhistory.org/the-velvet-kind-the-sweet-story-of-hendlers-creamery

https://www.baltimoremagazine.com/section/artsentertainment/

john-waters-on-keeping-the-memory-of-the-buddy-deane-show-alive/

https://en.wikipedia.org/wiki/Good_Roads_Movement

https://uboat.net/forums/read.php?3,47135,47177

https://explore.baltimoreheritage.org/items/show/398

https://www.baltimoresun.com/maryland/laurel/ph-ll-rosie-riveter-20110630-story.html

https://teachingamericanhistory.org/blog/the-long-controversy-over-alger-hiss/

www.josephkavanaghco.com/about.html

https://www.mdhistory.org/lost-city-baltimores-vibrant-automobile-show-rooms/

https://www.proquest.com/docview/536640730/346A4BDDE1AA49F0PQ/26?accountid=34685

https://mht.maryland.gov/secure/medusa/PDF/NR_PDFs/NR-943.pdf

https://timesmachine.nytimes.com/timesmachine/1982/06/20/issue.html

https://www.baltimoresun.com/news/bs-xpm-2003-02-22-0302220361-story.html

https://lib.guides.umd.edu/c.php?g=327119&p=2197762

https://explore.baltimoreheritage.org/items/show/690

https://content.time.com/time/subscriber/article/0,33009,754694,00.html

https://www.wypr.org/wypr-news/2021-09-16/searching-for-a-turn-around-on-the-highway-to-nowhere

https://apps.mht.maryland.gov/nr/NRDetail.aspx?NRID=1567

https://www.npr.org/2023/08/17/1194494775/legendary-baltimore-jazz-performances-are-brought-back-through-unearthed-recordi

Additional Sources

Maryland Historical Trust, multiple references, Maryland's National Register Properties

Maryland State Archives. https://msa.maryland.gov/

Oral History. "Meda Montana Brendall Collection", Library of Congress. https://www.loc.gov/item/afc2001001.04951/

R.L. Polk & Co. Baltimore City Directory, University of Maryland, digitized, various years.

"The Baltimore". You Tube video, retrieved at: https://www.youtube.com/watch?v=lo3WNYaL1RM

From the author's collection:

Baltimore Copper Paint Company, Paint Catalogs and Schedules.

Baltimore Museum of Industry. "Bendix: 60 Years in Baltimore." Presentation, April 21, 2016.

Bethlehem Steel Management Conference program, August 1977.

Canton Community Association. "A Timeline of Canton History." May 2019.

Cope Salt Company. History of Road Salt. Undated.

Labor Day Ceremonies program, Fairfield Shipyard, September 1942.

Photograph, The Chateau Hotel, April 1939, The Baltimore Sun.

Photographs, Launch of the Liberty Ship Samuel F. B. Morse II, Fairfield MD, May 1944.

ACKNOWLEDGEMENTS

I AM DEEPLY INDEBTED TO MANY individuals and several groups for their assistance and suggestions in the research and development of this book, and the lectures that preceded it. A partial list of persons who aided, informed, or advised follows, though doubtless I have skipped someone or some group, and for that I extend my apologies. A note to nativesonbaltimore@gmail.com will have your name added in subsequent editions.

Larry Bannerman, Baltimore Gas and Electric, Retired

Bill Barry, Labor Historian and Teacher

The Bendix Guys, retired Bendix radio employees at the Museum of Industry

Helen Bentley, Maritime and Port of Baltimore Advisor

Chris Bozel, Trucking Executive

Louis Campion, Maryland Motor Truck Association

Ralph Clayton, Researcher and Author

Charlie Conklin, Bethlehem Steel, Retired

Nathan Dennies, Historian

Holly Detwiler, Bundy Baking Solutions, Inc.

Jeremy Diamond, author, *Tastemakers: The Story of Baltimore Groceries*

Louis Diggs, Historian and Author

Sally DiMarco, Garment Industry Consultant

Ernie Dimler, History Specialist, Bromo Seltzer Arts Tower

Rachel Donaldson, Baltimore Museum of Industry

Tim Fabizak, Independent Historian

Nicole Fabricant, Towson University

Brigitte Fessenden, Baltimore Immigration Museum

Nicholas Fessenden, Baltimore Immigration Museum

Mike Franch, Historian

John Green, Educator, Baltimore Museum of Industry

Niada Green, Edgewood Arsenal Worker

Hays T. Watkins Research Library, B&O Railroad Museum

Edward Hawkins, Garment Industry Advisor; Educator, Baltimore Museum of Industry

Brian Helbing, Baltimore Gas and Electric, Retired

Christopher Hitch, Constellation Energy

Johns Hopkins, Baltimore Heritage

I.L.A. (Longshoremen) Staff Personnel

Chip Jewell, Fire Department Advisor

Ken Jones, Baltimore Museum of Industry

Anita Kasoff, Baltimore Museum of Industry

Joseph Kavanagh, Joseph Kavanaugh Company

James Keffer, Historical Society of Baltimore County

Eric Kelso, Maryland Fire Museum

Dean Krimmel, Museum and History Consultant

Rick Kuethe, Engineer, Northrop Grumman

Barry Larkin, Rail History Advisor

Jennifer Liles, Independent Historian

James Lynn, McCormick and Co., Retired

Luke McCusker, Irish Railroad Workers Museum

Maggie Marzoff, Baltimore Museum of Industry

Peter Menzies, Terminal Transportation

Scott Menzies, Terminal Transportation

Samya Murray, Freight Forwarding Advisor

Kathleen Bender O'Keefe, Museum Educator

Alexis Ojeda-Brown, Lillie Carroll Jackson Civil Rights Museum

Stan Piet, Glenn L. Martin Museum

Robert Pratt, Nautical Historian, Baltimore Museum of Industry

Diane Price, CJ International, Advisor on Shipping Practices

Rick Ralph, Bethlehem Shipbuilding Engineer, Retired

Wayne Schaumberg, Educator and Historian

Kurt L. Schmoke, Esq., Former Mayor of Baltimore; President, University of Baltimore

Rob Schoeberlein, Archivist

Matt Shirko, Baltimore Museum of Industry

Jerry Smith, Smith Shipyard

Mike Stillwell, Bethlehem Steel Engineer, Retired

Stacy Stube, Fashions Unlimited

Harrison Van Waes, Maryland Center for History and Culture

Rick Warfield, Bethlehem Shipbuilding, Retired

Deborah Weiner, History Consultant

Rovan Wernsdorfer, Independent Historian

John Zieman, Radio and Television Advisor, Retired

And most of all

My dear wife, Cynthia Horn Burkert

INDEX

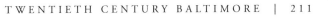

U

Union Station 28
United Garment Workers 45
United States Maritime Commission 78, 81

V

Veterans Administration (V.A.) 91
Victory Gardens 88
Victory Hour 52
Victory Villa 85

W

Waller, Thomas \ 69, 71
Walters Art Museum 144, 159
Walters, Henry T. 12
Walters Public Bath 12
War Memorial 37
War on Drugs 185
Washington, D.C. 9, 11, 18, 23, 26, 63, 70, 83, 86, 125, 126, 129, 156, 185
Waters, Ethel 41
Waters, John 137, 148, 165
Watson, Arthur 130
WCAO 51, 52
Webb, William \ 71
Welcome, Verda 150
Western Electric 55, 59, 83, 84, 130
Westinghouse 70
  Broadcasting 122
Whitcomb, James 19
White Coffee Pot 69
white flight 116, 117, 144, 147
white marble steps 40
White, McCall 83
Wilkie, Wendell 80
Willard, Daniel 47
Williams, Emily Raine 37
Willis, Jack 81
Wilmington, Delaware 11
Wilson, Woodrow 21, 22, 23, 30
Winans, Thomas 131
WKC 51
women in war industries
  Arnold, Elsie 85
  Eckley, Mae 85

Green, Niada 85
Meda Brindall 85
\"Rosie the Riveter\" 85, 93, 94
women's suffrage 13
Works Progress Administration (W.P.A.) 67

Y

Y2K 191

Z

Zambala, Dennis 188
Zamoiski, Calman 51
Zappa, Frank 151
Zemeral, Zim 166
Zion Lutheran Church 33